THE HAMLYN
Younger Children's
ENCYCLOPEDIA

Gillian Wilson
2 More Wood DRive
Burton in Kendal
Cumbaia

THE HAMLYN
Younger Children's
ENCYCLOPEDIA

Kenneth Bailey

HAMLYN
LONDON · NEW YORK · SYDNEY · TORONTO

First published 1972
Third Impression 1975
by The Hamlyn Publishing Group Limited
LONDON · NEW YORK · SYDNEY · TORONTO
© Copyright 1972 The Hamlyn Publishing Group Limited
ISBN 0 600 34366 9
Printed by Litografia A. Romero, S.A., Santa Cruz de Tenerife, Canary Islands, Spain.
D. L. TF. 288 - 1975

CONTENTS

Our Land and its People

The British Isles are a group of islands off the north-west coast of Europe. They include Great Britain and Northern Ireland and about 5,000 smaller islands, most of which are uninhabited.

Great Britain consists of England, Wales and Scotland. England and Wales were politically united in 1536. Union with Scotland took place in 1707. The inclusion of Northern Ireland with this group makes up the United Kingdom – the official name of the country.

Although Britain is a small country the people and the land which supports them vary a great deal. The first people on these islands probably came from continental Europe. Over a period of thousands of years many different races, chiefly Celtic and Saxon, have mingled with the original settlers. Today, the country is one of the most densely populated in the world, although there are still isolated areas to be found, mostly in Scotland, where few people live.

Above **Map to show the principal cities of England.**

Above **Some English cathedrals were originally parish churches and one of these is at Manchester. It is the lovely 15th-century cathedral of St. Mary once a collegiate church. Built in the Perpendicular Gothic style, its interior possesses some magnificent carved woodwork.**

England

England is the largest part of the United Kingdom and has an area of about 50,300 square miles *130,275 square kilometres*. It is divided into 39 counties, although there are plans to change the way they are organised.

On the whole, the countryside is made up of gentle, undulating hills, but there are flat areas in the south-east and some mountainous districts. The latter includes the Pennine Chain which extends from the Scottish borders to Derbyshire, the Cumbrian Mountains around the Lake District (which includes the highest mountain in England, Scafell Pike, 3,210 feet *978·3 metres*), and the Cotswold and Mendip Hills. Rivers include the Thames and Severn (the longest, each at about 200 miles *322 kilometres* long), the Great Ouse, Mersey, Trent, Avon and Dee.

Right **Motor car production is one of the most important of British industries having a large export market. In the early days of motoring, Herbert Austin and William Morris were pioneers of the industry and the cars they made were very popular and reasonably cheap. Today, the firms of Austin and Morris are important parts of the British Leyland Corporation. The picture shows Morris Marina cars being made on the company's modern assembly lines at its extensive factory in Oxfordshire, England.**

The basis of the economic life of the country is industry and fewer than 2% of the people are engaged in agriculture. Yet estimates of the total area of land used for agriculture have been placed as high as 80%. Although the nature of the farming varies from place to place, nearly every part of England is suitable for the growing of crops or as pastureland for animals.

At the end of the 19th century, England was known as the 'workshop of the world' as a result of the Industrial Revolution. Coal has always been very important and mining has been carried on intensively since

Above **St. Paul's Cathedral, London, designed by Sir Christopher Wren and completed in 1710. This was 44 years after fire had destroyed the first St. Paul's.**

Left **Piccadilly Circus in the heart of London's West End. Visitors from all over the world visit it each year.**

about 1750. Other important manufacturing industries are iron and steel, shipbuilding, woollen and cotton textiles, pottery and plastics. Many of the raw materials used in England's factories have to be imported and the export of manufactured goods to pay for these is vital for the country's economy.

The capital city is London—the home of the monarch and the seat of government for the United Kingdom.

Right **The M1 motorway in Toddington, England.**

Clyde, which include the great industrial regions centred around Glasgow. Scotland's other major cities, Edinburgh (the capital), Dundee and Aberdeen are in this area. In the South, the Cheviot Hills mark the boundary with England.

Left **Map to show the main cities of Scotland.**

Right **The Forth Railway Bridge in Scotland is about 5300 feet long,** *1624 metres* **and was opened in the year 1890.**

Scotland

Scotland occupies the northern part of the mainland of Great Britain and includes the island chains of the Inner and Outer Hebrides, and the Orkney and Shetland Isles. The total area is about 30,400 square miles *78,700 square kilometres,* and there are 38 county areas.

The Highlands of Scotland are the most mountainous part of Great Britain. There are many deep valleys containing freshwater and sea-water lochs, and the mountain ranges are formed from very ancient rock. The Highlands are divided into two parts by the Great Glen which runs from Fort William in the south to Inverness in the north, and contains the three lochs, Lochy, Oich and Ness, which are joined together by stretches of the Caledonian Canal. The country north of the Great Glen is thinly populated, has very little industry and contains some of the finest scenery in Great Britain. South of the Canal is the mountain range which contains Scotland's highest peak, Ben Nevis, 4,406 feet *1,343 metres.*

The Lowlands consist of the east coast and the valleys of the Forth and

Above and right **This is a picture of Edinburgh Castle and Princes Street. Castle Rock, on which the castle is built, is probably the site of an Iron Age fort. The castle was the home of Scottish monarchs but after the country was united with England, it was used mainly as a fortress.**

Right **Loch Shiel, one of Scotland's beautiful lochs. In the foreground is the Glen Finnan monument where Bonnie Prince Charlie raised his standard in 1745.**

Above **A Scottish soldier wearing traditional dress uniform and playing the bagpipes.** This is an instrument consisting of a number of reed pipes, a bag, and a chanter. The piper blows through the chanter into the bag and then squeezes this to force the air through the pipes. The bagpipes produce a very plaintive musical sound.

Below **The mountains and lochs of Scotland provide wonderful opportunities for pony trekking holidays.**

Left The map of Wales showing its principal cities and its border with England. To the west lies the Irish Sea and beyond that is Ireland. The Welsh are a Celtic people, many of whose ancestors were driven out of England during the invasions in pre-Saxon times.

Below The Welsh people have always been noted for their poetical and musical gifts. Here are officials – in their ancient Druidic robes – of the National Eisteddfod, an annual festival of music and poetry. Awards are made for the best recitals and original compositions.

Wales

Wales is a principality of the United Kingdom. At the time when Edward I crushed Welsh independence in the 13th century, he sought to appease the defeated nation by making his son (later Edward II) Prince of Wales. This title is still retained by the eldest son of the Sovereign.

Geographically, Wales is bordered on the east by England and on the west by the Atlantic Ocean and the Irish Sea. Its area is about 8,000 square miles *20,720 square kilometres,* and there are 13 counties, including Monmouthshire. Wales is a mountainous country, its highest peak being Mount Snowdon, 3,560 feet *1,085·2 metres.* Although much of the high ground is covered with rank grass, heather and bog, there are also well-wooded and fertile valleys which support a prosperous agriculture.

At the time of the Industrial Revolution, Wales ceased to be mainly a hill-farming community. This was the period when the great coal fields in the south were developed and the iron and steel industries set up. Today, fishing is a declining industry.

The population is made up of the small dark Iberians and the tall, fair or red-headed Celts. The Welsh language is totally different from the Anglo-Saxon of England, and the people are still fiercely independent and jealous of their national heritage. Cardiff is the administrative capital of the country.

Above **Although Wales has some lovely mountainous scenery, it is also very industrialised, especially in the south where most of the coal valleys are. This is a picture of an oil tanker at Milford Haven, the largest refinery in the UK.**

Right **This girl is seen wearing traditional Welsh national costume.**

Far right **A typical Welsh public house.**

Right **Welsh male voice choirs are renowned the world over.** This picture shows a choir of miners who are among the keenest singers of all.

Left **Some of the finest coal in the world is mined in South Wales.** This picture shows a typical coal mine set in one of the lovely Welsh valleys.

13

Northern Ireland

Ireland is a land of mountains and inland loughs. It is the second largest island in the British Isles. Northern Ireland consists of the six counties in the north-east – Antrim, Londonderry, Down, Armagh, Tyrone, Fermanagh – sometimes called Ulster. Ulster chose to remain part of the United Kingdom after the fight of Southern Ireland for Home Rule during the early part of the present century. In area, Northern Ireland

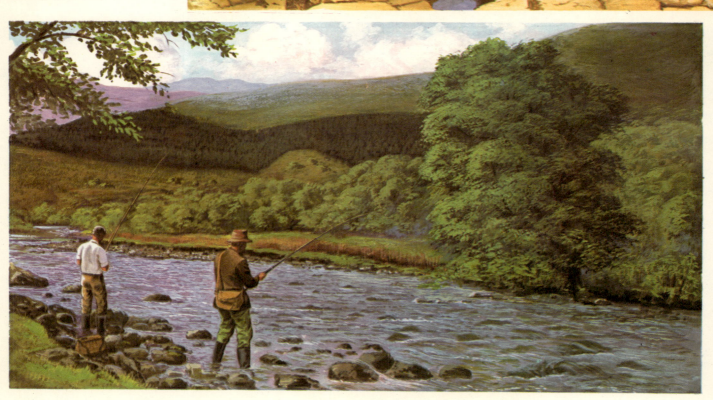

Above **Map to show the main cities of Northern and Southern Ireland**

Right **The Giant's Causeway, a headland in County Antrim with an interesting formation. The close-fitting columns of hard, dark-coloured basalt rock look like steps for a giant.**

Below **Ireland's rivers are a paradise for anglers.**

14

covers 5,450 square miles *14,115 square kilometres,* and its capital city is Belfast.

The Republic of Ireland

The Republic of Ireland occupies the major part of the land area of the island, about 26,500 square miles, *68,700 square kilometres.* It consists of 26 counties and its capital city is Dublin. She proclaimed herself a Republic in 1919 but was not formally recognised as such until 1949.

The land is one of exceptional beauty, and farming is still the chief industry. The highest point is Macgillicuddy's Reeks in Kerry (3,414 feet *1,040 metres*) and Ireland also contains, the longest river in the British Isles, the Shannon (250 miles *531 kilometres*).

Above **This is a view of the famous O'Connell Street in Dublin named after a former Lord Mayor of the City – Daniel O'Connell, who agitated for Catholic emancipation.**

Above **The City Hall, Belfast, the capital of Northern Ireland, has a most impressive setting.**

Right **Here are the docks at Northern Ireland's largest port, Belfast. Most of its exports, which consist mainly of potatoes and processed foodstuffs, are despatched from here.**

The landscape of Britain

Within the quite small area of land covered by the British Isles is a great variety of landscape and plant life. The most important thing to remember about it is that large parts of it are man-made. Except for the permanent features like mountains, lakes and rivers, nature has been tamed by man over a period of hundreds of years. This does not apply to the wilder areas, particularly in Scotland and Wales, but it is true of the places in which many people live and work, whether in industrial England or the quiet farmlands of the south.

The character of the land in prehistoric times was changed during the Ice Ages, which destroyed much of the existing vegetation. The exact causes of the Ice Ages are not known, but the whole of the British Isles, in common with most of northern Europe, was covered with sheets of ice as far south as the Thames and Avon valleys. At this time, the coasts of Britain were joined with those of Europe across the Channel and the North Sea and many plants migrated across the dry land from the mainland continent.

Before man evolved on earth, the British Isles was covered by vast tracts of forestland, and the nature of the plant life then was again changed by man's shaping of the land. Plants which thrived in forests and swamps were replaced by those which found the new landscape suited their needs. The flora of Britain would again be affected if man's cultivation of the land were to cease.

There are about 1,700 species of flowering plants which grow wild in the British Isles. This is not such a great number compared with some other countries of roughly the same size, and fossil remains of plants dug out of the ground show that Britain's flora used to be richer. The most important factors which control the growth of plants are rainfall and temperature. There are some plants, like daisies, which will grow almost anywhere, while others will only survive where the conditions are right for them.

The surface of the land is made up

Above **A typical collection of wild flowers found in Britain: daffodils, daisies, harebells and orchids.**

Left **The majestic sweep of the Welsh coastline, seen here, is one of the most beautiful stretches around the shores of Britain.**

Above **A woodland scene in Wales.**

Right **A typical Cotswold village scene.**

16

of rock and practically every important type of rock can be found in Britain. The oldest rock is in the north-west of Scotland and is over 2,500 million years old, whereas the sand and clay found in East Anglia may be less than a million years old.

The landscape of England is full of charm and beauty, its variety of small-scale scenes ranging from the bleak moors of Yorkshire to the rolling downlands of Sussex. Despite the demands of modern farming, which have tended to combine small farms and small fields into larger units, and of industrial development, there are still large areas of England where villages, woods and beauty spots, remain unchanged.

Some of the most beautiful parts of the British Isles are in Scotland, where there are large areas of mountainous, unspoiled and breathtaking country. Wales is also a mountainous country with wind-swept coasts and deserted beaches. Its most magnificent scenery is to be found in the north around the heights of Mount Snowdon. The Emerald Isle of Ireland has two very distinct coastlines – the gentler east coast which faces Britain, while on the west there are rugged cliffs and inlets pounded by the Atlantic Ocean. Between these two coastlines is a soft, green country with uncrowded roads.

Below **Pine trees by the edge of a Scottish loch. The Highlands of Scotland are famed throughout the world for their beauty and are a great attraction for anglers and mountaineers.**

Above **Cornwall is a land of fishermen. This is Polperro, a typical Cornish fishing village on the south coast.**

Below **Here are some of the best-known plants found in Scotland: harebells, heather and thistles.**

Right **The English countryside offers a great variety of styles. In general, it is less rugged than Wales and Scotland. Although it has a large plain in the East and a ridge of hills known as the Pennine Chain, England's countryside is loved for its gentle rolling hills and vales. The picture shows a representative view of rural England with its trees, green grass, hills and a village dominated by the tower of the parish church.**

The pictures on this page show a fallow deer (1) which has a spotted coat. The spots help to camouflage it in the open woodland where it lives. Next to it is the red deer (2), an inhabitant of the forests of North America, Asia and Europe. The grey squirrel (3) has almost ousted the red squirrel from many parts of Britain. The badger (4) lives in a set, like a burrow, and feeds on fruits, roots and insects. The fox (5) is a stealthy night hunter feeding mainly on voles and mice. The otter (6) is a water mammal with webbed feet and a thick tail.

Animals in Britain

Mammals. There are about 50 species of mammals in the British Isles and many of them have been introduced to this country from abroad during the last 100 years. The largest wild mammal is the red deer, which is found mostly in the Scottish Highlands and the north of England. Other deer are the native roe deer, which lives in woodlands and forests, and the fallow deer, which was brought into this country – possibly by the Romans – and is now common in parks and ornamental grounds, where it lives in semi-tame herds.

Other familiar mammals are badgers, otters, hedgehogs, moles, rabbits and shrews. Among the rodents are squirrels, mice, voles and rats. Carnivores, or flesh-eating mammals, include the rare pine marten and the wild cat, and the common red fox, stoat and weasel. There are a number of different types of bats, and among the mammals which live in and around the sea are seals, whales, dolphins and porpoises.

Reptiles and Amphibians. There are two harmless snakes in the British Isles, the ringed or grass snake and the smooth snake. The adder, or viper, has a poisonous bite, although few people are known to have died from it. The common lizard is found all over Britain, whereas the slow-worm and sand lizard prefer dry, open country.

Here are the weasel (7) a nocturnal hunter. The wild cat (8), now rare in Britain, is larger than the domestic variety and feeds on small mammals. In autumn, the jay (9) is very busy collecting its acorns and burying them in the ground. The robin (10) is a friendly bird but during the breeding season, one male will attack another found in its territory. The hare (11) is a solitary mammal but the rabbit (12) lives with others in warrens. The toad (13) secretes an irritating substance in its back which it gives off when attacked. The trout (14) and salmon (15) are both freshwater fish found in many British rivers.

Various newts, toads and frogs make up the number of amphibians, which can live on land or in water.

Birds. The climate of the British Isles is moderate compared with many other parts of the world, since it does not reach the extremes of heat and cold. This makes the islands a popular place for birds in which to live and breed. There are over 200 species to be found, although many of them are migrants which breed in the British Isles but fly to warmer lands for the winter, returning in the spring and summer.

Many of the woodland and garden birds, such as the blackbird, robin and thrush, are common in all areas. The house sparrow, perhaps the most familiar of all birds, has become almost a nuisance, so closely does it live to man and share his environment. Other birds select their breeding grounds carefully and can only be found in particular parts of the country. Some of the most attractive birds, both in appearance and in the beauty of their flight, are those which live on rocky coasts and cliffs, such as the guillemot, cormorant and herring gull.

Insects. The most numerous of all animals in the British Isles, and indeed in the world, are insects. It has been estimated that there are over 500,000 species of insects in the world and of these about 20,000 can be found in and around Britain. The most attractive of them are the butterflies, moths and dragonflies. Although all insects in the islands are practically harmless to man, most people fear and dislike

them. This is particularly true of cockroaches, beetles, flies, wasps and ants. Many insects, of course, do cause damage to crops and in the home and are rightly regarded as pests for this reason.

Spiders, which exist in the British Isles in great numbers and variety, are not true insects but belong to the family called arachnids.

Fishes. In many ways the greatest assortment of animal life is to be found in the sea creatures which live around the shores of the British Isles. There are also large numbers of freshwater fish which live in rivers and provide man with food and sport.

Right **Here we see Julius Caesar landing in Britain in 54 BC after he had made a brief reconnaissance trip the year before. The picture shows Caesar's main invasion when he came with five legions and a fleet of 800 ships. When Britain became a Roman colony the Romans brought with them many of the advantages of their civilisation and Britons gained the privilege of Roman citizenship.**

Britain and the ancient world

The nations of Europe have their roots in the ancient world. Their culture, laws, customs and behaviour have direct links with the past. In Britain these links are with the many people from other lands who invaded the islands at different times and, having conquered, stayed to become absorbed into the native population. In this way, people in Britain are a mixture of many races – Iberian, Celtic, Roman, Saxon and Viking.

When the great civilisations of Egypt and Mesopotamia were at their height, Britain was still living in the Stone Age, and her people practised a simple form of farming using flint and stone implements. Not until settlers arrived from the continent of Europe was there any knowledge of metals. Remains of monuments such as Stonehenge and Avebury built during this period, as the Stone Age advanced into the Bronze Age, can still be seen in Britain today.

Being an island race, the inhabitants of Britain have always been traders and sea-farers. Apart from the continental settlers the first people to reach her shores were the Phoenicians from the eastern shores of the Mediterranean. They traded in tin, found in the Scilly Isles and southern England, gold and pearls.

About 500 BC, during the Iron Age, Celtic people from Gaul (present-day Belgium and France) invaded Britain. They are described by Julius Caesar in

Below **Long after Caesar's invasions, Hadrian was the Roman emperor and Aulus Platorius Nepos was the governor of Britain. About AD 120 there was a revolt of northern tribes in Britain and Hadrian ordered the building of a boundary wall which was to stretch from the River Tyne to the Solway. The wall was manned by troops from about AD 124 until 383.**

Right **Bronze Age people** are seen here in one of their primitive settlements. They are so named because instead of using flints for tools and weapons, they used bronze, often hammering it into shape without heat. The Bronze Age in Britain lasted from about 2000–500 BC.

Below **Here** we see ancient **Phoenicians** trading. They settled in parts of those lands known as Syria, Lebanon and Israel about 3000 BC. The Phoenicians were a truly great people. They were wonderful colonisers and seafarers and had a love of culture. They were so skilled in navigation and commerce that they established sea trading routes right round the coast of Africa as far as the Red Sea. It is said they also traded with Britain.

his book *The Conquest of Gaul* after his two brief invasions of Britain in 55 and 54 BC. The real conquest of Britain began in AD 43 and the influences of the Roman Empire, of which Britain was a part until the barbarians invaded Europe in the 5th century, had a lasting effect on these islands.

Great events in British History

500 BC Celtic people from Gaul (now Belgium and France) migrate to Britain
300 BC Pytheas the Greek probably voyaged to Britain
55 BC First expedition to Britain by Julius Caesar
54 BC Second expedition to Britain by Julius Caesar
AD 43 Roman emperor Claudius sends expedition to Britain under the general Aulus Plautius
61 Britons under Queen Boadicea rebel against the Romans but are defeated
78 Julius Agricola appointed Roman governor of Britain
122 The emperor Hadrian visits Britain
122–27 Hadrian's Wall is built across Britain from the Tyne to the Solway to keep out the northern tribes
211 The emperor Severus visits Britain and dies at York
285 Carausius, Roman commander of British Fleet, proclaims himself Emperor of Britain
303 Martyrdom of St. Alban
410 Roman legions withdrawn from Britain to protect Rome. Soon after this the Jutes, Angles and Saxons begin to invade Britain and settle
449 Supposed landing in Kent of the Jutish chiefs, Hengist and Horsa
500 Saxon kingdom of Wessex founded
530 A Romano/British war leader, the supposed 'King Arthur', wages war against the invaders
563 St. Columba establishes his mission on the island of Iona
597 Landing of St. Augustine in Kent, sent by Pope Gregory to convert the English to Christianity
664 The Synod of Whitby, which allies the church in England to Rome

770 Offa's Dyke, named after the King of Mercia, is built as a defence against the Welsh
825 Wessex defeats Mercia at the Battle of Ellandun
828 Egbert of Wessex recognised as overlord of all England
844 Kenneth MacAlpine becomes first King of Scotland
850–80 The period of successive Danish invasions and victories
855 The Danes winter in the Isle of Sheppy
871 Ethelred defeats the Danes at Battle of Ashdown Hill. He dies, and is succeeded by Alfred the Great
878 Alfred defeats Guthrum, the Danish leader, and the Treaty of Wedmore is signed
883 Winchester becomes the capital city of England
901 Alfred dies and is succeeded by Edward the Elder
960 Dunstan becomes Archbishop of Canterbury
980 Renewal of Danish raids on England
1007 The Danes are paid large sums of money to stop them attacking England
1013 Sweyn, the Danish king, is acknowledged as King of England
1014 Brian Boru defeats great army of Norsemen in Ireland
1016 Canute, Sweyn's son, becomes King of England
1040 Duncan, King of the Scots, is murdered by Macbeth, who takes the crown
1042 Edward the Confessor, son of Ethelred the Unready, becomes King of England. Later, he names William of Normandy as his successor
1053 Harold, son of Godwin, becomes Earl of Wessex
1064 Harold pays homage to William of Normandy

1066 Harold becomes King of England. He defeats the forces of Norway at the Battle of Stamford Bridge. William of Normandy invades England and defeats Harold at the Battle of Hastings. William becomes king
1067 The Tower of London built
1069 Beginning of the feudal system in England
1070 Lanfranc becomes Archbishop of Canterbury and starts reform of the church
1072 Hereward the Wake submits to the Normans after his unsuccessful rebellion
1086 Survey of all land and buildings in Britain for tax purposes is completed and published in the Domesday Book
1093 Anselm becomes Archbishop of Canterbury
1095 Proclamation of the First Crusade
1099 Crusaders capture Jerusalem
1135 Stephen is crowned King of England. Civil war in England between Stephen and Matilda
1138 The Battle of the Standard, in which the Scots, invading on behalf of Matilda, are defeated by the English
1154 Nicholas Breakspear is elected pope as Adrian IV, the only Englishman to have filled this office. Henry Plantagenet becomes Henry II of England
1162 Thomas Becket becomes Archbishop of Canterbury
1166 The Assize of Clarendon sets up a jury system and the rule of 'Common Law' begins in England
1170 Thomas Becket murdered in Canterbury Cathedral
1187 Saladin captures Jerusalem from the Crusaders
1190 Richard I sets out on Third Crusade
1215 The signing of Magna Carta by King John. This lessened the king's power

Above **William the Conqueror, victor of the Battle of Hastings rides into London.**

Below **Joan of Arc, condemned to death by the English, bravely meets her death in Rouen.**

1258 At the Great Council of Oxford, Simon de Montfort imposes the Barons' will on Henry III. Civil war follows
1264 Battle of Lewes: Henry III defeated by Simon de Montfort
1265 Parliament sits at Westminster. Simon de Montfort killed at the Battle of Evesham
1284 Edward I conquers Wales
1290 Expulsion of Jews from England
1295 Model Parliament summoned by Edward I
1297 William Wallace defeats the English at the Battle of Stirling Bridge during Scottish struggle for independence
1298 Wallace defeated at Battle of Falkirk
1306 Robert Bruce is crowned King of Scotland
1314 Battle of Bannockburn. Robert Bruce defeats Edward II
1337 Hundred Years' War between England and France begins
1346 Battle of Crecy
1347 Calais captured by the English
1348–9 The Black Death
1356 Battle of Poitiers
1381 The Peasants' Revolt in which Wat Tyler is killed
1384 Death of John Wyclif, the religious reformer
1399 Death of John of Gaunt
1400 Owen Glendower rebels against the English and the battle for Welsh independence begins
1403 Death of Sir Henry Percy, 'Hotspur', at the Battle of Shrewsbury during rebellion of the Percy family
1415 Henry V invades France, takes Harfleur and wins Battle of Agincourt
1429 Siege of Orleans
1431 Joan of Arc is executed at Rouen
1450 Defeat of Jack Cade's rebellion
1455 Wars of the Roses between the rival Houses of York (white rose) and Lancaster (red rose)
1476 William Caxton sets up his printing press in England
1485 Battle of Bosworth Field. Richard III is killed. Henry Tudor becomes Henry VII
1487 Lambert Simnel's rebellion defeated. Court of Star Chamber established
1499 Perkin Warbeck, claimant to the throne, executed
1509 Accession of Henry VIII
1513 James IV of Scotland killed in the fighting at the Battle of Flodden Field between Scots and English
1514 Peace declared with France. Marriage of Mary, sister of Henry VIII, to Louis XII of France
1515 Wolsey becomes a cardinal and Lord Chancellor of England
1520 Meeting between Henry VIII and Francis I of France at the 'Field of the Cloth of Gold'
1526 Publication of Tyndale's translation of the New Testament
1529 Fall of Wolsey
1534 Henry VIII becomes head of the church in England and denies the authority of the Pope
1535 Execution of Sir Thomas More
1536 Union of England and Wales. The Pilgrimage of Grace, a Catholic revolt
1539 The great monasteries dissolved
1541 Henry VIII takes title of King of Ireland
1547 Death of Henry VIII
1549 The first Book of Common Prayer published
1553 Lady Jane Grey proclaimed queen by Protestants. Accession of Mary I
1554 Execution of Lady Jane Grey
1555 Protestant martyrs, Latimer, Ridley and Hooper, burned at the stake
1557 War with France

1558 Loss of Calais. Elizabeth I becomes Queen of England
1577 Drake starts voyage around the world
1587 Execution of Mary, Queen of Scots
1588 Defeat of Spanish Armada
1592 Presbyterian Church established in Scotland
1600 First charter granted to East India Company
1601 Earl of Essex executed
1603 Death of Elizabeth I. James VI of Scotland becomes James I of England and unites the two kingdoms
1605 Gunpowder Plot fails
1607 Virginia, first permanent British settlement at Jamestown
1611 First Authorised Version of the Bible
1616 Death of Shakespeare
1620 Voyage of the *Mayflower* to America with the Pilgrim Fathers
1629 Parliament is dissolved and Charles I governs country personally until 1640
1640 Parliament recalled
1642 Civil War between Charles and the Parliamentarians begins
1644 Battle of Marston Moor
1645 Battle of Naseby. Overwhelming victory of Cromwell's New Model Army
1649 Trial and execution of Charles I
1651 Charles II crowned at Scone in Scotland
1653 Three-day battle at sea between British and Dutch fleets
1657 Cromwell inaugurated as Lord Protector
1658 Death of Cromwell
1660 Restoration of monarchy with the return of Charles II
1665 The Great Plague
1666 Great Fire of London
1670 Hudson's Bay Company established
1678 The Popish Plot. Many Catholics put on trial
1679 *Habeas Corpus* Act, which makes it illegal to imprison anyone without trial
1685 Monmouth's rebellion ends with his defeat at the Battle of Sedgemoor. The Bloody Assize under Chief Justice Jeffreys
1688 William of Orange and his wife Mary accept the crown of England. James II flees to France
1689 Declaration of Rights establishes the rule of Parliament
1692 Massacre of Glencoe
1694 Bank of England established
1702 War declared against France and Spain. Marlborough commands in the Netherlands
1704 Battle of Blenheim
1707 The Act of Union with Scotland unites the two Parliaments and results in the United Kingdom of Great Britain
1708 Battle of Oudenarde
1709 Battle of Malplaquet
1711 Duke of Marlborough is dismissed from his commands
1713 The war between England and France ends with the signing of the Treaty of Utrecht

1715 Jacobite rising in Scotland and the north of England
1720 The financial scandal of the South Sea Bubble
1721 Sir Robert Walpole in effect the first Prime Minister of Great Britain
1739 John and Charles Wesley spread the message of the Methodist faith
1743 George II is present at the Battle of Dettingen against the French, the last English monarch to lead his troops in battle
1745 Prince Charles Edward Stuart lands in Scotland and leads the second Jacobite rebellion
1746 The rebellion ends with the defeat of Charles at the Battle of Culloden. Charles flees to France
1752 Reform of the calendar so that New Year starts on 1 January instead of 25 March
1756 The Black Hole of Calcutta
1757 Victory of Clive at the Battle of Plassey
1759 Capture of Quebec and death of General Wolfe
1760 Capture of Montreal and conquest of Canada completed
1768 Captain Cook's first voyage
1773 The 'Boston Tea Party'
1774 Warren Hastings becomes the first Governor-General of India
1775 American War of Independence
1776 Declaration of American Independence
1778 France intervenes in the war in America
1783 The Treaty of Versailles ends the American war and Britain recognises the United States
1788 Temporary insanity of George III. Regency Bill proclaimed
1789 French Revolution begins
1793 Britain goes to war with France
1797 Battle of St. Vincent. Mutinies at Nore and Spithead
1798 Battle of the Nile at which Nelson destroys French fleet
1799 Income Tax introduced as a 'temporary' wartime measure
1800 Parliaments of England and Ireland united by Act of Union
1801 Union Jack becomes the flag of the United Kingdom. First census of population taken
1805 Battles of Trafalgar and Austerlitz
1807 Slave Trade forbidden in Jamaica and on British ships
1808 Beginning of Peninsular War in Spain
1809 Battle of Corunna
1811 The Prince of Wales becomes Regent
1812 Britain at war with United States
1814 Congress of Vienna. Peace of Ghent between Britain and the United States
1815 Battle of Waterloo. Napoleon sent to St. Helena
1819 The 'Peterloo' massacre at Manchester
1820 Death of George III. Accession of George IV. Cato Street conspiracy
1832 First Reform Bill passed
1833 Factory Act forbids employment of children under nine

Right **The Battle of Waterloo lasted only one day in 1815 and Wellington's victory led to the abdication of Napoleon.**

Below **Scene from the Great Exhibition of 1851.**

1834 Tolpuddle Martyrs, first attempt to form trade union
1837 Accession of Victoria
1839 First Chartist petition calling for Parliamentary reforms
1840 Penny Post introduced
1841 New Zealand proclaimed independent colony
1845 Potato famine in Ireland
1851 The Great Exhibition opens in Hyde Park
1854-6 The Crimean War
1857 The Indian Mutiny begins
1867 Canada becomes self-governing
1869 Opening of the Suez Canal
1870 First Elementary Education Act. Irish Land Act
1875 Britain gains major interest in Suez Canal
1879 Zulu War
1882 Britain occupies Egypt. Married Women's Property Act
1885 Fall of Khartoum and murder of General Gordon

1886 Gladstone's Home Rule Bill defeated
1888 County Council Act establishes rule of local government
1891 Free elementary education established by Education Act
1892 Gladstone becomes Prime Minister for fourth and last time
1894 Parish councils created by Act of Parliament
1897 Diamond Jubilee of Queen Victoria
1898 Kitchener wins Battle of Omdurman and Sudan is conquered
1899 Beginning of the Boer War
1900 The Boxer Rising in China is crushed. Relief of Ladysmith and of Mafeking
1901 Australian constitution comes into force. Death of Queen Victoria
1902 End of Boer War
1910 Union of South Africa constituted

under the South Africa Act
1911 National Insurance Act
1914 Outbreak of First World War
1917 Balfour Declaration. Jewish National Home set up in Palestine
1918 Armistice signed to end First World War
1919 Treaty of Versailles between Allies and Germany
1920 League of Nations established
1922 British Protectorate in Egypt ends. BBC makes first regular broadcasts. Irish Free State established
1924 First Labour Government. British Empire Exhibition at Wembley
1926 General strike in Britain
1928 Women gain the vote on same terms as men
1931 British Dominions become sovereign states
1936 Abdication of Edward VIII who becomes Duke of Windsor

1938 Munich meeting between Hitler and Chamberlain
1939 Outbreak of Second World War
1940 British evacuate Dunkirk
1944 Allies invade the continent of Europe
1945 Second World War ends
1947 India and Pakistan become self-governing
1948 National Health Service introduced
1951 Festival of Britain
1952 Accession of Queen Elizabeth II
1965 Death of Winston Churchill
1969 Investiture of Prince of Wales

Below In 1940, British troops, in retreat from the German advance, were evacuated from Dunkirk in all kinds of boats.

Right **Map showing Egbert's kingdom in 827.**

Left **The statue of Alfred the Great commemorating the man who founded the English Navy and revised the laws of the country.**

Below **King Canute, surrounded by his court, has his feet made wet by the waves which refuse to obey him.**

Above **Egbert, who became the first king of a united England, is seen being crowned in the year 827.**

Left **Edward the Confessor is seen here at his devotions. He was a gentle, pious man whose authority was largely controlled by the powerful Earl Godwin.**

Kings and queens

In 827 the kingdoms of Wessex and Mercia were at war. Wessex won the battle and their king, Egbert, became 'the first king of England' in 828. This title is better applied to William I who took the country firmly under his control in 1066 after the Norman invasion. The monarchy in Britain has continued since that date until today, disturbed only by the Commonwealth Period, after the execution of Charles I, when Oliver Cromwell (1653–8) and his son Richard (1658–9) ruled Britain in succession with the title of Lord Protector. When Edward VI died in 1553, Lady Jane Grey was proclaimed queen by the Protestants, but she was never crowned.

Right **Saxon soldiers fight the invading Norman army at the Battle of Hastings in 1066. The death of Harold, caused by an arrow in the eye, sealed the future of England. William the Conqueror, seen above, was a brilliant soldier and a wise law-giver who soon set about bringing peace to the land.**

Left **Richard Coeur de Lion.**

Right **Henry VIII** and his wives – Catherine of Aragon, Anne Boleyn, Jane Seymour, Anne of Cleves, Catherine Howard and Catherine Parr.

Left **Charles I** and his son who later became Charles II.

Left below **Oliver Cromwell** who ruled England during the time of the Protectorate.

Below **Elizabeth I,** sometimes called Elizabeth the Great.

Bottom **Elizabeth II** being crowned in Westminster Abbey.

Kings and queens of England

Egbert	828–39
Ethelwulf	839–56
Ethelbald	856–60
Ethelbert	860–6
Ethelred	866–71
Alfred the Great	871–901
Edward the Elder	901–25
Athelstan	925–40
Edmund	940–6
Edred	946–55
Edwy	955–9
Edgar	959–75
Edward the Martyr	975–8
Ethelred the Unready	978–1016
Edmund Ironside	1016
Canute	1017–35
Harold I	1037–40
Hardicanute	1040–2
Edward the Confessor	1042–66
Harold II	1066
William I	1066–87
William II	1087–1100
Henry I	1100–35
Stephen	1135–54
Henry II	1154–89
Richard I	1189–99
John	1199–1216
Henry III	1216–72
Edward I	1272–1307
Edward II	1307–27
Edward III	1327–77
Richard II	1377–99
Henry IV	1399–1413
Henry V	1413–22
Henry VI	1422–61
Edward IV	1461–83
Edward V	1483
Richard III	1483–5
Henry VII	1485–1509
Henry VIII	1509–47
Edward VI	1547–53
Mary I	1553–8
Elizabeth I	1558–1603

Kings and queens of Great Britain

James I	1603–25
Charles I	1625–49
Charles II	1660–85
James II	1685–8
William III and Mary II	1689–94
William III	1694–1702
Anne	1702–14
George I	1714–27
George II	1727–60
George III	1760–1820
George IV	1820–30
William IV	1830–7
Victoria	1837–1901
Edward VII	1901–10
George V	1910–36
Edward VIII	1936
George VI	1936–52
Elizabeth II	1952–

Below left **Queen Anne**

Below **King George VI** who led his people through the Second World War (1939–45)

Government in Britain

In the early days of Britain's history the king governed the country himself, with a small body of advisers. Over the years a system of government has developed which has seen a gradual decrease in the power of the king and an increase in the power of the people. The laws which govern the United Kingdom today are made by Parliament, which consists of the House of Commons, the House of Lords, and the reigning king or queen. Members of the House of Commons are chosen by the people at elections held at least every five years. Members of the House of Lords have inherited their right to sit there or have been appointed for life. The king or queen has no real power today but always gives new Acts of Parliament the 'Royal Assent'.

Above **Sir Robert Walpole** who became the first British Prime Minister in 1721.

Above **King John**, who was forced by the barons in 1215 to sign Magna Carta. This was a document which said that the king was not above the law and had a duty to rule with the advice of his nobles. After the death of Oliver Cromwell parliament had to admit that the three-fold structure of Sovereign, Lords and Commons was too deeply rooted to be destroyed.

Centre **King John's seal on Magna Carta.**

Above **The Queen on her throne in the House of Lords reading her speech at the State Opening of Parliament.**

Below **Sir Winston Churchill.**

Right **This picture shows two Yeomen of the Guard** – often called beefeaters – who have their origins in Elizabethan days. Before the State Opening of Parliament each year, the beefeaters make a ceremonial inspection of the Houses of Parliament to ensure that no traitors are lurking there. Normally, the beefeaters are to be found at the Tower of London and are a great attraction to visitors to Britain.

Mr. Ian MacArthur (Perth and East Perthshire): No.

Mr. Mackintosh: I am quoting from a Government publication which I have here, and I shall now give the figures to support what I say.

Mr. Brewis rose——

Hon. Members: Sit down.

Mr. Mackintosh: The supporting figures show that wages in Scotland in 1960 stood at 91·6 per cent. of the United Kingdom average and went up by 1969 to 97·2 per cent. Unemployment, which had been running at twice the United Kingdom average, fell to 1½ times. Thus, during this period, the latter part of the 1960s, the key point is that Scotland did better than the other development areas.

Above **Hansard is a record of all parliamentary debates.**

Right **A man recording his vote.**

Below **The Chancellor of the Exchequer makes his economic proposals.**

SMITH.A.L. (CON)
WALKER.D (LAB)
BULL.J.T. (LIB)
MOORE.S (IND)

Above **The House of Commons.**

Right **The Houses of Parliament.**

Left **The Mace which rests in front of the Speaker – that is, the chairman – when the House is in session.**

British Empire and Commonwealth

The driving forces which led to the formation of the British Empire were the British love of the sea, a spirit of adventure and an eagerness for trade. In 1600 the merchants of London collected £30,000 and secured a charter from Queen Elizabeth I to found the East India Company. Several trading companies were formed during this period, the most successful being the East India Company. To protect their interests, forces were sent to the various countries with which Britain was trading and a struggle for power began.

In India this struggle for trading posts was mainly between Britain and France. The French tried to drive the rival British out of India by forming friendships with the Indian princes. In the 18th century Robert Clive led a small British force to victory against overwhelming odds and captured the city of Arcot. In another part of India the British fortified Calcutta against possible attack by the French. The city was captured by the Nabob of Bengal and Clive was sent to relieve Calcutta. Again he achieved victory against a mighty Indian army with a force of only 3,000 men.

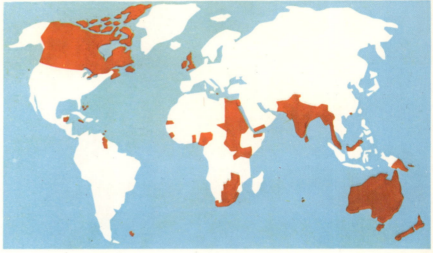

Top **The proclamation of Victoria as Empress of India.**

Above **Map to show the British Empire at its greatest extent during Queen Victoria's reign.**

Below **To show the greatness of Britain, the Great Exhibition was held in 1851 at Joseph Paxton's Crystal Palace, a building of glass and iron set up in Hyde Park, London. In 1854 the Crystal Palace was moved to Sydenham Hill.**

In 1773 Warren Hastings, one of the founders of the British Empire, became the first Governor-General of India. By the middle of the 19th century Britain had control over most of the sub-continent.

The early settlements in America were founded by Englishmen seeking to escape religious persecution in the 17th century.

Canada was won for Britain by battle, again with the French, who had founded New France to the north of the British settlements, and also a colony to the south in Louisiana. The French wished to unite their two settlements but to do this it was necessary to drive the English out. The English suffered many defeats until, in 1759, General Wolfe captured Quebec. This led to the taking of Montreal and finally, in September 1760, the Governor-General of French Canada also surrendered.

Captain Cook played his part in the formation of the British Empire

Below **In the 18th century, the British and French fought for supremacy in India and later, in 1857, the Indians mutinied. This is a picture of Delhi being stormed.**

during the 18th century. He explored and mapped Newfoundland, Labrador and New Zealand. When he landed on the east coast of Australia he named the land New South Wales and claimed it for Britain. Cook also discovered some of the smaller islands of the Pacific. Later, other Englishmen settled in parts of Africa.

At the end of the 18th century the American colonies united and broke away from Britain in favour of self-government. Thomas Jefferson, on 4th July, 1776, read to Congress the famous Declaration of Independence, while George Washington was appointed Commander-in-Chief of the forces which finally defeated the British in 1781.

Canadian colonists then became discontented and the British North America Act of 1867 set up provincial governments. During the next 50 years the constitutions of other countries in the Empire were reviewed and amended. After the First World War the relationship between Britain and the Dominions was clearly defined. Countries were free to govern themselves and, if they chose, to leave the Commonwealth. Those countries which remain in association with Britain today do so upon the foundation of trade and friendship.

Top **Here are some Commonwealth imports into Britain.**

Centre **The Queen surrounded by some of the Commonwealth Prime Ministers including President Kenyatta of Kenya, Mrs Indira Ghandi and Mr Edward Heath.**

Left **A scene from the Commonwealth Games.**

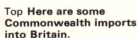

The British Commonwealth of Nations had its beginning when Canada ceased to be a colony and assumed Dominion status in 1867. Since then, most of the British colonies have become independent, self-governing members of the British Commonwealth.

Britain in the modern world

Economic depression at the end of the old colonial empire, a rise in power outside Europe, and two world wars helped to sap Britain's strength.

Although she is no longer a world power in the sense that she once was, Britain still has an important part to play in the making of history.

In an age of technology Britain's engineers and scientists often lead the world in the discovery of new techniques. Unable to afford a space programme of her own, British craftsmen are responsible for the manufacture of many components that go into spacecraft. Her universities are among the greatest in the world and one of her largest 'exports' is the brain power developed there.

Today, Britain is pulling away from her old ties and moving closer to Europe, believing that her future strength will lie in a united continent.

Below Many new colleges have been built recently in Britain – like Leicester University shown here.

Below Britain's gas-cooled nuclear power station at Windscale, Cumberland.

Below centre **The VTOL Hawker Siddeley Harrier, an example of Britain's advanced technology.**

Save the Children Fund

help OXFAM fight

hunger and disease

Although Britain is losing many of her old ties with countries abroad, she still gives economic aid to under-developed lands where living standards are much lower than in the West.

Such organisations as Oxfam and Save the Children Fund have been set up so that people in Britain can make their own personal contributions towards helping the sick and needy.

SUMMARY

The Mysterious Universe

Look into the sky on a clear night, and what do you see? Little pin-pricks of light that are some of the millions of stars in the universe. No one knows how many there are, but the universe is so enormous that it will always be mysterious. Even today, when man can travel in space, we have only scratched the surface of the mystery. A journey to the moon is like a few paces compared with the distance from the earth to the closest star.

When you look at the sky through a telescope, or read what scientists tell you about the universe, two things will amaze you: size and distance. The heavens are filled with a countless number of stars, and astronomers using radio telescopes have detected objects in outer space millions of miles away. There seems no end to the size of the universe or to the distance

of objects from the Earth.

To all of us who live on it, the Earth is a large place. One man seems a tiny creature on its surface. Yet the Earth is only a small part of the system of planets and satellites which circle the Sun. And the Sun itself is like a speck of dust in the great void of space.

It is very easy to fall into the trap of thinking that the Earth is at the centre of things, and very natural, since our world is important to us. But in fact the solar system to which the Earth belongs is a tiny part of a star system, or galaxy, called the Milky Way, which contains about 100,000 million stars. And the Milky Way is just one of a million, million galaxies in the universe.

It is difficult to understand or have any real picture of the great distances in space if they are written in ordinary

Right **The elliptical orbit of Halley's Comet. The small white dot on the left represents the earth.**

Below right **How Halley's Comet appeared to the earth. Sir Edmund Halley, who lived at the same time as Newton, felt that a comet must travel on an elliptical course. He noticed that the comet of 1682 was similar to those of 1607 and 1531 and guessed that it was the same one making return visits. His prediction that it would appear in 1759 was proved correct. Halley's Comet is due to be seen again in 1986.**

Below **Our galaxy of stars, of which the sun is a member, is only one of an infinite number of galaxies in the universe. This picture shows how they vary in shape. Some are spiral or elliptical while others are quite irregular.**

Above **A simple diagram showing how insignificant man is in relation to the rest of the universe. He is a creature of the earth (1) which is part of the solar system (2). This is in its turn a part of our galaxy of stars (3). And this is just one of the infinite number of galaxies in the whole of the universe (4).**

Below **An eclipse of the sun. This has been caused because the moon has passed in front of the sun, hiding it from view. The bottom picture shows an eclipse of the moon caused when the earth is between the sun and the moon, thus cutting off the reflection of the sun's light from the moon. Most eclipses are partial as total ones are very rare. Eclipses do not occur every month as the plane of the moon's path is slightly different from the earth's.**

Facts about stars. The total number of stars that can be seen with the naked eye on a clear night is from 2–6,000. Although there are too many stars in the heavens to count, most of the universe consists of empty space. The largest star to be measured is *Epsilon Aurigae*, which is 2,500 million miles, *4,000 million kilometres* across. The nearest star to Earth (excepting the Sun, which is a star) is *Proxima Centauri*, about four light-years away. The brightest star is *Sirius* in the constellation Canis Major. Stars shine by their own light and vary in colour from whitish-blue to shades of red. The colours are very faint and not easily seen.

words or figures. For this reason astronomers use another form of measurement, based on the speed of light, which travels at about 186,000 miles, *300,000 kilometres* per second or about 6 million, million miles, *9½ million, million kilometres* in a year. This unit is called a light-year and it is simpler to express distances in it. For example, the Great Galaxy in Andromeda, which is the most remote heavenly body that can be seen with the naked eye, is about 2,200,000 light-years distant from the Earth.

The speed of light sounds very fast, and indeed it is. You cannot see light travelling in the same way that you can see a car travelling but, just as it takes a car a certain period of time to get from one city to another, so light takes time to travel from an object to your eye. This is just as true of things seen over very short distances as it is for the faraway stars. In this sense you are always 'seeing' into the past. Which makes the picture of the universe even more mysterious, since no one can ever see it as it is – only as it used to be a number of light-years ago.

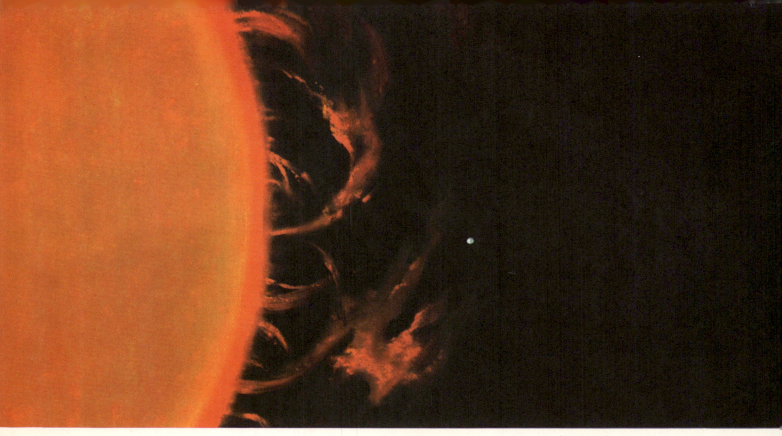

Sun, Moon and Earth

The Sun is at the centre of all things in our solar system. Its light and heat give life to everything on Earth. Without it there would always be night on our planet and we should all die from the cold.

Although it is so important to us, the Sun is just another star, like thousands of millions of other stars. If the Sun and the whole solar system it supports were to vanish, the effect on the universe would be no more than if a small star had ceased to shine. Like any other star, the Sun will not remain bright for ever. Gradually, it is cooling down, and in billions and billions of years it will die out altogether.

All the planets probably began life as swirling clouds of gas and dust. The Earth has cooled down so that parts of it have become solid rock and water, but the Sun is still a mass of hot, glowing gases. Its temperature is about 6,000° C. on the surface, from which great flames of gases shoot out, sometimes for hundreds of thousands of miles. Sun-spots, which were first observed by Galileo in 1610, are cooler areas which move about on the Sun's surface and show up as dark spots.

Below **The ancient Egyptians and the Aztecs were sun worshippers. The Egyptian sun god Ra stands before an Aztec temple to the sun.**

36

Right **It is now possible to take photographs of the earth from satellites in space. The accuracy of this map of the Middle East showing Aden and the Red Sea is demonstrated by a photograph of the same area.**

More is known about the Earth than any other heavenly body.

It is not a true sphere but is slightly flattened at the north and south poles. Around the equator it measures 24,902 miles, *40,075 kilometres*, while around the poles it is 24,860 miles, *39,908 kilometres*. Its mass, or weight, is nearly 6 thousand, million, million, million tons, *tonnes*. Surrounding the Earth is an atmosphere of gases which extends for hundreds of miles. The Earth rotates once on its axis in slightly less than 24 hours, and revolves around the sun once a year, a distance of 600 million miles, *960 million kilometres*, at a speed of $18\frac{1}{2}$ miles, *29·7 kilometres* per second. The Earth has no light of its own but is lit on one side by the Sun. As the Earth rotates on its axis from west to east the Sun seems to move from east to west.

Left **A familiar view of the surface of the moon as seen through a telescope.**

Below **This dramatic shot shows the earth rising above the horizon of the moon.**

Bottom **This diagram shows how the moon, rotating round the Earth, causes its own eclipse and the eclipse of the sun.**

Earth's nearest neighbour is the Moon. In the vastness of space, it is just across the street, a mere 216,420 miles, *348,291 kilometres* away when it is closest to Earth. It moves around the Earth, not in a circle but in an oval-shaped path called an ellipse, which means that its distance from the earth varies according to its position. Because the Moon rotates on its axis in about the same time as it takes to go round the Earth, it always keeps roughly the same face turned towards us.

The surface of the Moon is covered with enormous plains, which are called seas because early astronomers thought they were filled by water. There are great mountain ranges and the ground is strewn with rocks. The best-known features of the Moon are its craters, which were most likely caused either by rocks bombarding the Moon or by volcanic action.

Because it is smaller than the Earth, the Moon's gravity is much less, and astronauts on the Moon have found they weigh only one-sixth of their normal weight. The Moon has no atmosphere, no sound and no life. It is very hot in daytime (more than 100° C.) and very cold at night (150° C. below zero).

Since man landed successfully on the Moon, many of the astronomers' theories about it have been proved right. But those who look upon the Moon from afar as a romantic place now know that it is – as the first astronauts discovered – a cold, dead world of black dust and silence.

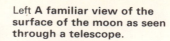

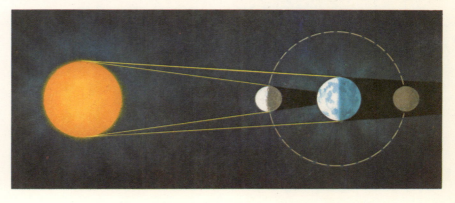

The solar system

The mysterious force of gravity keeps us all firmly on the surface of the Earth, so that we do not 'fall off'. The same force from their central Sun holds the family of planets together in their orbits. There are nine planets in the system, including the Earth, with their moons or satellites, as well as asteroids, comets and meteors.

Asteroids are minor planets, most of which circle the Sun somewhere between Mars and Jupiter. Comets are made up of gases and solid metallic pieces, which develop a 'tail' when they approach the Sun as they travel through space. Meteors are very small pieces of matter which move round the Sun in swarms.

In all this swirling mass of matter the only place where life is known to exist is on Earth. This and the fact that the Sun and stars appear to circle the Earth led to the early belief that the Earth was at the centre of the heavens. It was only in the 16th century that scientists recognised the Sun to be at the centre of the solar system. Our family of planets is only a small unit in a universe which may contain other similar systems.

Above **The nine planets of the solar system are shown in scale with one another and in relation to the sun around which they circle. They are (1) Pluto (farthest from the sun); (2) Neptune; (3) Uranus; (4) Saturn; (5) Jupiter; (6) Mars; (7) Earth; (8) Venus; (9) Mercury (nearest the sun).**

Left **Ptolemy, an astronomer who lived in the 2nd century AD, believed the earth to be the centre of the universe. This diagram illustrates his theory.**

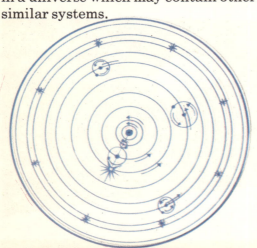

Below **Ancient Egyptian drawings showed the goddess Nut stretched across the sky.**

The nearest planet to the Sun is Mercury, which is also the smallest in the solar system. It has one side always turned towards the Sun and the other facing away in constant darkness. For this reason it is at the same time the hottest and the coldest planet.

Venus is about the same size as the Earth and comes closer to us than any other planet. Little is known of its surface because it is surrounded by clouds which reflect sunlight and make it one of the brightest objects in the sky.

Mars, or the 'red' planet, has very little atmosphere and astronomers have been able to make quite detailed photographs of its surface. These show canyon complexes and evidence of dust drifts formed by frequent dust storms. There are also icy white patches at its north and south poles which are a mixture of dry ice and water vapour.

Jupiter is the largest planet, about ten times larger across than the Earth. Its surface has distinct mark-

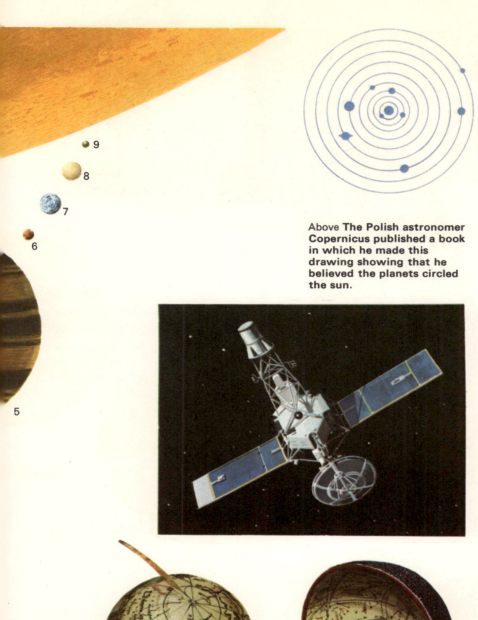

9

8

7

6

5

Above **The Polish astronomer Copernicus published a book in which he made this drawing showing that he believed the planets circled the sun.**

ings, including a curious red spot, which moves at different speeds as it rotates. Because of this it is believed to be made up mostly of gassy clouds surrounding a solid central body.

The most familiar and beautiful planet is Saturn, with its rings. These are made up of millions of small rocks and other fragments which circle round the planet and have never formed themselves into proper satellites. The rings can only be seen through a telescope, although the planet itself appears in the sky as a bright star.

The last planet which can sometimes be seen with the naked eye is Uranus. It is about four times as large as the Earth and appears in the sky as a very faint star. Like most of the planets it has a number of satellites which revolve around it.

The other two planets, Neptune and Pluto, can only be seen through a telescope. Neptune, because it is so far from the sun, moves very slowly in its orbit around the mother star. It was discovered in 1846 and will not complete its circuit and be back at the position where it was first observed until the year 2011.

The most mysterious planet in our solar system is Pluto, discovered as recently as 1930. Its orbit around the Sun takes about 250 years. It may be that Pluto is not the last planet in our 'family', although the discovery of new planets would be very difficult, even with powerful modern telescopes.

Above **In the centre of the page is a drawing of the spacecraft *Mariner II*, which the Americans launched from Cape Canaveral in 1962 to make observations of the planet Venus. Below this are examples of terrestrial and celestial globes. Terrestrial globes are maps of the earth's surface projected on to a globe, while celestial globes – which were made much earlier than terrestrial ones – perform the same function in mapping the position of heavenly bodies in the sky. The particular globe of the earth shown opens up to reveal a celestial one inside it.**

Below **This is a mechanical device called an orrery which illustrates the movements of the planets and their moons in the solar system.**

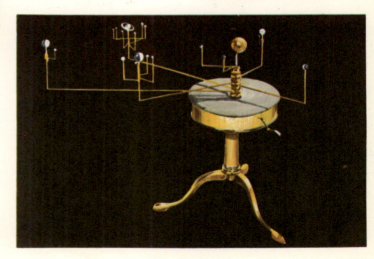

Astronomy

Man has studied the stars since the beginning of his time on earth. Even primitive man must have looked up into the heavens and been influenced by what he saw. In the ancient world the stars were supposed to govern men's lives. The horoscopes of early astrologers are echoed today in newspapers and magazines which tell their readers what experiences await them each week under their sign of the zodiac. The twelve constellations of the zodiac, which form the path of the sun as it appears to cross the sky, are very ancient.

Astrology led to astronomy, and it was often difficult to separate the two. This was particularly so in China where the first astronomers were very important people. They were called upon to make forecasts of such things as an eclipse of the sun, and if they made a mistake in their predictions they were condemned to death.

The ancient Greeks from the time of Thales of Miletus, a philosopher who lived in the 6th century BC, began to look at the universe scientifically. Euclid invented geometry; Eratosthenes measured the distance round the earth; and Hipparchus, the first real astronomer, made a close study of the heavens and established the position of over 850 stars.

After the Greeks, the Arabs took up astronomy. According to their religion all true believers must kneel and face in the direction of Mecca, the sacred city of Arabia, when they pray. One of the most important reasons why Arabic astronomy developed was to establish the geographical position of Mecca for the faithful, wherever they were in the world.

Modern astronomy began with

Nicolas Copernicus, a Polish astronomer who lived from 1473 to 1543. It was he who first demonstrated that the sun was at the centre of the solar system and not the earth, as had been previously believed. Tycho Brahe, a Danish scientist, who also lived in the 16th century, became so famous that the king of Denmark built him the finest observatory in the world on an island near Copenhagen, and called it the City of the Heavens.

But the most famous name in the history of early astronomy was that of Galileo, who died in 1642. Although he did not invent the telescope, Galileo was the first man to make proper use of it, and in 1609 he became the first person to see an object in the sky as it really was. When he published his astonishing discoveries about the universe he was put on trial by the pope, who said that his views were against the teaching of the church.

Another genius who devoted his life to science was Isaac Newton 1642–1727, who is remembered for the story of the falling apple in his garden, which is supposed to have set his mind thinking about the problems of gravitation. He probably did more than any other man to show that astronomy is a science based on scientific reasoning. He invented the principle of the reflecting telescope, which is now used in the world's largest optical telescopes.

Today, astronomers reach far beyond the range of ordinary telescopes which 'see' into the heavens. Radio telescopes, which receive radio waves from bodies in outer space, were first experimented with in the 1930s. The principle of the original bowl-type radio telescope has now been developed into new types which use many aerials and extend over large areas.

On these two pages, we see Sir Isaac Newton (1) whose work contributed much to science. In 1668, he made the first effective reflecting telescope (2) for observing the heavens. The orrery (3) was an apparatus for representing the motions of the planets and at (4) we see an armillary sphere used by early astronomers to represent the positions of stars. Tycho Brahe (5) was a 16th-century Danish astronomer who built an observatory (6) and made most of his own instruments. His quadrant (7) determined the altitudes of stars. Copernicus (8) was one of the founders of modern astronomy. Figure (9) shows a terrestrial sphere made by Cushee in London in 1731 and (10) is another armillary sphere. The Great reflector (11) is from the telescope at Mount Palomar in the United States and (12) is the famous radio telescope at Jodrell Bank in England. It has been able to send back valuable messages about the progress of recent space probes. (13) The largest refracting telescope in the world at Yerkes Observatory in the United States.

Below A diagram explaining the difference between the two kinds of telescope. In the refracting kind (A) the image goes straight through the two lenses. Figure (B) shows the mirror in use in the reflecting type of telescope.

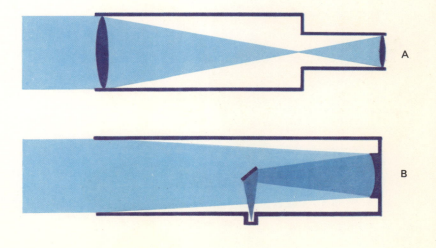

The Story of the Earth

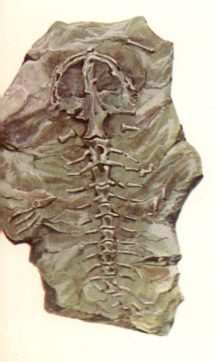

Above **This is a fossil of a salamander. Fossils, which are found in certain kinds of rocks, show us how plant and animal life developed on our planet.**

The earth began its life about 5,000 million years ago. No one knows for certain where it came from, but in the very beginning it was probably a mass of tiny particles and flaming gases, which may either have broken away from the sun or simply come together out of space. Over a very long period the earth cooled down and a crust hardened over its surface, forming into areas of land and water. How life began is a mystery. Scientists think it must have started from various natural substances in the oceans, perhaps about 2,500 million years ago.

The crust of the earth, with its mountains, trees, seas and rivers, varies in thickness between 10 miles, *16 kilometres* under the oceans to about 35 miles, *56 kilometres* under parts of the continents. Beneath it is an area of iron-hard rock about 1,800 miles, *2,900 kilometres* thick, called the

mantle. At its centre, the earth is thought to be still in very hot, liquid form, giving off great pressure.

Primitive man thought of the earth as a flat disc, or as an island rising out of the waters from the floor of the universe. When man realised that the earth hung suspended in space he devised other supposed methods for its support, such as the god Atlas who, in Greek mythology, carried the heavens on his shoulders. Other peoples pictured the earth being borne on the backs of four elephants, who were themselves carried by a tortoise.

It is only in modern times that the great age of the earth has been established, by methods which examine and date radioactive substances in rocks. In the ancient world the earth was thought to be some tens of thousands of years old. But geologists have found that certain natural features have

taken hundreds of millions of years to be formed.

Lying in the fields on a warm, still summer's day, it is difficult to imagine the great forces which are at work within the earth. The fearful destruction caused by the action of earthquakes and molten lava erupting from volcanoes is a reminder of the fiery inner depths of our world.

The main zones where volcanoes and earthquakes occur are grouped together in lands which border the Pacific Ocean. It has been estimated that about 1,000 earthquakes cause damage somewhere in the world every year. Many of the most terrible disasters have been in Japan where, in 1923, 180,000 people were killed and 575,000 houses destroyed in Tokyo and Yokohama.

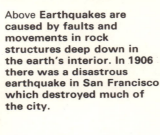

Above Earthquakes are caused by faults and movements in rock structures deep down in the earth's interior. In 1906 there was a disastrous earthquake in San Francisco which destroyed much of the city.

Left The supposed structure of the inside of the earth consists of four basic layers: the inner core, the outer core, the mantle and the crust.

Some volcanoes, such as Mount Etna in Sicily, erupt from time to time over a long period. Etna's first recorded outburst was in 475 BC and as recently as 1971 its lava flow once again threatened nearby villages. Other volcanoes grow almost overnight, such as the one at Paricutin in Mexico. It began one afternoon in February, 1943, as a crack in the surface of a farmer's field which belched forth smoke and dust. By the next day a baby volcano over 25 feet, *7·5 metres* high had been formed by hot rocks that shot out from the crack. Within a year the volcano was 1,000 feet, *300 metres* high and the village of Paricutin had disappeared beneath the ashes.

Earthquakes occur when rock layers beneath the surface of the land break up, causing the ground to shudder violently and great cracks to appear. Earthquakes can also happen under the sea, creating huge ocean waves which may reach the land.

Left Diagram showing the eruption of a volcano.

Left These chalk cliffs are formed from sediment deposited by glaciers during the Ice Age. Successive layers of sediment are clearly seen in the rock in the foreground.

Mountains, rocks and minerals

Nothing looks more permanent than the solid bulk of a huge mountain. Yet the surface of the earth is always changing. New mountains are formed, old ones are worn away, rivers change course and dry up, islands appear and disappear in the oceans. All this takes place so slowly that it is almost impossible to see it happen. Yet the

Below Monument Valley Arizona. Like all other landscapes of our planet, it is a ruin of earlier landscapes and the remains of former worlds. These worlds are separated from our own by almost unimaginable stretches of time. For instance, the Colorado River has taken about two million years to cut the Grand Canyon. This is twice as long as man's existence on Earth, and it is several hundred times as long as all written human history.

results of change can sometimes be seen, at the seaside for example, when part of a cliff face breaks away and slides into the water.

There are several ways in which mountains can be formed. The most common mountains are composed of sediments of such things as pebbles, sandstone and clay which collect in hollows, sometimes beneath the sea, and build up into mountains. Others are made of lava, which pours out of the earth's crust from volcanoes and eventually hardens into cones or shield-shaped masses. Block mountains are great sections of the earth's crust forced upwards in a process called faulting. Sometimes, the crust on high, flat ground sinks to form valleys and new mountain heights.

The face of the earth is covered in solid rock. This is true even though there may be soil or water above it. Dig down deep enough anywhere on land or beneath the oceans and there will be rock. Rocks are divided into three types. They are: igneous, which are rocks formed from lava; sedimentary, which are rocks formed by lots

Left A comparison of some of the newest and oldest mountains in the world. The round, smooth mountain is typical of the Highlands of Scotland. The high, jagged mountain comes from the Swiss Alps. It takes millions of years for the effects of climate (heat and cold, wind and rain) to become really noticeable and alter the shape of mountains.

Left Here is a diagram to show how high, jagged mountains become worn down into smooth, rounded shapes over millions of years.

of tiny pieces of rock building up and hardening into a solid mass; and metamorphic, which are rocks that are changed from one form to another by heat or pressure.

Soil is, in fact, rock that has been worn down and weathered into very fine particles. Microscopic animals and plants help to break the soil down and give its familiar look. There are also various types of soil, depending on the original materials from which it was formed. Soil is very important to man, both for his crops and his animals, and there is very little of it in the world – its average depth is only about one foot. Soil is vital to life and should be treated with care.

Rocks are made up of minerals, which are substances in the ground formed by combining the basic elements of nature. There are over 90 of these elements, such as oxygen, mercury and iron, which can exist as a gas, a liquid or a solid.

Every civilisation uses and needs minerals. Without them we could not exist. Primitive man used clay to create pots and vessels, and stone to make weapons and tools. Minerals give us our building materials in the shape of sand, cement and stone. Among metals contained in minerals are tin, lead and copper. Coal, oil and gas are all mixtures of minerals, and another mineral, uranium, is the source of atomic energy. There are precious minerals such as gold and silver, and gem minerals – diamonds, emeralds, rubies – which for thousands of years have been used to fashion beautiful jewellery.

All these things have to be dug out of the earth, and mining is one of the world's oldest industries. At first, man chipped away at rocks on the surface, but in the New Stone Age simple mining pits were made, particularly in chalk. The ancient Egyptians had stone quarries to produce the massive blocks from which the pyramids were built.

Below Here is a collection of some of the world's most precious minerals, including salt and coal – two very essential minerals. The gems are shown in their natural form and as we see them as polished stones.
(1) Opal; (2) Emerald; (3) Diamond; (4) Salt; (5) Ruby; (6) Coal; (7) Gold.

Above **This stretch of the Cornish coast shows typical rock formations caused by the action of water and wind.**

Below **The bulk of the water covering the earth's surface is centred on one side of the globe, as illustrated in these two drawings.**

Right **Glaciers are like frozen rivers of ice and they move slowly towards water where lumps break off and form large icebergs.**

Bottom **St. Michael's Mount off the south coast of England becomes an island when the tides are high.**

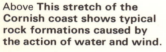
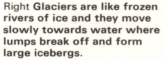

Oceans, seas and rivers

Over two-thirds of the surface of the earth is covered by water: in other words, there is more than twice as much water as there is land. Most people live in crowded cities and towns and we are used to seeing maps of the world which are covered by the continental masses of Europe, Asia, the Americas, Africa, Australia and Antarctica. But, looking at the side of the globe centred in the middle of the Pacific Ocean, nearly the whole area is taken up by the seas. Life began in the oceans and man has only just started to explore in earnest beneath their surface: food and mineral wealth are to be found there.

There are four principal oceans – the Pacific, Atlantic, Indian and Arctic

Above **Islands are formed by the tops of underwater mountains which appear above the level of the sea.**

Above right **The Pacific is dotted with thousands of such islands.**

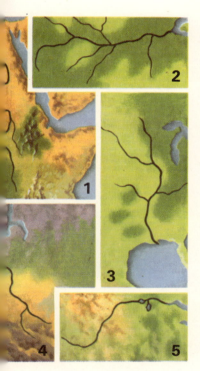

Above **The longest rivers in the world are 1 Nile (Africa), 2 Amazon (South America), 3 Mississippi/Missouri (North America), 4 Irtysh (Russia), 5 Yangtze (China).**

– and the biggest of them by far is the Pacific, which covers nearly 64 million square miles, *165 million square kilometres*. The deepest part of the oceans is a point in the Marianas Trench in the Pacific, which is over 36,000 feet, *11,000 metres* down. It was here that a United States bathyscaphe (an underwater ship designed for exploration) touched bottom in 1960.

The floor of the oceans is covered with great mountain chains and deep trenches. If all the water were taken away, the ocean bed would look very much like the rest of the earth. The highest mountain in the world would then no longer be Everest, but an extinct Hawaiian volcano called Mauna Kea, which rises over 31,000 feet, *9,140 metres* from the bottom of the sea. At present about 13,800 feet, *4,200 metres* of this appears above sea level.

When you look at a contour map of the Pacific Ocean you can see that all the thousands of tiny islands which are scattered across it are in fact the tips of great mountain ranges. There is a theory that the moon was once torn from the bed of the Pacific Ocean. Now that astronauts have succeeded in landing on the earth's satellite, perhaps they will bring back rock samples which will enable scientists to link the moon with her mother earth.

Of the natural forces which slowly change the appearance of the earth's crust, water is the most important. Rivers, swollen by rain, carve paths through the rocks. Glaciers, which are frozen rivers, carry tons of material from one place to another. The oceans themselves are constantly battering at our shores and eating away the land. Every force that acts upon the earth's crust tends to level things out, to fill in the valleys and bring down the mountains: in this process water plays the chief part.

Erosion, or the wearing away, of the land by water causes the spectacular scenery of places like the Grand Canyon in the United States, where the Colorado River runs. Here the rocks have been exposed in layers which have taken millions of years to form. Geologists are able to tell from these layers how long it took such deep gorges to be carved out. These areas are also valuable because they contain fossil remains of prehistoric animals and plants. Water in the form of rain also causes the steady wearing away of rock into weird shapes. Some of these rock forms, which are also carved by the action of the wind, are known as goblins.

Water can be found everywhere, even below the ground in the middle of a barren desert. Some water below ground is under internal pressure and when found forms an artesian well by rising naturally to the surface. Most of this water comes from rain which seeps through to a particular water level according to the conditions of the soil. Underground water also forms caves and submerged rivers.

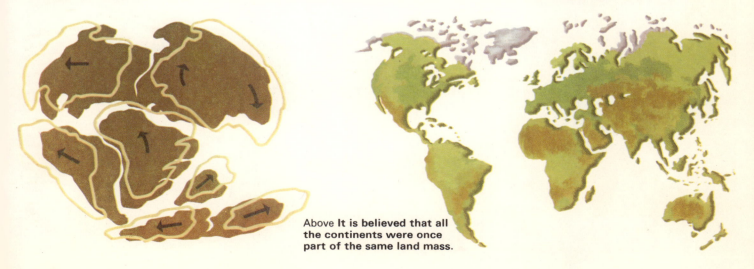

Above **It is believed that all the continents were once part of the same land mass.**

Weather and climate

There is a difference between weather and climate. Weather is what we experience daily in any particular area – how much sun, or rain, or wind, or frost. The weather in one place can change not only from day to day but from hour to hour. Climate refers to the general weather conditions which are usual in one place over a long period. On average, the climate in a country may be warm and dry in the month of June, but on a particular day in June the weather may be cold and wet.

All around the earth is a vast, invisible globe of air called the atmosphere, which extends upwards for many miles. On the ground the air is heavy and compressed by the weight of all the air above it, but as it goes higher it gradually gets thinner and thinner, until it fades away altogether. The lowest part of the atmosphere near the earth is always in motion and this is where weather effects build up.

The atmosphere is made up of gases which behave like a fluid and exert pressure on the earth at the rate of about 14 pounds-force per square inch, *1 kilogrammes-force per square centimetre*. We do not feel this pressure because the weight of the air presses equally in all directions. Variations in air pressure, which are measured on

Right **Types of clouds** –
(1) Cirrostratus;
(2) Cirrocumulus;
(3) Altocumulus;
(4) Stratocumulus;
(5) Cumulus; (6) Stratus;
(7) Cirrus;
(8) Cumulonimbus;
(9) Altostratus;
(10) Nimbostratus.

Below **A weather man**

an instrument called a barometer, cause air to move and so set up winds.

Most of us know very little about winds, perhaps because they cannot be seen or easily measured like rain or snow. But they are very important to the study of weather. The two things to note about winds are their speed and direction. Wind speed is measured on an instrument called an anemometer, although it is possible to judge speed roughly by comparing the natural effects of the wind with a table known as the Beaufort Scale. For example a moderate breeze which raises dust and moves small branches on trees is force 4 on the scale, and its speed is about 15 m.p.h., *24 k.p.h.*

Perhaps the most common weather experiences for all people in the world is the effect of temperature and the presence or absence of the sun. Air is

Above **A diagram showing how water vapour is drawn up from the sea to form clouds. These turn to rain which falls on the land and is drained back into rivers and seas.**

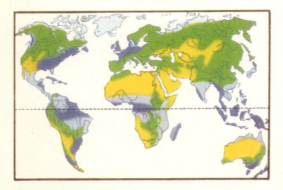

Left **Map to show the distribution of rainfall throughout the world. The dark blue shows areas of greatest rainfall, the yellow indicates desert regions.**

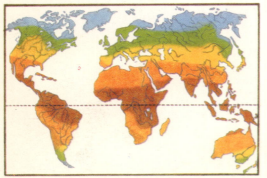

Left **Map to show where the heat from the sun is greatest in the world. The orange areas are the hottest, the blue areas the coldest.**

Right **Here a woman operator is seen reading the records of a weather box at a meteorological station.**

not heated directly by the sun's rays but by radiation back from the earth's surface. This is why the temperature of the air gets lower as you rise higher above the land. Places near the equator receive the sun's rays directly overhead and they have, accordingly, a hot climate. Places near the north and south poles, which the sun's rays reach only at an angle, are cold.

Rain is often considered an inconvenience to some people, but without it the land would dry up and nothing would grow. Snow is often more welcomed, although it eventually melts and becomes water before going away. Both rain and snow come from water vapour, which rises into the air when the heat of the sun causes water to evaporate from the surface of oceans, seas, lakes and rivers. These clouds of water vapour are, for various reasons, forced to rise over the land, where they become cool and condense into a liquid or a solid and fall on the earth as rain or snow.

Thunderstorms are caused when masses of air of different temperatures meet or when hot air rises suddenly and upsets the balance of the atmosphere. Clouds often contain static electricity and the flashes of lightning are the result of negative charges in the upper layers clashing with positive charges in the lower layers. This clash also affects sound waves and causes thunder. Since sound travels about a mile in five seconds, much slower than the speed of light, it is possible to estimate the distance of a storm away from you by timing the interval between the flash and the clap of thunder.

Below **Weather ships like this are equipped with instruments to measure weather conditions and atmospheric pressures.**

Below **Forked lightning across the sky always makes a very spectacular display. It is in fact nature's way of discharging millions of volts of unwanted electricity.**

The World of Plants

Below All plants are made up of cells. This drawing shows in diagrammatic form the progression from simple cells to the highest forms of plant life. It takes in the various major groups of fungi, seaweeds, mosses and liverworts, ferns, conifers and flowering plants. This development corresponds to the geological time-scale so that seaweeds and fungi are seen as plants of Pre-Cambrian times whereas flowering plants belong to a period within the last 150 million years.

The earliest living things on earth were simple cells. No one knows how they began but they probably became plants by attaching themselves to rocks under the water and then eventually growing out of the sea on to the land. At some stage in evolution simple living things branched in two directions, one to remain plants and the other to become animals. Again, no one knows how or when this happened.

The difference between an elephant and a dandelion may be obvious but it is not always so easy to decide whether a living organism is a plant or an animal. Generally speaking the difference between them is that a plant is able to manufacture its own food supply and an animal is not. This is why plant life is so important to man and other animals, for without it they would die. Animals which are carnivorous, that is meat-eating, live on animals which are plant eaters, and if there were no plants the food chain would break down.

At the heart of all life on earth is the sun, for plants and animals depend on it for their existence. Plants require food in order to stay alive, just like animals. They make this for themselves from carbon dioxide, which is a gas in the air, and from water in the ground. Before the plant can make its

liverworts and mosses

ferns

gymnosperms

algae

angiosperms

fungi

bacteria

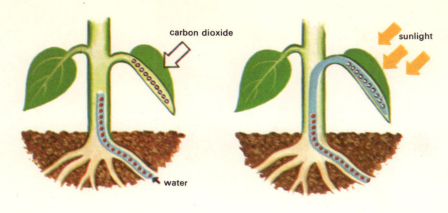

carbon dioxide

water

sunlight

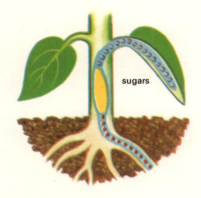

sugars

Above **This diagram shows the way plants are able to manufacture their food by a process called photosynthesis.**

Below **A close-up of the cellular structure of the root tip of a plant.**

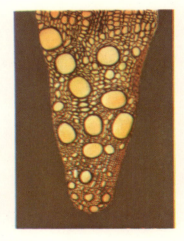

Below **The simple development of a bean seed into a plant is shown in water contained in a jar. The process of growth is similar to that which takes place underground.**

The kingdom of plants is divided into four principal parts, which in turn are broken down into a system of classification which enables scientists to identify a particular species. As there are about 350,000 different types of plants in the world, some system is necessary. The one we use now was developed from that invented by the Swedish botanist Linnaeus in the 18th century.

The four groups have long and complicated names which are taken from Greek words. They are thallophytes, which include seaweeds, fungi and bacteria; bryophytes, which are mostly mosses and liverworts; pteriodophytes, which include ferns and horsetails; and spermatophytes, which are the most familiar of all and comprise all the seed-producing plants. The reason for the word spermatophytes, for example, is easily explained when one knows that 'sperm' comes from the Greek word for 'seed', and 'phytes' from the Greek word for a plant, hence seed-plant.

The seaweeds, fungi and bacteria are the most primitive types of plants and have been on earth almost since life itself began. This is also true of mosses and horsetails. The common horsetail, which is such a nuisance as a garden weed, is a survivor of a very ancient group of plants which grew to giant size (over 40 feet, *12 metres* high) over 250 million years ago.

food it needs light. The chemical called chlorophyll in its leaves, which gives them the familiar green colour, uses the energy from the sun's rays to convert the carbon dioxide and water into food. This is a process called photosynthesis.

Another way in which plants and animals depend on each other is illustrated by what is called the oxygen cycle. Animals need to take in oxygen in order to live. Plants give off oxygen and help to renew the supply in the air. Since animals breathe out carbon dioxide, which is used by plants in food-making, the circle is complete.

Unlike animals, which move about to find food, most plants stay in one place, where they grow and die. There are exceptions such as certain primitive plants in water which swim about like animals.

Flowers

The earliest plants on earth had no flowers. The colour, scent and shape of flowers as we know them today have taken millions of years to develop. In the world of plants, flowering plants hold the same position as mammals do in the world of animals, for each represents the highest form of life within its kingdom.

Like all living things, plants are born, reproduce themselves, and then die. As there are male and female animals, so there are male and female plants, although more often the male and female parts occur on the same plant. In order to produce seeds from which new flowers can grow, pollen – which is a dust-like powder, usually yellow, inside the flower – must be carried from the male part of one flower to the female part of another, or between the parts in the same flower.

Most flowering plants depend on insects to transfer their pollen, and so reproduce more plants. In the fight for survival in the natural world the most successful plants have been those with the brightest flowers and the sweetest scents: for the whole purpose of these is to attract insects. Stored at the base of the flower petals is a fluid called nectar, which is the food of many insects. In searching for it, attracted by colour or scent, the insect's body collects pollen from the flower, and as it flies from flower to flower it transfers the pollen to the organs of another flower and so makes reproduction possible. Flowers can also be pollinated by wind, which

Above **The wild flowers in these drawings belong to the temperate areas of the northern hemisphere, but their names do vary from one place to another. 1 Lily of the Valley is a perennial herb with globe-like flowers which have a heavy scent. 2 Heather grows on moorlands, and ranges in colour from white to purple. 3 Bluebells fill the woodlands with colour in spring. 4 Primroses, too, are woodland plants and are among the earliest to flower each year. 5 Forget-me-nots used to be known as Water Mouse-Ear Scorpion-Grass. 6 Spotted Orchid, which grows in damp places in woods and pastures. 7 Ragged Robin, which produces honey, is a popular name for** Lychnis. **8 Poppies are one of the most familiar and colourful of all wild flowers. 9 The Michaelmas Daisy grown in gardens has been developed from the wild** Aster. **10 Cowslips grow abundantly in meadows.**

blows and scatters pollen over a wide area; or by water, on which pollen floats from one plant to another; or by animals, which carry pollen on their bodies.

The beauty and variety of wild flowers can be overlooked. Although the dramatic colour of a field of massed red poppies or yellow buttercups cannot be missed, many flowers grow unseen in hedgerows and forests.

Flowers are adapted for use in many different situations. Mountain flowers with tiny, delicate petals are, in fact, very hardy and well-suited to grow in exposed conditions. The typical heathland plant is heather, which likes sour (acid) soil, while in meadows nearly every type of plant, from daisies to lilies, grows well. Special sorts of flowering plants grow in or near water, and in woodlands early flowering primroses and bluebells thrive under the shade of the trees.

Above **Garden flowers have been developed by man from wild flowers and are usually much showier and brighter. Among those seen above are 1 Tulip; 2 Dahlia; 3 Lupin; 4 Chrysanthemum; 5 Rose; 6 Gladiolus; 7 Scabious; 8 Sweet Pea; 9 Montbretia.** Above left **Two mountain plants, Violet** left and **Edelweiss** right.

Even in the depths of winter, nature is never still and while plants die, new life can be seen forming in the shape of buds and seedlings.

Flowers were not created just so that we could enjoy their beauty. They are an essential part of the continuing life of nature. But man has improved on nature and for his own pleasure has cultivated plants with bigger, brighter and more colourful flowers than exist in natural wild growth. This can easily be seen by comparing the rich beauty of a cultivated rose with the common wild rose of the hedgerow.

For centuries, garden flowers have been developed from wild flowers growing all over the world, so that rare blooms from tropical lands may find themselves transformed into hardy flowering plants, bringing colour to city back gardens. Unlike wild flowers, which have to depend on insects and other animals, or forces of nature such as wind and water, not only to pollinate themselves but also to disperse their seeds, garden flowers are scientifically developed to produce the best possible results.

Above **Most flowers with bright colours and strong scents are pollinated by insects. This status flower is pollinated by butterflies.**

Ordinary wild plants which grow where they are not wanted are called weeds. Some of the most common in cultivated land are, thistles, dandelions and daisies.

Left **Ferns are called tracheophytes because they have tubes for drawing water, food and minerals up to their leaves. Ferns have played an important part in the evolution of life on our planet. They were the first large land plants and often grew to an enormous size. In Europe, we are more familiar with the smaller kinds of fern like the cultivated Maidenhair Fern and the wild bracken to be seen in the country, although there are some tall tree ferns still in existence in warm moist regions. This picture is of an Australian tree fern which can grow to about 50 feet, *15 metres* in height. The inset shows how the plantlets grow on the parent fern.**

Trees

Trees are the largest of all living plants and they share the features of many other smaller plants. It is usual to regard a tree as a plant that can develop a single woody trunk.

Trees of the world fall into two main groups. There are flowering trees and conifers. Most flowering trees are deciduous, and are so called because they live in temperate climates and shed their leaves in autumn, remaining bare during the winter. There are some flowering trees in the tropics that bear leaves all the year round. Generally, flowering trees have broad, flat leaves and their wood is hard and strong. Because of this they are known as hardwoods. The oak, elm, ash, maple and sycamore are all flowering trees.

Conifers are cone-bearing evergreens with hard, strong needle-like leaves. They are called softwoods.

Below **This is a Japanese miniature tree. These are cultivated for indoor use by careful pruning of the roots and stems.**

perilous years of its life. During these early years, in which losses are heavy, the tree can be subjected to drought, wind, snow, sun-scorch, fire and suppression by weeds. If a tree survives these dangerous years, it may live for a very long time. Oaks are considered ready for felling after 150 to 200 years. It has been known for a yew tree to live over 1,000 years.

The age of a tree is determined by the pattern of growth in its trunk. The trunk is made up of alternate layers of porous wood (formed during the spring and summer) and dense wood (formed in autumn and winter). These layers appear as circles when the trunk is cut across and the number of them will tell the age of the tree.

A tree must have sunlight, and any branches that are overshadowed by other trees will be lost. The practical height limit is about 400 feet *122 metres,* but the tallest tree known today is a redwood growing in California in the United States which

These pictures show (A) 'Shrubby Hollyhock' and its flower; (B) a weeping willow and (C) a beech tree.

Although they are dressed in leaves throughout the year, they do shed their leaves sometimes. The leaves of evergreens remain on the tree for two or three years, and each spring paler leaves grow where some of the older leaves have fallen off.

Conifers grow in colder parts of the world or on high ground and are very hardy. The hard or leathery leaves of the softwoods ensure that water vapour does not escape during very cold or dry spells. Winter can also be a time of drought for these trees, as they cannot absorb water from the soil if it is frozen.

The life span of a tree can exceed that of any other living thing, providing it can live through the first

Below **Here is the popular domestic tree, the laburnum, whose yellow flowers make a lovely display in the spring.**

reaches 365 feet *112 metres*. The eucalyptus of Australia is another giant tree.

Like other plants, trees make food in their leaves, but because they are so huge they need vast amounts of water to do so. The water is carried through tubes in the trunk. These tubes are very tough and packed closely together, making the tree very strong. To protect such an important part of the tree the trunk is covered with bark made mainly from cork. New layers of cork are produced as the trunk gets thicker, with the outside bark splitting and perhaps flaking off. Just as trees can be distinguished by their leaves, so they can also be identified from their bark patterns.

Some plants, such as hawthorn and privet, although cultivated as hedging shrubs, are really trees. If left alone, they will develop single trunks just like the giant trees of the forests.

Below **The man standing beside this Californian redwood tree gives some idea of its girth. The rings show its great age.**

Below **A Californian redwood tree displays its enormous height when compared with an average tree. Some redwoods are over 300 feet, *90 metres*, tall.**

Right **Here we have a Scots pine and (above) a new shoot growing out of the pine cone.**

Centre **A lilac tree in full bloom.**

Below **An oak tree (1); a white poplar (2); a mountain ash in the fruiting season (3) and a Norwegian maple in leaf (4).**

1

2

3

4

Fruits and vegetables

Man relies on fruits and vegetables as foods which keep his body healthy, for they are rich in minerals and vitamins. Some contain protein and starch and other useful things.

Most of the fruits we eat are the seed vessels of plants but when we eat nuts, we are, in most cases, eating the seeds themselves. Fruits are constantly being improved by careful selection and cultivation, and the luscious fruits now so familiar to us have all been produced by man from the small fruits that once grew wild in different parts of the world. In respect of size and flavour they far surpass the wild ancestors from which they came.

Perhaps the most valuable fruits of all are the semi-tropical ones known as citrus fruits, which include the orange, lemon, lime and grapefruit. Some soft fruits such as blackcurrants, gooseberries, raspberries, strawberries and blackberries still grow abundantly in something like their wild state.

Fruits such as peaches, melons, grapes and apricots, which grow in warm climates, are now as familiar as the pear and apple, due to the high speed at which they can be transported from one country to another. Figs and dates are two fruits which have a high food value. Nuts are also very good to eat, although they vary enormously in their formation, from the tiny beech-nut to the large coconut of the Philippines, the trees of which can bear fruit for 80 years or more.

As well as being able to eat fresh fruit of one sort or another all the year round, we can also eat it as jam or marmalade, from cans, frozen, or in a variety of other ways so that it is always available, in or out of season.

Vegetables as well as fruits grow in

Left The fruit is a vital part of a plant since it protects the seeds from which new plants will grow. Fruits take on many different shapes and sizes. They may be either fleshy — as the peach or the apple, or dry — as the nut or the fruit of such vegetables as peas or beans. The fruits that we eat have been bred and cultivated from wild plant ancestors. Many reach us in tins or frozen packs, but due to modern methods of packing and transport it is possible for fruits from one part of the world to be available in another land where they would not grow naturally. The fruits shown on this page are
(1) Paw-paw; (2) Apples;
(3) Pineapple; (4) Grapes;
(5) Avocado pear;
(6) Aubergine; (7) Bananas;
(8) Strawberry; (9) Lemon;
(10) Gooseberry;
(11) Red-currants.

Below **Some of the vegetables we eat include (1) Cabbage; (2) Tomatoes; (3) Celery; (4) Spring Onion; (5) Beetroot; (6) Sweetcorn; (7) Cucumber; (8) Pepper.**

Of the vegetables mentioned, most have to be cooked before they are eaten, but there are a number of vegetables that we prefer to eat uncooked and these are the summer vegetables used for making salads, such as lettuces, cucumbers and spring onions. A few vegetables are used only as flavouring and for decoration and these include horseradish and parsley. Some of the more uncommon vegetables are artichokes, aubergines, chicory, sweet corn and peppers.

Fruits and vegetables blend well and are found together in sauces, pickles and chutneys.

Below **Individual seed potatoes are planted in the ground. Each of these will develop into a potato plant which will produce leaves and flowers above ground and a mass of new potato tubers in the soil.**

a number of ways. Some, like turnips, swedes, carrots and radishes, grow beneath the soil with the flower growing above ground. The potato also grows in this way. Potatoes have an interesting history and it is traditionally believed that Sir Walter Raleigh introduced them from the Americas to his estates in Ireland in the 16th century.

Some vegetables such as peas, beans and lentils are called leguminous plants because the seeds are housed in legumes, or pods. These are not only valuable from the food point of view but also because they restock the soil with nitrogen, which is essential to growth. Of some beans, such as the haricot and butter bean, we eat the seeds themselves, while of others like the scarlet runner and French bean, we eat the pod as well as the seed.

Cabbages, cauliflowers, marrows, Brussels sprouts, broccoli, kale and asparagus are vegetables that grow in the same way as many other flowering plants; that is, they have roots beneath the soil and the part that is eaten grows above the ground.

Above **An arid desert scene. It is in deserts like this in America that the Joshua tree (right) grows. About 35 feet, *11 metres*, tall, it holds most of its water in its tough leaves.**

Above **These are Bottle trees of the Australian grasslands. They get their name from the shape of the trunk which acts as a water storage tank.**

Unusual plants

In the animal kingdom there are strange creatures that strike the imagination because of their immense size or weird form, and this is also true of the plant kingdom. There are some plants that are not able to build up sugar and starch from carbon dioxide in the air and which have to rely on other matter for their food.

Fungi are such plants, and the most familiar of all fungi is the common mushroom, which lives on organic matter in the soil. The main part of the fungus is called mycelium, which is hidden in the soil with only the fruit bodies appearing above the ground. If the fruit bodies are picked to eat others will appear after a day or two.

Left **Here are some fungi. They are (1) Sulphur Polyporus; (2) Cup Fungi; (3) Fly Agaric; (4) Meadow Mushroom and (5) Lurid Bolete. Some of these fungi are very poisonous.**

Some flowering plants are parasites which feed off living hosts. One example is the mistletoe. This is really a partial parasite for it has leaves and can make sugar but it has no roots and must depend on its host for its supply of water and mineral salts. Other plants such as dodder rely entirely on their hosts for their living.

There are plants that 'eat' insects. One is the sundew. This has numerous tentacles round the edges of its leaves which produce a sticky substance. When a small insect is caught on the sticky fluid, the tentacles and edges of the leaf curl over and trap it. Another insect-eater is the pitcher plant, which has a slippery, urn-shaped leaf that collects rainwater. The insects slip into the water and drown, to be digested later by the plant.

Venus's fly-trap has leaf blades with

Above **Nature uses various methods of propagation. The familiar mistletoe, like many others, has its seeds carried by birds on their beaks. Mistletoe is called a parasite as it takes its food from the trees from which it grows.**

sharp spikes on their outer rims and sensitive hairs on either side of a hinge in the centre of the leaf. When an insect alights on the hairs it causes the leaf to snap shut on the insect, which the plant then digests.

Cacti are unusual inasmuch as they have thorns instead of leaves. Because they grow in areas where water is scarce they have learned to conserve what water they do get by producing leaves which do not present a large surface area to the sun, therefore reducing the normal rate of evaporation. Other unusual desert plants are the tumbleweeds, which in a dry season will detach themselves from the ground and be blown by the wind to more favourable soil in which to put down roots.

Among the giants of the plant world must be included the Amazon Water Lily which can support a child on one of its leaves.

Toadstools look very similar to mushrooms but one must remember that some are extremely poisonous, such as death cap fungus and fly agaric, a toadstool with a scarlet cap flecked with white. One non-poisonous toadstool is called the blusher because its flesh turns pink when broken. The fairy ring fungus is so called as it is the cause of 'fairy rings' on lawns.

There are many fungi that cause dry rot in timber and some called bracket fungi that project themselves on to tree trunks and fencing. One of these is called beef-steak fungus because it looks like a piece of raw meat. Some fungi are small and grow on damp bread and rotting fruit. From these comes a family called *Penicillium* from which the life-saving drug penicillin was discovered.

Lichens are some of the most curious plants of all, being part algae and part fungus. They often grow in dry places or on such surfaces as bare rock. Most of them are a grey/green colour but some are brightly coloured.

Above **The Welwitschia which grows in the deserts of S.W. Africa is a living fossil.**

Below **These plants trap and 'eat' insects. They are (A) Sarracenia; (B) Venus's Fly Trap and (C) Bladderwort. The inset shows a tiny insect unable to escape from the trap of the bladderwort.**

The World of Animals

The living world is divided into two mighty kingdoms, the kingdom of plants and the kingdom of animals. Plants manufacture their own food; but animals rely on plants or other animals for their food, and this is one way we can tell them apart. Because animals have to find their own food supply, they are equipped with certain senses, such as smell, sight, taste and touch. In this respect, they are far more advanced than plants. They also have mouths to take in the solid food they use as fuel for growing and moving about. Any waste food is passed out of the body.

Right A zebra's hoof compared with a house mouse.

Below A shrew, a tiny mammal which is common in Britain.

Animals reproduce by laying eggs or by giving birth to miniature copies of themselves. The size of animals can vary from that of the microscopic amoeba to the great Blue Whale, the largest animal in the world.

There are about a million different types of animals known to man, and they are grouped into sections for the purposes of study and identification. First, the animals are placed in a group called a genus. For instance, all the breeds of dog make up a genus. More than one genus makes up a family. The wolf belongs to the same family as the dog. Families are grouped into orders. The dog and the wolf are both meat-eaters and belong in the order Carnivora along with all the other meat-eaters, such as lions and tigers, which are members of the cat family. Orders are then grouped into classes. The dog belongs to the class Mammalia (mammals), the songthrush belongs to the class Aves (birds), the frog belongs to the class Amphibia (amphibians), and the pike to the class Pisces (fishes).

The animals in these classes have one very important feature in common: they all have backbones and so belong together in the largest group of all called a phylum. In this case the phylum is known as the Chordata. Another important phylum is Mollusca, which includes such animals as

Above A chimpanzee, the most advanced of the apes, is found wild in Africa.

Below The coelacanth was believed to be extinct until it was re-discovered in 1938. Its history can be traced back more than 300 million years by fossil remains.

Some 440 million years ago the first primitive vertebrates (animals with backbones) appeared. Then came the age of fishes, so called because of the many types of creatures which lived in the sea. From them developed the first animals to leave the water entirely, to live on land and eventually to lay eggs there. These amphibians were the ancestors of the enormous dinosaurs.

Alongside these first land animals there grew up an abundant plant life, on which most of them fed. Insects, too, thrived and they were much bigger than they are today. In the water lived the sea-monsters, the ichthyosaurs and plesiosaurs. When they died out, turtles, sharks and rays took over the seas. In the skies there were flying reptiles called ptero-dactyls.

When the mammals took over from the dinosaurs, they multiplied rapidly. Their warm bodies, efficient reproduction and the protection of fur helped them to survive. In some present-day mammals we can still recognise their ancestors from long ago.

Above **Here is a blue whale and beside it is a basking shark. The whale is especially interesting as it is the largest mammal to become adapted to a marine existence. Whales breathe the air and suckle their young like other mammals.**

oysters, mussels, snails and squids. Yet another is Arthropoda (insects, crabs, spiders and scorpions).

The animals in the world today have evolved from creatures living on earth millions of years ago. The period about 500 million years ago was the age of shellfish – trilobites, sea-urchins and corals – which all lived in the sea. There also existed numerous molluscs, from which the present-day squid is descended.

Fossils have played an extremely important part in building up a picture of the evolution of plant and animal life on earth. This diagram shows how the fossil remains of important animals are found embedded in rock. The earliest fossils, like jelly fish of the Cambrian period of 570 million years ago, are in the red band at the bottom of the page, whilst the most recent, like the mastodon of the Pleistocene period of 2 million years ago, are in the brown band at the top of the page. Owing to movement in the earth's Crust, rock strata shift about so that they often do not lie in chronological sequence. However, modern methods of telling the age of fossils are very accurate and, in fact, fossils play a large part in recording the age of the rock they are found in.

Prehistoric animals

Scientists find out about animals of past ages by studying fossils, which are remains of living things that have been preserved in rocks. Fossils have been found which are believed to be about 2,500 million years old and it is probable that life began even before this, although there are few traces of the very earliest plants or animals. The first animals lived in the sea, which is where all life on earth developed.

The period of pre-history about 600 million years ago is known as Cambrian, after Cambria, the Roman name for Wales, where some of the earliest fossils were studied. From this time fossils have been found in large numbers, particularly of animals called trilobites, which had many legs, looked rather like wood-lice and crawled about on the bottom of the sea. Other animals which lived in the sea in the early periods of time were cephalopods, which were rather like giant squids, and crab-like sea scorpions.

In a later period called Devonian, named after the English county of Devon where very ancient rock formations are found, sea-animals took to the land. This period is also known

Above **One of the heavily armoured dinosaurs was *Stegosaurus*, protected all along its back by rows of bony plates.**

Below **The flesh-eating *Tyrannosaurus*, killed its prey by tearing at it with its terrible teeth.**

as the Age of Fishes, because there were so many different varieties swimming in the sea. Some of these are called lung-fishes, because they crawled out of the water and learned to breathe on land. In time their fins turned into legs and arms and they developed into amphibians, animals that can live on land or in water.

Reptiles developed next and it is to this class of animal that the popular dinosaurs, which most people think of as typical prehistoric animals, belong. In fact the dinosaurs were only one kind of prehistoric animal in the vast pageant of creatures which have developed over the last 2–3,000 million years. But because of the size of some of them their 'fierce monster' image has made them very famous.

Right **The mammoth was a type of elephant living during the Ice Ages some 2 million years ago. It was about the size of an Indian elephant and had long spiral tusks.**

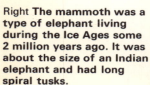

Many of the dinosaurs, which is a name made up of two Greek words meaning 'fearful lizard', were quite small, no bigger than an average-size dog. But the largest of them, such as *Diplodocus*, was about 90 feet, *27 metres* long from head to tail. Most dinosaurs were plant-eaters, although one group were hunting, flesh-eating animals. The most terrible looking of these was *Tyrannosaurus*, a great heavy animal which lumbered about on its hind legs. Some skeletons of them have been found which are over 50 feet, *15 metres* long. They had enormous skulls with powerful jaws and sharp teeth, about four inches, *10 centimetres* long.

Other dinosaurs were armoured, with heavy bony plates which made them look like walking tanks, and

Above **This plaster cast of a skull of the fierce and rhinoceros-like *Triceratops* was made from remains of its skeleton.**

great rhinoceros-like horns. They were so bulky that they probably had only to lower their heads and stand firm to put off any attacker. There were flying reptiles called pterosaurs, which probably glided through the air supported by bat-like wings rather than flew. About 150 million years ago they developed into the first bird-like creatures, such as *Archaeopteryx*, which had true feathers and wings.

The dinosaurs died out about 75 million years ago to be replaced by the mammals which, although they had been in existence for a long time, had never progressed while the dinosaurs ruled the earth. Most of the earliest mammals were marsupials, that is they had a pouch in which the baby animal developed. This type died out and was replaced by the placental mammal, in which the young are born fully developed. Some marsupials, such as the kangaroo in Australia, still exist today.

Above **This group of prehistoric animals includes *Iguanodon* (standing upright); and *Moschops* (crouching alongside); on the left are flying *Pterodactyls*; and on the right, the largest of all the dinosaurs, *Diplodocus*.**

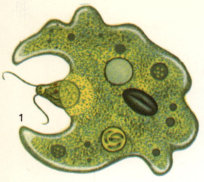

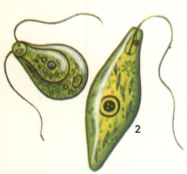

Primitive animals

Most primitive forms of animal life are found in water. The simplest animals are the Protozoa whose bodies consist of a single cell. Protozoans are so small that they can be seen only through a microscope.

Sponges are the simplest of the many-celled animals that live in the sea. Many of them, except for causing movement in the water around them, show no sign of life and were once thought to be plants. Other creatures that look like plants, which are often very beautiful to look at, are sea-mats, sea-squirts, sea-anemones and coral.

There are many types of worms that live in the sea and on the seashore and some, like the earthworm, have their bodies divided into segments. Unlike the earthworm, most marine worms have tentacles on the head and some have eyes. Those living in muddy conditions sometimes have gills to help them breathe where there is a shortage of oxygen. Some worms have scales and others are equipped with paddles. The rag-worms can give a nasty bite if handled roughly.

Molluscs are creatures which have either one shell or a pair of shells. Limpets, sea-snails, winkles and whelks are all single-shell molluscs, which are called gastropods. Some molluscs which have a pair of shells are the edible mussels, oysters and cockles.

Above (1) The amoeba, a tiny creature consisting of only one cell. It is constantly changing its shape because it absorbs food with any part of its body. There are more protozoa (2) than other forms of life except bacteria.

Right A section of the sea anemone showing its many 'fingers' which wave about.

Below Here are some marine sights which an aqualung swimmer might see. They are (1) pieces of coral; (2) a sea urchin; (3) a plumrose anemone; (4) trelia crassi cornis; (5) a hermit crab and (6) parasite anemones.

Right A diagram showing a section through a simple sponge. Unlike the amoebas, they are small multi-celled animals and live in the sea.

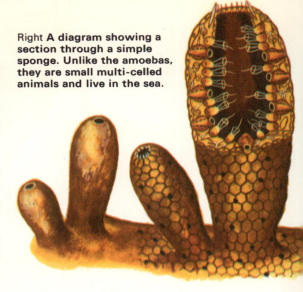

Right **A garden slug which is like a shell-less snail, and is destructive to small plants.**

Below **The earthworm has a segmented body and no bones.**

Below **Crabs belong to the group known as crustaceans. This one is the common crab and it has ten legs. There are many types of crab and they vary greatly in size, shape and in some of their habits.**

family of arthropods, one of the main divisions of the animal kingdom. Arthropod is a Greek word meaning 'jointed legs'.

Arthropods are divided into seven classes, of which crustaceans are second in importance to insects. Crustaceans owe their name to the external skeleton which covers and protects their soft bodies. The shells of some crustaceans do not grow with the animal so, when a shell becomes too tight, the crustacean will shed it, then hide away in crevices until a new one has grown. Some, like the crab, have the power of regeneration–that is, if a limb is lost the crab will grow another one to take its place.

· Cuttlefish, octopuses and squids are also molluscs, although their shells are either very small or almost absent. These molluscs have a number of arms and a siphon through which water can be forcibly expelled, providing them with jet-propulsion. These molluscs are called cephalopods, which is a Greek word meaning 'head-footed'.

Octopuses have eight arms and practically no shell on the body. On their arms are rows of suckers. Some octopuses have only one row of suckers on each arm while the Common Octopus has two rows. Cuttlefish and squids have ten arms. Two of these, called the tentacles, are much longer than the rest and are used for capturing food while the other arms enable the animal to hold on tightly to its victim. The cuttlefish can change its colour when alarmed and like the squid can squirt out an inky fluid which confuses an enemy. Cephalopods are more active than other molluscs.

Crustaceans (crabs, lobsters, shrimps and prawns) belong to the

Right **The lobster, another crustacean. Its forward movement is slow but it can move backwards quite fast.**

Above **The common octopus is relatively intelligent for experiments show that it can learn by experience.**

Right **A few sea shells which were once inhabited by various forms of marine life.**

Fish and other marine animals

Nobody knows for sure exactly how many species of fish there are in the world, but we do know that they first took form some 450 million years ago and were the first backboned life to appear on earth. Fishes live in the salt water of the sea or the fresh water of rivers and lakes, and some live in both. In fact, they have adapted themselves to almost every variation of water environment.

Like man, fish need oxygen in order to live and they get their oxygen from the water by taking it in through their mouths and then forcing it out over the gills through the gill slits. The oxygen in the water is thus absorbed by the tiny blood vessels in the gills and carried to other parts of the body. Fishes that live in water with little oxygen, such as guppies, have learned to gulp in oxygen from the air above the water.

Water is very much denser than air and this fact determines the general shape that fish have taken. Active fish that rely on speed in order to live have developed into streamlined forms. The powerful Bluefin Tuna can

Some of the species on this page are tropical fishes while the remainder are to be found in colder seas in various parts of the world. The ones shown here are (A) rock beauty; (B) clown triggerfish; (C) coral beauty angelfish; (D) neon tetra; (E) Arabian snapper; (F) boxfish or trunkfish; (G) common clownfish; (H) cleaner wrasse; (I) regal tang; (J) eel; (K) sperm whale; (M) powder blue surgeonfish; (N) crayfish; (O) bottle-nosed dolphin; (P) common whelk; (Q) heart urchin or sea potato; (R) cowrie; (S) pike and (T) perch. Many of the tropical species shown here are quite suitable for keeping in fish tanks at home, provided that they are heated and aereated adequately.

move at a speed of 45 m.p.h., *72 k.p.h.* for a short distance. Fish that live at the bottom of the water such as mud-skippers, catfish or scorpionfish, do not need to be so streamlined.

There is no uniform method by which fishes swim, and swimming is not the only way that fishes have evolved of moving about. Some crawl, climb, leap, soar or hop, and some even use jet propulsion, like the flying-fishes of tropical oceans.

Not all fishes survive by eating other smaller fish. A great many fish live entirely on small green plants and minute animals called plankton. Others live on plankton only when they are young and small. Some live on fish and plankton and some, called predators, live by hunting down and eating other fish. Even a fish as large as the Basking Shark, which is 45 feet, *13·7 metres* long, can live on a diet of plankton alone.

The fish that are hunted by predators have some clever ways of protecting themselves. Sharp or poisonous spines are good protection for some fish, while others camouflage themselves by blending in with their background colours. Some fish have armoured skin and scales and there are some that can mimic other fishes that are not likely to be attacked by predators. In a world so full of hazards it is not surprising that the senses of fish are so acute.

Most ray-finned fishes have a sense of colour, and sharks and eels have a particularly good sense of smell. The underwater world is surprisingly noisy and fish use sound in much the same way as birds.

Above **In this picture a velvet swimming crab is seen with an octopus in the background. Surprisingly, the octopus has a complex nervous system and its eye is highly developed. The crab belongs to the family called crustaceans, the largest of which is the Japanese spider crab.**

Below **Chrysaora isosceles is a kind of jelly fish with a very powerful sting. The common sunstar fish feeds mainly on small shell fish.**

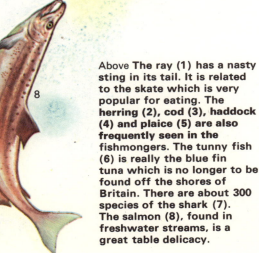

Above **The ray (1) has a nasty sting in its tail. It is related to the skate which is very popular for eating. The herring (2), cod (3), haddock (4) and plaice (5) are also frequently seen in the fishmongers. The tunny fish (6) is really the blue fin tuna which is no longer to be found off the shores of Britain. There are about 300 species of the shark (7). The salmon (8), found in freshwater streams, is a great table delicacy.**

Unlike fishes, other animals that live in the water do not have backbones and they take on many forms. Some look like plants, such as sea-anemones and corals, but in fact they are flesh-eating creatures. Jellyfishes are shaped like umbrellas and move about by slowly opening and closing their 'umbrellas'. Starfish, of which there are nearly 2,000 species, live at the bottom of the sea in great variety of form and colour.

Generally speaking, water animals without backbones are harmless to man but there are a few exceptions. The Portuguese Man-of-War looks quite pretty as it rides on top of the warm sea but underneath the water are scores of long tentacles waiting to do their deadly work.

Below **This is a beadlet anemone. Its delicate waving tentacles are poisonous barbs which paralyse tiny creatures.**

Reptiles and amphibians

Most people think of reptiles as horrible, slimy creatures and their very name causes a shiver. Yet few of the 5,000 species are dangerous to man and they play a useful part in the balance of nature.

The reptile family is divided into five sections: Crocodilians, the Tuatara, Lizards, Snakes, and Turtles. Reptiles represent a higher form of life than amphibians, from which they have developed.

Reptiles are animals with backbones and they breathe air through lungs. One very useful feature they have is that their bodies, which are covered with scales or plates for protection, can change to the temperature of the air or water around them. Apart from the tortoises, all reptiles have ribs and teeth. In most cases the females lay shell-covered eggs but sometimes they produce live young.

Of the Crocodilians (alligators, cay-mans, crocodiles and gavials), by far the most dangerous are the man-eating Nile and Salt-water Crocodiles, which grow to an average length of 20 feet *6 metres*. Alligators are wary of man and will attack only when cornered.

The Tuatara is a peace-loving animal, which can only be found on a few small islands in New Zealand. It is probably the oldest and rarest reptile to have survived from prehistoric times.

Above **At the top of the page is a Flap-necked Chameleon, a lizard which uses its long tongue to capture insects for food. Beneath it is a Leopard Tortoise.**

Below **In this drawing are seen American Alligators and a Nile Crocodile.**

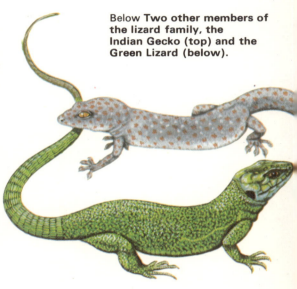

Below **Two other members of the lizard family, the Indian Gecko (top) and the Green Lizard (below).**

The most numerous of all reptiles are the lizards, which number about 2,500 species. Iguanas, perhaps the best-known lizards, with 300 species, live only in the western hemisphere; yet the chameleons, with their fast-changing colours and rolling eyes, number less than 50 species and roam much farther afield. As its name suggests one of the fiercest of all the lizards is the Gila Monster.

Snakes, despite their bad reputation, are generally harmless. There are, of course, exceptions, and some snakes are poisonous. Constrictors and pythons are so large that they can include goats and leopards in their diet. The most dangerous of the poisonous snakes is the King Cobra, which will attack man if disturbed.

Scientists call the entire turtle family Chelonians, and this includes terrapins and tortoises as well as turtles. The turtle lives in the water and has flippers instead of legs. The tortoise is a land creature, while the terrapin divides its time between water and land.

The largest tortoise is the Giant Tortoise which lives on the Galapagos Islands. It is so big that a child can ride on its back. Some turtles are called Snapping Turtles and live in freshwater streams. There are also Sea Turtles and Mud Turtles.

Amphibians, unlike the reptiles, breathe mainly through their skins. They begin life in the water as eggs protected by a jelly-like substance. Then they develop into limbless tadpoles and later into creatures with legs, lungs, and eyelids. Salamanders, newts, frogs, toads and caecilians (worm-like amphibians) form the 1,800 species. Like every animal family, salamanders have their giants, found in Japan and China, and they are the largest of all the amphibians. Frogs and toads are able to live anywhere in the world except the extreme north near the Arctic Circle.

Above **Shown here, from top to bottom, are an Iguana, the Common Frog and a male Mid-wife Toad with eggs attached to its body. On the right are seen four snakes, from top to bottom, the European Grass Snake, the Scarlet King Snake, the Puff Adder and a boa constrictor, the Anaconda.**

Right **Butterflies and moths are the most popular and attractive insects. They exhibit a wide range of colour and size. Some are beautifully marked as can be seen in these drawings of a selection of species from various parts of the world. They are (1) Garden Tiger Moth; (2)** *Ornithoptera priamus*; **(3)** *Acraea anemosa*; **(4)** *Actias maemas* **Moth; (5)** *Pereute leucodrosime*; **(6) Small Copper; (7) Marbled White; (8)** *Peliconius amaryllis*; **(9) Atlas Moth; (10)** *Papilio ulysses*; **(11) Owl Butterfly.**

Below **These drawings illustrate the life cycle of a Swallow-tail from chrysalis stage to the final butterfly.**

Insects and spiders

An insect is an animal with a body made up of three segments: the head, the thorax (which is between the head and the abdomen and bears legs and wings) and the abdomen. Even flying insects have their bodies arranged in this way. They breathe in air which travels directly to the tissues where it is needed. Insects eat all kinds of food, plant or animal, fresh or decayed, but they have two main ways of feeding: there are those that bite and chew, and those that suck.

After mating, female insects lay eggs and when the larva inside is ready to hatch it will break out of its shell by pushing hard with special 'egg-bursters' on its head. Most insects' larvae behave in this way.

Not much is known about the brain-power of insects, but we do know, for instance, that ants have highly developed senses. When they go off on hunting trips they find their way home by noting the direction of the sun or the light that comes from the sky. Ants never live alone but in great colonies where they follow a strict pattern of communial life.

Some insects migrate in the same way as birds. Many moths migrate but the best-known migrants are the Monarch butterflies of North America. In the summer they are scattered over the countryside but when the cold weather comes they all gather together and move southwards.

Some insects cause a lot of damage and this is mainly the outcome of their feeding habits. Plant-feeders such as grasshoppers, caterpillars and saw-flies do untold damage to cultivated crops. Insects that feed from rotting material carry germs on their feet which they leave behind when they settle on fresh food that we are about to eat. Flies are the worst culprits for doing this. Other insects, such as mosquitoes, pass on disease by biting. The 'parasite' insects do not just bite man or other animals but stay attached to their 'host' for a long time.

Fortunately for us, most insects are harmless and some even do a useful job of work for man. The Praying Mantis eats some of the harmful insects and so do the colourful lady-birds and graceful dragonflies. Butter-flies and bees pollinate our flowers. The bee also gives us honey and the silkworm moth supplies man with silk for clothing.

Spiders and scorpions are not classed as insects, as they have only two body segments. Spiders do not start life as larvae, but hatch out as tiny copies of their parents, rather like the babies of mammals.

They help to keep down the insect population. Like man they are capable of making artificial traps to catch their food. Not all spiders build web traps, though. Some are hunters and catch food by running, jumping and pouncing on their victims. All spiders have one thing in common and that is they kill or paralyse their victims with a poisonous bite which is injected through two fangs.

Scorpions, which are related to spiders, are found mainly in the deserts of hot countries. They have a pair of powerful claws at the head and a 'sting' in the tail. When attacking or defending, the tail curves right over the scorpion's back so that it faces forwards.

On this page are seen a number of different species of insects, spiders and scorpions. They are (1) African Beauty Dragonfly; (2) Honey Bee; (3) Wasp; (4) Ladybird; (5) Rhinoceros Beetle; (6) Great Longhorn Beetle; (7) Scorpion; (8) Argiope; (9) Jumping Spider; (10) Cat Flea; (11) Bluebottle; (12) Stick-tight Flea; (13) Leaf-cutter Ant; (14) Termites. Also shown at the top of the page is a spider's web and at the bottom a termite hill, some of which are built up above the height of a man.

Birds

Birds are animals which have feathers and most of them can fly. These are the important differences between them and all other animals, although bats, among the mammals, are also capable of true flight. Like reptiles, birds lay eggs in which their young develop, but they do much more than most creatures in the care and protection they give to their offspring.

Birds are divided into various classes in the same way as all other animals but there is no simple or clear-cut system of grouping into which they fall. In a very general sense there are land birds – which either live on the ground in trees or bushes or spend most of their time in the air – and water birds. Land birds include what are called the 'perching birds'. Among these are the common garden birds, such as sparrows, finches and thrushes, which have feet specially adapted to grip on to branches. Also in this group are the crow family and the highly coloured birds of paradise. Another 'land' bird which, although it nests on the ground, spends most of its time in the air, is the skylark, which will sing for long periods while on the wing.

Game birds, including the turkey, pheasant and grouse, which are shot for sport and are eaten, are also land birds. Others include the toucan of Central America with its enormous beak; woodpeckers, which will chip away tree bark in search of insects; and the cuckoo, which sometimes lays its eggs in another bird's nest, leaving them to be reared by foster parents.

Birds that live on the wing are those which hunt for their food while

Birds' eggs vary in colour and size but they are mostly oval in shape. The colouring and markings on the eggs help to camouflage them 1 Ostrich, 2 Duck, 3 Puffin, 4 Golden Eagle, 5 Blackbird.

Many birds which breed in the colder northern lands of the world will seek warmer climates as winter approaches. They fly in great flocks across oceans and continents, and cover hundreds, sometimes thousands of miles. When summer comes again they return to their old haunts, pin-pointing their destination with astonishing accuracy. The amazing thing about bird migration is not only the distances involved but the fact that flights both to and fro begin and end at the same time each year, as if to a time-table. The routes taken appear to be fixed and it is believed that birds have an instinct for using the sun and the stars to help them find their way across the globe on their long journeys.

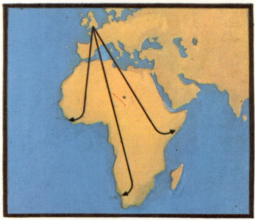

Above **Swallows migrate from northern Europe in winter to the warmer climate of South Africa, and they always travel during the day.**

Above **There are over 8,000 different species of birds and something of their great variety of shape and colouring can be seen in these drawings of birds from different parts of the world. The birds are 1 Puffin; 2 Herring Gull; 3 Golden Eagle; 4 Tawny Owl; 5 Pintail Duck; 6 Grey Parrot; 7 Humming Bird; 8 Kookaburra; 9 Robin; 10 Swallow; 11 Blackbird; 12 Kingfisher.**

Right **Bowerbirds live mostly in Australia and the males build bowers or playing grounds which they decorate with shells, stones and flowers to attract the females. These bowers are not nests but are used solely for mating.**

Below **When the male peacock displays its tail it is a shimmering fan of colour.**

flying. They may be either birds of prey or insect-catchers.

Water birds may be wading birds, swimming birds or sea birds. Wading birds are generally tall and dignified creatures, like the flamingo and the heron. Swimming birds are the familiar and friendly ducks and geese, as well as the most graceful bird of all, the swan. Geese are also excellent fliers and can travel thousands of miles in the air. Some of the brilliantly coloured kingfishers are water birds, although Australia's kookaburra, or laughing jackass, which belongs to the same family, is a land bird. Sea birds, like the gulls, auks and guillemots, nest on rocky cliffs and sea shores in vast colonies.

Flightless birds are those which have lost the ability to fly. They are mostly the largest and heaviest birds such as the ostrich, rhea and emu, which live in the southern parts of the world. Penguins, too, belong in the south, mostly in and around the Antarctic continent. Although they cannot fly they use their wings as flippers when swimming underwater.

Above **Among the birds which can no longer fly are the penguin, ostrich and the kiwi, which lives in New Zealand.**

Mammals

In terms of evolution mammals are the most successful of all land animals. The basis of their success is the way they care for their young. The word 'mammal' comes from the Latin *mammilla*, which means breast, and tells us that young animals are fed on milk from the mother.

The most advanced mammals are the primates, which include monkeys, apes, lemurs and man. All primates

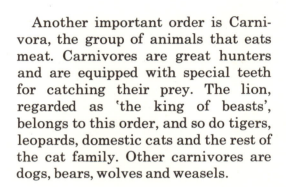

Below **The duck-billed platypus, an egg-laying mammal which lives in burrows on the river banks and hunts all its food in the water.**

Below **The walrus, of which there are two species, one living in the Atlantic and one in the Pacific. It has a thick layer of blubber and a very tough hide to combat the cold. The walrus dives for its food and eats great quantities everyday.**

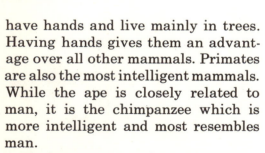

Another important order is Carnivora, the group of animals that eats meat. Carnivores are great hunters and are equipped with special teeth for catching their prey. The lion, regarded as 'the king of beasts', belongs to this order, and so do tigers, leopards, domestic cats and the rest of the cat family. Other carnivores are dogs, bears, wolves and weasels.

Right **A kangaroo is a marsupial, which means it has a pouch. The baby can be seen resting in its mother's pouch.**

have hands and live mainly in trees. Having hands gives them an advantage over all other mammals. Primates are also the most intelligent mammals. While the ape is closely related to man, it is the chimpanzee which is more intelligent and most resembles man.

The largest order of mammals is the Rodentia. Rodents are rapid breeders and are difficult to control. They are gnawing animals and have to gnaw in order to keep their teeth at the right length. Squirrels are climbing rodents, and beavers, the great rodent builders of the animal kingdom, live in water. Rats and mice are happy to live anywhere near food, and hamsters and marmots like to stay near the ground and tunnel beneath it.

Left **The hoofed mammals. The giraffe which lives in herds in Africa, feeds on acacia trees, stripping the leaves with its long tongue. In front of the giraffe is a springbok, now a rare animal. The other mammal in the picture is a gnu.**

Left **The anteater which is a toothless primitive mammal. It has a long, tapering snout, a sticky tongue and extra long claws which it uses for breaking open ant hills when searching for food.**

Below **The largest of the big cats, the tiger, which kills by biting its victim's throat.**

Marsupials are mammals with pouches used for carrying the young, and nearly all species live in Australia. These include kangaroos, wombats and the cuddly-looking koalas. Australia also has a marsupial cat and a marsupial squirrel called the Cuscus. Other mammals living in Australia, such as cattle, sheep and rabbits, have been introduced by man.

Also natives of Australasia are the two primitive egg-laying mammals, the Platypus and the Echidna, which are a living link between the reptiles of the past and ourselves.

Above **A beaver, a rodent that lives in the rivers and lakes chiefly in North and Central America.**

The order of Ungulata consists of those mammals having hoofs. Horses, rhinoceroses, deer, antelopes, camels and cattle are ungulates, and they are divided into families according to the number of toes they have on each hoof. Most ungulates are fleet of foot and are vegetarian. The edentates are an odd collection of mammals with no visible teeth, including armadillos and pangolins, which live mainly in Africa and South America. Elephants are the largest land mammals. Bats, the only flying mammals, belong to the order Chiroptera.

Sea-dwelling mammals include whales, dolphins and porpoises. Whales may look like fish but the unborn babies of whales show many mammal-like characteristics which die out in the adult animal. Dolphins are intelligent sea mammals with a built-in 'sonar device' which enables them to move about in darkness without knocking into anything.

Above **An armadillo and a bat, both of them mammals.**

Right **A Mandrill.**

Left **Dogs have lived with man since prehistoric times and no other animal has so strong a place in man's affections. The variety of breeds is enormous, there being well over a hundred different types. Those shown here are (1) Greyhound, which has been used for racing and hare-coursing since the time of Elizabeth I; (2) Afghan Hound, one of the oldest breeds; (3) Alsatian or German Shepherd Dog; (4) St. Bernard, famous for its life-saving exploits; (5) Chihuahua, one of the smallest breeds.**

Pets and domestic animals

Man has kept pets probably since the time when he first made a home for himself and his family. The first animals to live with man were dogs, and today perhaps the most popular household pet is still the dog. This is partly because a dog can be chosen to fit in almost exactly with the needs of the particular home and family it is to live with.

The variety of the different breeds is enormous, and size is perhaps the most important element in the choice of a dog as a pet. They can vary from the Chihuahua, only about six pounds, *2·7 kilogrammes* in weight, to the great St. Bernard, which can weigh up to 200 pounds, *90 kilogrammes*.

Alsatians and poodles are among the most popular breeds today but

Above **The domestic cat is a member of the Cat family which includes the 'big' cats such as the lion and the tiger. Although cats have been kept as pets by man certainly as long ago as the time of ancient Egypt, they have changed very little and do not show such a great variety of breeds as dogs. The cats shown here are (1) Long-haired Blue Persian and (2) Siamese.**

there are many other dogs, such as the rough collie, golden retriever, labrador and red setter, which make excellent companions and will regard themselves as members of the household rather than mere pets.

Cats are usually a lot more independent than dogs, but nevertheless they will respond to love and affection. There are three main groups of pure-bred cats. First, the very graceful Orientals, which include the Siamese, Burmese, Abyssinian and Russian blues. They all have a lean, elegant look, with taut, smooth muscles. The second group is the Persians, which are long-haired, thick and well-muscled, with short and powerful necks. The third group of pure-bred cats is the European, domestic or British short-haired. This group has short but dense coats, and included in the breed is the tail-less Manx cat, which is said to be the greatest hunter in the cat family.

The vast majority of cats are not pure-bred at all and may have features belonging to one or more of the three main groups. Although cats have a slightly shorter life span than dogs, both can live for 12 years or more.

Because of the increasing number of dwellings being built, such as blocks of flats, where dogs and cats are often not allowed to live, people are choosing smaller pets that can be kept in cages. The hamster is perhaps the most popular of these. The first hamster was not discovered until 1930, during a scientific expedition in Syria and, in fact, all our pet hamsters are the descendants of an original mother and her twelve babies. Hamsters are particularly suitable as house pets for they are nocturnal, that is, they sleep during the day and wake up in the evening, when the family has more time to play with them.

Guinea-pigs and rabbits are natural outdoor pets and will live happily in a weather proof hutch in the garden. The guinea-pig is a gentle creature descended from a relative that lives wild in Brazil. Rats and mice need a lot of exercise and therefore their cages should be as big as possible.

Not to be forgotten in the list of domestic animals are the creatures that help man in his work and also provide him with food and clothing. Elephants work hard for their living in Burma, where they are trained to transport timber. Oxen are used for tilling the land and sheep give us wool. Other farm animals, such as goats, pigs, chickens and cattle keep man supplied with meat, eggs, milk and other dairy produce.

Below **Among the animals which work for man is the Indian elephant (1), which is still used in the East for haulage. Farmyard animals which give us meat, milk, wool, and eggs are (2) Tamworth Pig; (3) Gayal; (4) Bantam Fowl; (5) Jersey Cow; (6) Romney Marsh Sheep.**

Below **All kinds of animals may be kept as pets, though some are obviously more suitable than others. Among the smaller animals which make good pets are (1) Dutch Rabbit; (2) Greek Tortoise; (3) Golden Hamster; (4) Budgerigar; (5) Canary.**

Above **The horse of today has developed from a creature called Eohippus (1) which lived about 70 million years ago. Man domesticated the horse in primitive times. Also shown in the picture are (2) Clydesdale; (3) Przewalski's or Mongolian Wild Horse; (4) Thoroughbred Racehorse.**

The History of Man

It is only in the last few hundred years that man has come to realise how small he is in the vast expanse of the universe. Science has taught him that the earth he lives on is like a mere speck of dust in the air. And the span of man's life on earth is very short compared with the estimated age of the planet. The earth was formed about 5,000 million years ago but man has lived on it for only about 500,000 years. In other words, if the whole period of the earth's life was divided into 10,000 equal parts, man would have existed for only one of them.

The other fact about man which is now accepted by nearly everyone is that he is part of the great chain of life which began on earth thousands of millions of years ago. He has evolved, or developed, within the animal kingdom and is classified as a mammal. He belongs to the group called primates, which includes the apes and monkeys, to which he is related. Most biologists believe that man and the ape had a common ancestor.

The fossil remains of bones, skulls, tools and weapons buried in the earth and discovered by scientists have made it possible for many of the

Below Man is a meat-eating creature and he used to hunt for his food. In the early days of his existence, he had to use primitive weapons like clubs and lumps of rock.

Left **Some stages in the development of man. They are (1) Southern Ape-man; (2) Peking Man; (3) Neanderthal Man and (4) *Homo sapiens*.**

Right **Man learnt in time to shape flints by chipping flakes off them. The picture shows some tools and weapons made of flints. At the bottom of the picture, a flint is being used as a saw blade to cut through a piece of wood.**

various stages of man's development to be plotted. But there are still missing links and it is not easy to decide which animal was the first true man. Certainly, man is the most successful of all animals. He has a large and complex brain, can use tools, has the power of speech and the ability to reason. He has adapted himself to live in almost every natural condition found on earth, and in space itself.

The oldest man-like primates are called australopithecines, and they lived in southern Africa from 1–2 millions years ago. They were probably cave-dwellers and may have used simple tools. About 500,000 years ago more developed creatures such as Java Man and Peking Man existed. There is evidence that they used fire for heating and cooking. Neanderthal Man lived in parts of Europe about 100,000 years ago, and was skilled in the use of weapons and tools.

Man, as a tool-making animal, was given the name *Homo sapiens*, or 'Man, the wise one'. During the Old Stone Age, before the discovery of metal, he wandered about from place to place, living 'off the land', hunting animals, eating wild vegetation and learning to fish. These early men probably had rough shelters and some form of

clothing made from skins. Man's first permanent homes were caves, and it was about 10–12,000 years ago that the famous cave paintings of animals and people, discovered in France and Spain, were done.

The term Stone Age (usually divided into three periods, called Old, Middle and New) does not apply to a fixed period of time. When the early civilisations of the ancient world were very advanced and highly organised, people in Britain were still living in the Stone Age. In the same way, certain primitive people still live in Stone Age conditions today, and it is possible to see the way man behaved thousands of years ago by studying the everyday life of such people.

The Ice Ages were periods when large areas of the globe were covered with ice. They began about 1 million years ago. When the last of them was over, about 10,000 years ago, and the land became warmer again, man began to settle down and live by farming. The practice of agriculture formed the basis for society as we know it today, and it first began in the fertile valleys of Egypt and Mesopotamia.

Below **Most children know that by creating friction near dry material like tinder, you can make a fire. Early man's discovery of this meant that he could become more civilised. He soon preferred to eat cooked instead of raw meat.**

River valley civilisations

History begins only with the records man was able to leave behind him. The earliest civilisations grew up around four great river valleys: the Tigris/Euphrates in Mesopotamia, the Nile in Egypt, the Yellow River in China and the Indus in India. In these places, so far as we know, men first created organised societies and, what is most important, made lasting records of what they did.

Above **The earliest Egyptian boats were made from bundles of papyrus reeds tied together.**

Above **Wall paintings found at Knossos, capital of an ancient civilisation on the island of Crete, suggest that athletes performed a dangerous form of bull-baiting as a popular public entertainment.**

Key dates in world history
4000 BC Sumerians established on Plain of Shinar.
3500 BC Sumerian cities, Ur, Erech etc. established.
3400 BC Upper and Lower Egypt joined. 1st Dynasty.
2500/1500 BC Indus valley civilisation.
2500/1400 BC Minoan civilisation in Crete.
1760/1122 BC Shang Dynasty in China.
1750/550 BC Persian Empire.
1225 BC Israelites leave Egypt.
1100/612 BC Assyrian Empire.

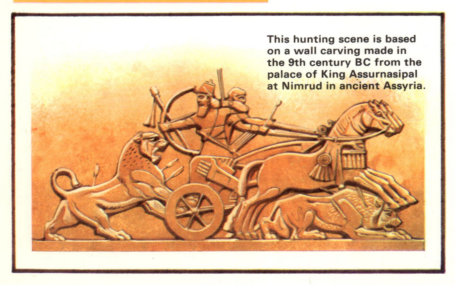

This hunting scene is based on a wall carving made in the 9th century BC from the palace of King Assurnasipal at Nimrud in ancient Assyria.

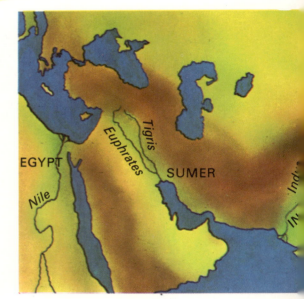

No one can give an exact date when these civilisations began. As with every stage of man's development, the formation of these civilisations took a long time; the gradual coming together of people into social groups on a large scale, however, is thought to have happened about 5000 BC. The Indus valley civilisations at Mohenjo-daro and Harappa in India are later, perhaps about 2500 BC; and there are no records before the beginning of the Shang dynasty, about 1750 BC, of Chinese civilisation, although it goes further back than this.

Mesopotamia, which means 'the land between two rivers', was known in ancient times as Sumer, and its people as Sumerians. It was an area of independent city-states, the most famous of which is Ur. The people who first settled there came from the flat, high country we now know as Iran, or Persia. They were already farmers and they began to cultivate isolated areas of fertile land where the earth was rich. As these communities grew, the city-states did not band together but lived in a state of constant war with each other.

The Sumerians were skilled metal workers, particularly in bronze, which is an alloy (mixture) of tin and copper: this is why the period is often called the Bronze Age. The Sumerians were also one of the first peoples to use writing. They invented a system called cuneiform, in which marks were made on soft clay with a stylus, because they needed to keep a record of their possessions and such things as taxes collected from the people.

The first true nation was Egypt. Here the conditions for early settlement were roughly the same as in Mesopotamia, and life was centred around a great river, the Nile. Each year, rain on the tall mountains of Ethiopia, through which the Nile passes, causes the river to flood. This leaves a top layer of rich, black mud on the land in which crops grow well.

Above **The headdress of a Sumerian queen discovered in the royal tomb at Ur.**

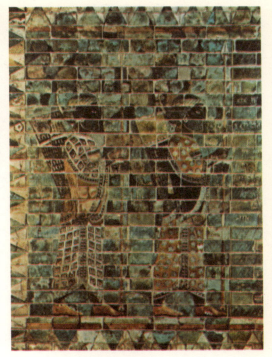

Above **The archers of King Darius are pictured on enamelled tiles on the palace at Susa (6th century BC).**

River Valley Civilisations

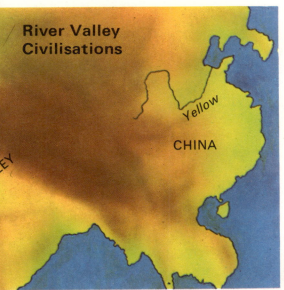

Yellow

CHINA

Right **A three-legged bronze cauldron dating from the Shang dynasty in China.**

Below **This bronze figure of a dancing girl was made by people of the Indus valley about 4,000 years ago.**

At first, the floods did not go down naturally and some way of distributing the water had to be found. This need for irrigation (a system for watering the land) made the people work together for the common good, and it was this fact, more than any other, which probably led to the first united nation of people.

Egypt was made up of two distinct areas. The oldest part, called Lower Egypt, was the rich delta land where the Nile branches out and flows into the Mediterranean. Upper Egypt ran from the delta along the narrow valleys which follow the course of the Nile, to Aswan in the south. The history of

Egypt really begins about 3400 BC when the two lands were united under one king, called the pharaoh. He ruled from Memphis and his symbol of power was the double crown, which combined the white crown of Upper Egypt with the red crown of Lower Egypt.

The early people of China and India also depended on the fertile land of river valleys. The Chinese discovered for themselves many of the things which had been 'invented' in Egypt and Mesopotamia. The most striking thing about the early cities of India is their carefully planned streets and buildings and their 'modern' drainage system.

Above **The ruins of Athena's temple – the Parthenon – on the Acropolis in Athens.**

Below **Rival city states of Athens and Sparta were constantly at war during the 5th century BC.**

Greeks and Romans

The first wandering tribes to settle in in the mountain peninsula of Greece came from the north about 2000 BC. They were an Indo-European people called the Achaeans. Before they came, highly developed civilisations existed in some of the islands in the Aegean Sea, on the coast of Asia Minor (where ancient Troy was situated) and, most important of all, on the island of Crete, where the Minoans already had links with the older civilisations of Egypt and Mesopotamia. Early Greece owes a great deal to the Minoans, who were mysteriously wiped out by a fire which swept the island about 1400 BC.

Because Greece has a chain of mountains running down its spine and its coastline is cut into a jagged

Below **This map shows how the Roman Empire expanded until, at the height of its power in AD 117, it included all the lands around the Mediterranean Sea.**

Above **Pericles, the most brilliant statesman of the Golden Age of Greece, had the temples on the Acropolis built.**

Below **A golden funeral mask found at Mycenae by the German archaeologist Heinrich Schliemann. He called it the 'Mask of Agamemnon'.**

Below **Here is an example of early Greek jewellery. It is part of a gold belt from Thessaly and is dated about the 3rd century BC.**

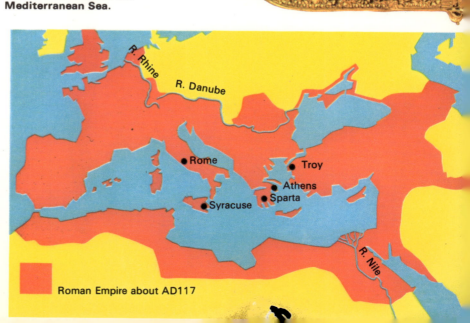
Roman Empire about AD117

pattern of inlets by the sea, it was often difficult for people in one place to communicate with those in another. This is one of the reasons why Greece became a country of city-states, such as Athens, Thebes and Sparta.

Although Greece was split into self-governing city-states, the people were bound together by many beliefs and traditions which they had in common. This was the origin of the Greek spirit, which was based on a fierce feeling for personal independence. At first, the city-states were ruled by kings but gradually a system grew up called democracy (a word which comes from the Greek for 'people', *demos*). Unlike 'democracies' in the modern world the Greek city-state was a small unit. Athens,

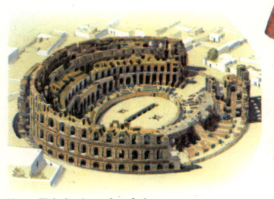

Above **This is the ruin of the Colosseum which was a Roman amphitheatre built in AD 72–80. It was in the Colosseum that the gladiators would fight wild animals. The first games held there lasted a hundred days and thousands of men and beasts were killed.**

Below **A Roman aqueduct at Segovia in Spain.**

for example, had only about 40,000 citizens and of these every freeman was entitled to speak and vote at meetings of the Assembly, or parliament. So the Greeks did not elect other people to represent them, but each freeman took a personal part in government.

During the greatest period of Greek history, in the 5th century BC, called the 'classical' period, Athens was the centre of the world. It was at this time that the temples of the Acropolis, which exist today as noble ruins, were built under the direction of the great leader, Pericles. The art, literature, science and philosophy of the 'classical' Greek period have had more influence on western civilisation than that of any other period in the history of man.

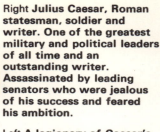
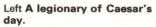

Right **Julius Caesar, Roman statesman, soldier and writer. One of the greatest military and political leaders of all time and an outstanding writer. Assassinated by leading senators who were jealous of his success and feared his ambition.**

Left **A legionary of Caesar's day.**

Below **A Roman charioteer.**

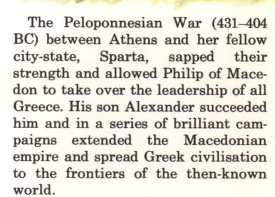

The Peloponnesian War (431–404 BC) between Athens and her fellow city-state, Sparta, sapped their strength and allowed Philip of Macedon to take over the leadership of all Greece. His son Alexander succeeded him and in a series of brilliant campaigns extended the Macedonian empire and spread Greek civilisation to the frontiers of the then-known world.

The power of Greece passed eventually to Rome. At the time of Alexander the Great, this Italian city already controlled the whole of Italy. She was then to engage in a bitter struggle with Carthage in the Punic Wars which lasted, on and off, for over 100 years. Rome emerged the victor and spread her entire empire along the shores of north Africa and to the coasts of Britain.

The Greeks had given the world great art and thinking; the Romans, who were practical men, gave it good government and good laws. Wherever the Romans went on their conquests they tried to allow the people as much freedom as possible, while encouraging them to live in the Roman way. The Romans were also great engineers and evidence of the long-lasting strength of their buildings can still be seen all over Europe. Roman rule lasted for about 500 years and it brought many benefits to people within the Empire. There was a time in the 1st and 2nd centuries AD when for nearly 100 years there was no war and the whole world was at peace.

The Dark Ages

The Dark Ages is the name given to a period of history following the collapse of the Roman Empire, when western civilisation was overrun and Christian ideas were challenged by the barbarians. Who were these barbarians and where did they come from? The word 'barbarian' is Greek and means 'foreign', and the Romans applied it to anyone who did not share their way of life. The barbarian hordes were made up of a number of different races from the north and east of Europe and Asia. They included the Goths, Vandals, Franks, Saxons and, fiercest of them all, the Huns, who came from central Asia. They overran the western part of the old Roman Empire and brought a period of darkness to Europe.

Below **Early books were hand written by monks. They were beautifully decorated with bright colours and gold leaf.**

476	Fall of Roman Empire in the West
563	St. Columba lands on Iona
570	Birth of Mohammed
597	St. Augustine's Christian mission to England
619	T'ang dynasty in China
622	Moslem religion founded
664	Synod of Whitby
711	Moslems invade Spain
800	Charlemagne crowned as Holy Roman Emperor
871	Alfred the Great, king of Wessex
c. 1000	Vikings discover Nova Scotia
1066	Battle of Hastings. William of Normandy becomes king of England

Left **These gilt bronze horses which now stand before St. Mark's Cathedral in Venice are part of Crusading history. They once stood on Trajan's Imperial Arch in Rome. Constantine took them to Constantinople, but when the city was attacked by Christian crusaders in 1204 the horses were moved to Venice.**

Below **This is a Viking longship built about the 10th century. It was in warships like this that the Vikings invaded Britain and western Europe between the 8th and 10th centuries.**

One of the most important dates in the history of the breakdown of Roman power is AD 364, when the Empire was split into two parts. In AD 330 the emperor Constantine had already moved the capital to Byzantium in Asia Minor and renamed it Constantinople. Then it was decided that the Empire was too big to govern from one place and two capitals, one in the east and one in the west, were set up. This and other signs of weakness were seized upon by the barbarian tribes in the north who were eager to attack Rome.

Only in the monasteries were the traditions of learning guarded. In AD 380 the emperor Theodosius I had decreed that Christianity should be the official religion of the Roman state. Even before this the Christian faith had spread to the outermost limits of the Roman Empire, where it had developed and flourished in spite of the confusion of the Dark Ages.

Despite the invasions, during the next two centuries the power of Christianity grew and the Bishop of Rome, whom Christians believed had inherited the mantle of St. Peter himself, became known as pope, or father, of the Catholic Church. Pope Gregory sent St. Augustine to England in AD 597 to bring the pagan Saxons back to the Christianity which the British had known in Roman times. On the continent of Europe the warrior-king Charlemagne came to the throne and in AD 800 founded the Holy Roman Empire, which united large areas of central Europe and lasted for 1,000 years.

The pagan people of north Germany made a final bid to challenge the Christian world of the west when the Vikings, or Danes, attacked Europe's coasts and rivers from the sea. This 'Viking Age' lasted from the 8th to the 10th centuries, and after many fierce battles the Vikings settled in the lands they had come to conquer and became a part of them. In England, the Danish invaders mixed easily with the Saxons who had taken over the country after the fall of the Roman Empire, for they had many of the same customs. The final settlement of the Vikings came when Canute became

Below (1) Saracens fighting Christians in the Crusades. (2) shows a Saracen sword which could be opened up like scissors. Armour once had jewels on it like this Celtic shield (3). King Alfred's jewel is seen in (4).

Above Here is a typical Viking warrior of the 10th century. The Vikings were clever seafarers and brave soldiers who served as a volunteer army under leaders of great ability. They were very well disciplined but brutal and were allowed to keep what they had looted from those they had captured or killed.

king of England in 1014 and for a time ruled over England, Denmark and Norway.

Another great event of the Dark Ages was the coming of the Arab peoples upon the scene of world history. In the 7th century Mohammed became the prophet of Islam and united the Arab people in one faith. Their conquests, which were spurred on by a burning desire to convert the whole world, extended over the Middle East, along the coast of north Africa and into Spain.

Above **The jousting tournaments of medieval knights provided a very entertaining sport. Sometimes, however, they were fought in earnest and the lance became a lethal weapon.**

The medieval world

During their campaigns in the Middle East the Arabs captured Jerusalem, the Holy City of Christianity. At a Council in 1095, Pope Urban II called upon the Christian knights of Europe to band together in a great fighting Crusade to recapture the city. This led to a series of Crusades in which there were many brutal battles but few positive results. Jerusalem was taken by the Christian armies in the first Crusade, only to be re-taken by the Arab sultan, Saladin, after which it remained an Islamic city until the Allied armies captured it during the First World War in 1917.

After the barbarian invasions had died away and the northern peoples had found a place in western society, life in Europe was based on a way of government called the feudal system. The word 'feudal' comes from the Latin, meaning 'a fief', which is an area of land held by someone in return for service, either in the fields or as a soldier in time of war.

The most important thing to everyone was the land, and farming occupied the mass of the people. The peasants were poor and their lives and property belonged to a local lord. They tilled the land and produced food for themselves and for their master, in return for his protection. Each district, or manor, had its village, church, manor house and mill, set amid woods and pastureland.

The lord of the manor was usually a knight, and he in turn was a tenant or vassal of one of the powerful

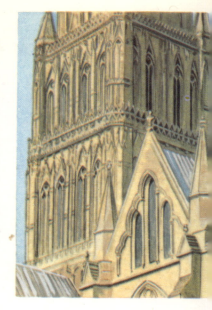

Above **Salisbury Cathedral is built in the Gothic style.**

Below right **Medieval towns had cobbled streets and overhanging wooden houses like this.**

Right **Here is Edward, the Black Prince, son of Edward III.**

Far left **These are Lombards who were bankers from Italy.**

Below **A map showing the Third Crusade of 1189. Its aim was to defeat Saladin and win back Jerusalem from the Moslems. Three important European rulers took part— Richard I (the Lion-heart) of England; Philip II of France and Frederick Barbarossa of Germany. Frederick was drowned on his way to the Holy Land.**

1095 First Crusade
1099 Capture of Jerusalem by Christian armies
1170 Murder of Becket
1187 Saladin captures Jerusalem
1215 Magna Carta signed
1260 Kublai Khan conquers China
1290 Jews expelled from England
1338 Beginning of 100 Years War
1349 Black Death
1415 Battle of Agincourt
c. 1200–1400 Hanseatic League of German cities
1431 Execution of Joan of Arc
1206 Genghis Khan founds Mongol Empire

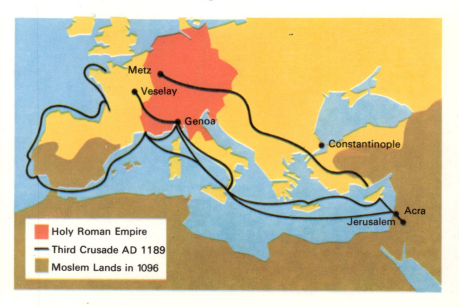

Metz
Veselay
Genoa
Constantinople
Acra
Jerusalem

Holy Roman Empire
Third Crusade AD 1189
Moslem Lands in 1096

barons who controlled the country on behalf of the king. Even so, the peasants, or serfs, were not allowed to leave the district or even get married, without the lord's permission. This meant that conditions for the peasant in the Middle Ages depended upon what kind of master he had. If the lord was just, things were bearable, but if he was not then life was hard and miserable.

The peasants' lot began to improve when it became the custom to allow them to pay their lords money instead of working for them. The most dramatic event in the Middle Ages, which affected the peasants' lives more than anything else, was the Black Death which swept across Europe in 1347–50, killing a third of the population. This meant that there were many more jobs available than men to fill them. Wages rose and so did the peasants' standard of living.

The Crusades lasted for about 200 years. This encouraged the profession of knighthood, and when the knights were not fighting the infidel abroad, they fought among themselves, either in serious battles or in mock tournaments. The sons of noblemen were trained not only to fight with lance and sword, but to be chivalrous and well-spoken and to behave in a

Below **Many noblemen retained minstrels to entertain them.**

Bottom **Medieval lovers swore undying faith to their ladies.**

Above **A peasant scene by the Flemish artist, Peter Bruegel.**

'knightly' fashion. When they had grown up to be proper knights they took serious vows to serve God and be true and valiant.

Everyday life in the Middle Ages was ruled not only by the knights and barons but by the Church. Each village had its place of worship and its priest, and the religious festivals were the only holidays the peasants had. As well as the parish churches there were the many large monasteries which grew up at this time. Into them the monks withdrew to lead a self-contained life of worship away from the world. But many of these same monks also looked after people by teaching them and caring for the sick. They also kept alive the tradition of art and learning as it was practised in the classical world, until it flowered again in the Renaissance.

Renaissance and Reformation

Towards the end of the Middle Ages, merchants began to take the place of knights, and commerce became more important than wars of honour and glory. As men moved about more from place to place, the traders of Europe became a powerful new class. Cities grew in strength and importance upon the basis of trade, and the fortunes of the principal Italian city-states – Venice, Florence, Rome, Milan – all at the very heart of the movement known as the Renaissance, were gathered from trade.

The Renaissance has been called the greatest period in the history of art and man. The word Renaissance means rebirth, and it is used principally to apply to the new surge of interest in the arts and in the importance of man as an individual. It was an age which looked back to the classical era of Greece and Rome for its inspiration. It developed in Italy in the 15th century and during the 16th spread to the rest of Europe.

One astonishing thing about works of art in the Renaissance is their universal appeal. Every age and every culture recognises the genius of Michelangelo and Leonardo da Vinci. Much of their work and that of other great artists of the period was done against a background of conflict, cruelty and great social change. It could not have existed without the rich patronage of the popes and monarchs of that extravagant age.

Above **Henry VIII met Francis I of France in 1520 on the Field of the Cloth of Gold to settle disputes between them.**

Below **These pictures show (1) Charles V the Holy Roman Emperor; (2) Frederick the Wise and (3) Pope Paul III.**

Yet these artists speak directly from the heart to all men in every place and at any time.

Gutenberg's mid-15th-century invention of movable type and the growth of printing meant that knowledge, in the shape of printed books, was available to more people. Libraries were set up and households began to be able to afford a row of books on their shelves. Education spread and with it, curiosity. As well as being a period of rebirth in the arts and learning, the Renaissance produced men who were prepared to challenge the narrow traditional views of mankind and the universe. They were the scientists and explorers who trod new ground, either in the minds of men or on the shores of undiscovered lands.

Alongside the Renaissance there grew up a great challenge to the single authority of the Catholic Church in Rome. In medieval times Christianity had succeeded not only in spreading its message throughout the civilised world but in remaining united. Now a movement which came to be known as the Reformation caused many churchmen to break with Rome. One reason for this was that the Church had become rich, imposing taxes on poor people, and also the fact that several of the bishops, who in turn filled the office of pope, had become too involved with matters of state and were not good men.

The chief voice raised against the authority of the Church was that of

Right **Sir Thomas More, Lord Chancellor of England,** who would not recognise Henry VIII as head of the English Church. He was arrested on a charge of treason and beheaded in 1535.

Martin Luther, a German monk, who openly challenged Rome in a practical way by pinning up on the door of a church in Wittenburg a paper which listed 95 points on which he claimed the Church was wrong. He and his followers set up a rival 'reformed' church and because the chief reason for doing this was one of protest, the upholders of the new faith became known as Protestants.

Another strong feeling that grew up around the time of the Renaissance was the feeling for nationhood. Out of the confused state of Europe in the Middle Ages separate nations emerged, the first and most important being England, France and Spain.

Below **Martin Luther** a German religious reformer of the 16th century.

Below left **A page from Gutenberg's 42-line Bible.**

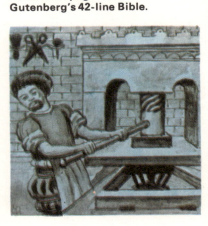

Above **Johann Gutenberg** was the first man to use moveable type in Europe. Here he is printing his Bible.

The expanding world

The age of expansion, when the frontiers of the world were extended beyond Europe and the Mediterranean lands, began at the end of the 15th century. This reaching out across unknown seas was led by Portugal. In 1418 the wealthy nobleman, Prince Henry of Portugal, began his life-long interest in exploration and discovery, which gave his country the finest ships and seamen in the world. He spent money freely in paying for expeditions and improving methods of ship-building and systems of navigation. The first quest was for a sea route to the East, and for years his tiny ships tried again and again to sail their way along the west coast of Africa.

1468 Renaissance of art at its height in Italy
1478 Inquisition begins in Spain
1486 Diaz rounds Cape of Good Hope
1492 Columbus lands in West Indies
1493 Moors defeated at Granada in Spain
1509 Accession of Henry VIII of England
1519 First circumnavigation of the world
1535 First English printed Bible
1558 Accession of Elizabeth I as queen of England
1571 Battle of Lepanto
1572 Massacre of Hugenots on St. Bartholomew's Day
1588 Spanish Armada defeated
1603 Union of the crown of England and Scotland
1620 *Mayflower* sails to America
1643 Louis XIV, king of France
1694 Bank of England founded
1696 Peter the Great, czar of Russia
1704 Battle of Blenheim
1759 Wolfe takes Quebec

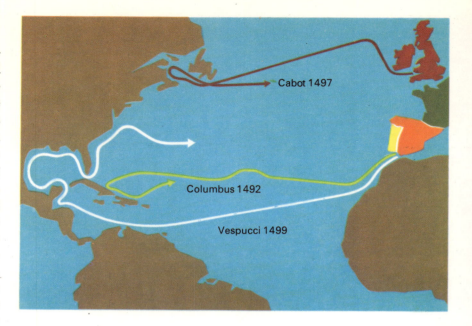

Above **This map shows the voyages of Cabot from England to Nova Scotia, 1497; of Vespucci to America, 1499 and of Columbus to the West Indies, 1492.**

Below **The Puritans were English Protestants who did not think the Reformation had gone far enough in doing away with rituals of the Catholic Church. A group of them joined the Pilgrim Fathers and sailed in 1620 to America so that they could practise their religion in peace. Here they are seen disembarking from their ship, the 'Mayflower', on to the shores of New England.**

It was after Prince Henry's death that Bartholomew Diaz finally found a way round the Cape of Good Hope, at the southern tip of Africa. This was in 1488, and before the end of the century Columbus (in 1492) had made his landfall in the West Indies, Cabot had reached Newfoundland (1497) and Vespucci had explored the northern coast of South America (1499).

This series of landings in the Americas brought Europe into contact with the New World. At the beginning of the 16th century voyages were undertaken in greater number with the object of securing new territories. The Spanish soldiers, Cortes and Pizarro, uncovered the unknown civilizations of the Aztecs in Mexico and the Incas in Peru. The first successful journey right round the world was made in 1519–22 by Magellan's expedition, although he himself was killed during the voyage. Merchant adventurers scoured the seas for new areas of trade and profit.

In the period between the end of the 15th century and the middle of the 17th, not only were new areas of the world opened up, but individual nations grew stronger and fought with each other over the new lands. Command of the seas meant home shores were safe from invasion. This was to be shown dramatically in the defeat of the Spanish Armada by the English fleet whose captains' superior seamanship won the day.

In England, particularly, the Elizabethan age saw a glittering procession of great statesmen, sailors and poets who brought fame and fortune to their country. Sir Humphrey Gilbert and Sir Walter Raleigh attempted to found colonies on the East coast of North America and so built the foundations of Britain's empire.

After the conquest of Central and South America by Spain and Portugal, the continent of North America was colonised by several European powers, chiefly Britain and France. The coastal areas, rivers and lakes were explored by the French, and in

Below **Here Hernando Cortes is seen in Mexico with some Aztec Indians whom he massacred brutally.**

1608 Champlain founded Quebec. The Pilgrim Fathers settled in New England in 1620. They were a company of Puritan exiles who sailed from Plymouth in England in the *Mayflower* to find a new home where they were free to practise their religion.

The British extended their rule in India through the East India Company, which was founded in 1600 to exploit the country's resources. In Australia, colonisation began in 1788 when the first batch of convicts sentenced to transportation were landed in New South Wales. The Dutch built up an empire based on trade in the East Indies during the 17th century, and the French settled in south-east Asia.

The 17th century has been called the 'golden age of France'. She was prosperous and powerful under the rule of an absolute monarch, Louis XIV. This concentration of power in the king led directly to the French Revolution in 1789.

Above **Christopher Columbus who sailed in 1492 to find a western route to India but found the West Indies instead.**

Below **The search for gold was one reason why so many voyages of discovery were made. This picture shows Spanish soldiers fighting pirates who were constantly plundering ships carrying gold and other valuable treasures.**

6

Left **Sir Francis Drake (1540?–96) was the first Englishman to sail round the world.**

Far left **This is a medal commemorating Drake's voyage.**

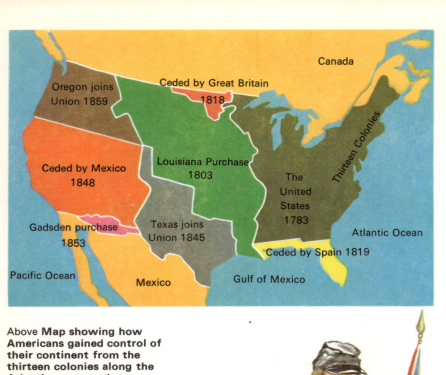

Above **Map showing how Americans gained control of their continent from the thirteen colonies along the Atlantic coast to the Pacific ocean.**

1764 Beginnings of Industrial Revolution
1776 American Declaration of Independence
1783 Treaty of Versailles
1789 French Revolution
1801 Union of Great Britain and N. Ireland
1804 Napoleon emperor of France
1805 Battle of Trafalgar Death of Nelson
1808 Peninsular War
1812 Napoleon's armies retreat from Moscow
1854/6 Crimean War
1857 Indian Mutiny
1861/5 American Civil War
1889/1902 South African War
1901 Death of Queen Victoria

Revolution and new ideas

At the time of the Revolution in France, the country was ruled by an all-powerful king and even the nobles had little part in the government of the country. They led an extravagant life at the royal court, paid no taxes, and had nothing to do with the common people. The prosperous merchants and bankers and, of course, the peasants, paid the taxes which allowed the king and his aristocratic court to lead their life of luxury. In 1789, Louis XVI decided to summon the States General, France's parliament, which had not met for 175 years. He was short of money and needed them to agree to new taxes. But the harvests had been bad for several years and the streets of Paris were full of people demanding food.

The king's last minute attempts to try and settle the unrest in his country

Below **Napoleon, emperor of France and, for a time, master of Europe.**

failed. It was too late to hold back the tide of feeling which was to sweep the king from his throne. On 14th July, 1789 a mob stormed the Bastille, the royal prison in Paris. This was the beginning of a wave of violence which spread over the whole country. In 1792 the common people had won and France became a republic. There followed a 'reign of terror' when the revolutionaries sent thousands of aristocrats, including the king and his queen, Marie Antoinette, to be beheaded by the newly-invented guillotine.

The Revolution ended the monarchy in France but out of the chaos which followed it created a new emperor – Napoleon. Between 1799 and 1815, when his armies were finally crushed at the Battle of Waterloo by the

Above **The Industrial Revolution was a time of great change and progress for industry, but life was hard for people in factories. They worked long hours in crowded and badly-lit buildings. Workers who were not satisfied with their lot formed the first trade unions in order to force employers to grant them better conditions.**

Far left **The soldier in the foreground is wearing the uniform of the Union Army at the time of the Civil War in the United States, while the two men in the background show the more casual dress of the southern Confederacy. Alongside is a portrait of Abraham Lincoln. Below left are two scenes from the French Revolution: the storming of the Bastille, the royal prison in Paris; and an execution performed by the dreaded guillotine.**

Below **The picture shows Nelson at the Battle of Trafalgar. The sailor is hoisting Nelson's famous message to his men: England expects that every man will do his duty.**

British and the Prussians, Napoleon dominated Europe.

Britain was at war with France for most of the 18th century and in Canada there was a constant struggle between the two countries. In 1759 General Wolfe and the British forces won Quebec in a surprise attack and went on to capture Montreal. Canada submitted to British rule but the thirteen colonies in North America, which were to become the original United States, rebelled against long-distance government from Britain.

The War of Independence between Britain and the colonists had been in progress for a year when the Declaration of Independence, which has remained the charter of American liberties ever since, was drawn up in 1776 by Jefferson, Franklin and other American statesmen. George Washington led the revolt and with the help of the French triumphed over the British forces. Britain recognised the United States of America as an independent country in 1783 and Washington became its first president.

During the next 70 years the American pioneers pushed westwards across their vast continent to the Pacific Ocean and established their northern boundary with Canada. Because some of the states believed in slave labour and others did not, a Civil War resulted between south and north. It lasted for four years (1861–5)

Above **In the early days of Communism, Lenin was a leading member of the Bolshevik party. After the Russian Revolution in 1917 and the overthrow of the provisional government which had been set up, Lenin was elected president of the first Soviet government.**

and ended with victory for Lincoln and the northern armies.

The Industrial Revolution, a period of great technical advance, began in Britain in the 18th century. It revolutionised industry by the introduction of new methods and machines. Britain was changed from an agricultural community to an industrial one, and similar developments took place later all over Europe and in the United States. In the 19th century Britain's industrial strength coincided with her greatest period of political power.

93

Two world wars

Man has made war against man probably since the beginning of his time on earth. But only in the 20th century have the weapons of mass destruction been so efficient and so terrible. In a curious and hopeful way the very power of modern weapons has made their use less likely – for no nation could hope to escape the consequences of an all-out attack.

The First World War (1914–18) happened because the nations of Europe were envious and frightened of one another. Ever since 1900 they had spent large sums of money arming themselves and making treaties so that different powers became grouped together as allies. The single event which sparked off the fighting seemed

Above **Three military leaders of the 1939–45 war – (1) Field Marshal Montgomery; (2) Field Marshal Rommel and (3) General Eisenhower.**

1914 Outbreak of First World War
1915 Gallipoli campaign
1916 Battle of Jutland
1916 Battle of the Somme
1917 Revolution in Russia
1918 Armistice signed
1922 Irish Free State founded
1924 First Labour government in Britain
1933 Hitler comes to power in Germany
1936 Civil War in Spain
1939 Outbreak of Second World War
1940 Evacuation of British army from Dunkirk
1941 Japanese attack on Pearl Harbour
1944 Allied armies land in France
1945 Germany and Japan surrender

Below **Tanks are an essential feature of modern warfare. At the beginning of the First World War, armoured cars had been used but their wheels could not cross the trenches. After the invention of caterpillar tracks, the tank was evolved. Britain's secret weapon first appeared in 1916 in Flanders. The picture shows the British Mark I tank.**

unimportant at the time but it set in motion a chain of events which no one seemed able to halt.

Archduke Ferdinand, heir to the Austrian throne, was murdered in Serbia in June, 1914. Austria declared war on Serbia, and Russia came in on the side of Serbia. Germany declared war on Russia and invaded Belgium and France and because of Britain's previous promises to aid those countries, she joined Belgium and France. America entered the war on the side of the Allies in 1917.

At first, everyone went to war with enthusiasm and said 'it will be over by Christmas'. In fact, the 'Great War' dragged on for four weary years, millions of men were killed and, in the light of what followed in Europe, solved very little.

Despite the determination of the Allied powers that there should never again be another war, the Second World War (1939–45) followed the

Above **A French 75 mm gun of the 1914–18 war.**

Below **The atom bomb, the first nuclear bomb ever to be used. When in 1945 one was dropped first on Hiroshima and then on Nagasaki, Japan immediately asked for an armistice.**

Left **A German tri-plane of the First World War, Richthofen's Fokker Dr.I.**

First, after a short and troubled period of only 20 years. Many will say that the peace terms imposed on Germany after the First World War made it certain that such a man as Adolf Hitler would appear, demanding to make his country strong again. This time, Germany, Italy and Japan lined up against Britain, France, the United States and Russia.

Unlike the First World War, in which troops spent years fighting over the same ground in France, there was very little trench warfare in the Second. It was a war of movement, of ships, aeroplanes and armoured vehicles, during which for a long period it seemed certain that Germany would win. It was also a war in which civilians were as exposed as the fighting men to danger and death. Massive air-raids took place on both sides, and it was from an aeroplane that the fearsome atomic bomb was unleashed by the Americans upon cities in Japan.

While the war was still in progress, Churchill and Roosevelt planned an Atlantic Charter of human rights and laid the foundations of the United Nations Organisation.

Below **Two fighter planes of the Second World War. The Vickers Supermarine Spitfire (in foreground) and the German Messerschmitt Me109.**

Above **War tactics were very different in the First World War from those used in the Second. In 1914–18 the troops dug themselves into trenches in the ground, firing at the enemy over the top. In the second war, there was much more movement of armies with a greater use of armoured vehicles.**

Below **A German 8·8 cm gun.**

Right **Field Marshal von Hindenburg who became Supreme Commander of the German Armies of the Eastern Front during the First World War.**

The modern world

All over the world there is social and scientific change, and everywhere patterns of conduct are being altered and old traditions discarded. A vast network of communications allows people of different cultures to come together, and the speed of modern transport is breaking down barriers that once existed. In this sense the world has become smaller, with many nations uniting for the common good.

It has always been the aim of man to strive for a united world. As the ancient Greeks spread their influence through many lands, they tried to unite peoples by commissioning ambassadors to settle the questions of war and peace. Believing in a common culture they standardised such things as money, weights and measures. The Roman system was quite different, for they believed that people in the countries they had conquered should have their own individual cultures, although they all abided by a common law. This system worked successfully for about 500 years and there has since

Above **The General Assembly of the United Nations Organisation in session in New York. Shortly after the Second World War, the organisation was formed to promote peace on earth through the delegates of its member nations.**

Above right **The League of Red Cross Societies established in 1924 an organisation to send food, clothing, shelter and medical supplies to areas stricken by national disasters.**

Below **This is a section of the Berlin Wall erected by the Communists to divide the city. Throughout its length it is defended by barbed wire and machine gun emplacements.**

Below **Three world leaders of modern times: (1) Richard Nixon (United States); (2) Alexei Kosygin (Soviet Russia) and Mao Tse-tung (Communist China).**

Above **Concorde in flight.**
This aircraft is the joint
product of British and
French technology and is
the first passenger plane
that can fly faster than the
speed of sound. When it
reaches this speed it goes
'through the sound barrier'
and makes a supersonic
boom which can be heard
on the ground.

Right **Computers, which do
much of the 'thinking' for
man, are being used
extensively in industry.
This picture shows a large
factory computer used for
mass production.**

Above **Two examples of the
modern world – (4) the City
Hall in Toronto, Canada, and
(5) electronic machines
which are now being used
to teach children in day
schools.**

Above **Although man is very
clever, he has not yet learnt
how to feed all the hungry
people of the world. That is
why hundreds of children
like these are under-
nourished.**

been no world government to equal
that of Rome.

Part of the world is a land of plenty,
but there are still areas where people
go hungry or have not kept pace with
20th-century developments. The fact
that people unite to build dams, or
to preserve animal life, or to study
art and science, is a hopeful sign.
Although the nations of the world
draw closer together, they still exist
under the fear of a third world war –
this time with nuclear weapons.

After the Second World War,
Germany was split into two halves and
an 'iron curtain' dropped between the

divided forces of East and West. This
created a state of tension in the world
which came to be called the 'Cold War'
–cold because it is a political war
rather than a fighting one. The Soviet
Union emerged as a leader in international affairs and other countries
near her borders came under the
Communist 'umbrella'. China, too,
another huge Communist power,
spread her influence in the Third
World.

The United Nations Organisation
was formed in 1945, so that the various
nations of the world could put forward
their points of view and argue out their
differences of opinion. But tension
continued to mount between the
United States and the Soviet Union.
With both powers balanced by
military force and the possession of
nuclear weapons, conflict has been
avoided. Now the countries are trying
to bridge the gap between them. Efforts
are being made to work together on a
joint programme of space exploration.
China, too, has relaxed her attitude
and has more contact with the western
world. These are pointers to the world
unity which must exist if mankind is
to continue to survive.

Exploration and Discovery

The search for food and shelter dominated the life of early man. Family and tribal movements from place to place were the extent of man's first steps in exploration. Whatever he discovered in his quest for new hunting grounds and better places of shelter he discovered accidentally. There would not have been the same incentives of trade and curiosity which drove explorers of later ages to find new lands and peoples.

The first true travellers or explorers were the Phoenicians, a race of people who lived on the east coast of the Mediterranean. They are celebrated in history as boat-builders and seafarers. Between about 1400 BC and 400 BC they traded with settlements on the coasts of the Mediterranean and founded several important cities, including Carthage, Tyre and Sidon. They sailed out of the Mediterranean and into the Red Sea and the Indian Ocean, and even rounded the southern coast of Africa.

At the time of the Persian wars, Greek soldiers made many extraordinary journeys on foot into unknown lands. But there is no more exciting story than that of the march of 10,000 Greeks from Babylon to the southern shores of the Black Sea under Xenophon in 401 BC.

Alexander the Great was not only a mighty conqueror and leader but was also a great explorer. The motives which drove him forward were conquest and the enlargement of his empire, but in the course of this he uncovered great marvels and mysteries in the East and spread the influence of Greek culture throughout a new world.

The Romans were less interested in exploration than they were in colonisation, but they made their influence felt on all the people in their vast empire.

During the 9th to the 11th centuries the Vikings, who came from lands around the Baltic Sea, sailed into the

Above **Head of Alexander the Great.**

Below **Hernando Cortes who conquered the Aztec Indians.**

Above **Ferdinand Magellan** and (right) **Francisco Pizarro who destroyed the Incas.**

Above right **A Peruvian vessel.**

Right **From the 9th to 10th centuries AD, the Vikings colonised much of Europe and traded with the East. Later, they set foot in the New World having sailed in a boat like the one below.**

Right **This is a scene from the adventures of Marco Polo (1254–1324) who went as a merchant and an ambassador of the Pope to the Mongol Empire. His travels in Mongolia and China took him 25 years.**

Above **After Ferdinand Magellan had suffered severe storms, he sailed into a sea so calm that he called it the Pacific. This map shows his route.**

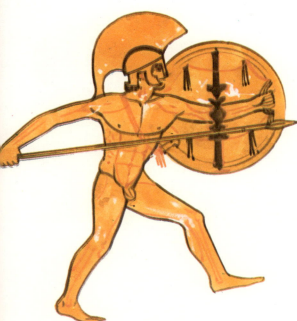

Above **An ancient Greek soldier with a shield and armour of the times.**

Right **The 15th century was an exciting time for exploration. Here are some of the important names of the period – (1) Bartholomew Diaz; (2) Vasco da Gama; (3) Amerigo Vespucci and (4) John Cabot.**

heart of Europe to conquer and settle. Their most remarkable achievements were the voyages of discovery in the 11th century when their longships sailed as far as Iceland, Greenland and the shores of North America.

After Marco Polo's many years spent in China at the court of Kublai Khan, when he helped to reveal the people of eastern lands to the western world, there followed in the 15th century a great age of exploration and discovery led by the seaman, soldiers and navigators of Portugal and Spain. The Cape of Good Hope was rounded, Columbus made his epic voyages to the West Indies, and the American mainland was explored.

Right **Christopher Columbus who discovered the Bahamas and (above) his ship, the Santa Maria.**

One driving force behind the history of exploration has been the desire to find new trading areas and new routes. Expeditions, such as the one conducted by the British sailors Willoughby and Chancellor in 1553 to find a North-east Passage to India, were often backed by merchants seeking trade. The results of these voyages were such enterprises as the Muscovy Company and the Hudson's Bay Company, founded in 1670 by Prince Rupert of the Rhine, to trade in furs with the American Indians.

Reaching out from the northern shores of the American continent and, at the other extreme, rounding Cape Horn and finding the Pacific Ocean, explorers pressed westwards across the vast expanse of sea to the East Indies and the exciting discovery of the great new continent of Australia.

It was in the 18th century that one of the greatest seamen and navigators of all time made a series of voyages in the extreme southern hemisphere which placed Australia and New Zealand firmly on the map. This was Captain Cook, whose chief aim was the search for new knowledge and experience rather than gold or trade. Cook's expeditions were genuine voyages of scientific discovery, and he took with him botanists, geographers and artists, all of whom brought back detailed and accurate records of the lands they visited. Cook himself was killed by natives on the islands of Hawaii when he and a party of marines landed on the island to retrieve a stolen boat.

Below This is an octant which is used in both astronomy and navigation. It gets its name because its curved part and two sides enclose a sector which is one eighth of a circle — *octo* being the Latin word for 'eight'.

Below A theodolite like this is used for measuring angles.

It was during the 18th century that the overriding motives of trade were replaced by a growing interest in the people and the flora and fauna of the new lands. Science was more often than not at the heart of voyages of exploration. One outcome of this was the formation of the theory of natural selection arrived at independently by Darwin and Russel Wallace as a result of their observations among the islands of Malaya and South America.

Later still, in the 19th century, man's great curiosity and sense of daring and adventure came to the fore. It was an age when to set foot on new land was justification in itself, because no one had done it before.

Above right Eskimos paddling their kayaks. These are canoes made of sealskin stretched on a wooden framework

Right The 'Endeavour' in which Cook explored the South Seas and New Zealand

Below **Here** Eskimos are trading with a ship of the Hudson's Bay Company. It was towards the end of the 15th century that John Cabot discovered what is now Hudson Bay, named after Henry Hudson who explored it in 1609. In 1670, the Hudson's Bay Company was formed to find the north-west passage, to occupy the nearby lands and to do business. Only the fur trade, however, really flourished and after 1870 the company dealt mainly in the retail trade.

The 19th century was also a period when the dark continent of Africa was opened up and exploited. One of the major themes which drove explorers into the heart of Africa to face the perils and unknown dangers was the search for the source of the Nile. This quest attracted such colourful characters as James Bruce, Richard Burton and John Hanning Speke. The most famous story of all in 19th-century Africa is that of the meeting between Dr. Livingstone and the journalist H. M. Stanley at Ujiji on the shores of Lake Tanganyika.

Right **These** are some of the great seafarers and explorers of the 16th and 18th centuries. They are (1) Sir Francis Drake; (2) Matthew Flinders; (3) William Dampier; (4) Sir Walter Raleigh and (5) Captain James Cook.

101

The desert areas of Asia and Australia and the African Sahara presented quite different problems to the explorer than did central Africa, with its dense jungles and abundant tropical life. Travelling across a desert is rather like being at sea. There are few landmarks and navigation is by the sun and the stars. Men voyage across deserts for the same reason they set out across uncharted seas – to find out what lies on the other side.

The Russian, Nicolas Prjevalsky, crossed the Gobi desert in Mongolia towards the end of the 19th century and visited Peking and Tibet. Other men, such as the Englishman Younghusband and the Swedish explorer Sven Hedin, covered thousands of miles in parts of central Asia which were then completely unknown to the rest of the world.

Australia's desert areas are often more barren and unfriendly than anywhere else on earth. They support little animal or plant life and the ground is comparatively featureless. The most primitive mammals, the marsupial or pouched mammals, live in Australia,

as do one of the most primitive peoples on earth, the aborigines, who have survived for centuries in natural surroundings which give their lives little support or comfort.

There are many tragic stories in the history of Australian exploration, none more so than that of the expedition of Burke and Wills, who made the first south to north crossing of the continent but died on their return journey in 1861.

The first explorer to penetrate deep inside the Australian continent, and sometimes called the 'father of Australian exploration', was Charles Sturt. After a lifetime spent in the Australian interior he lost his sight through

Below **Before the white man started colonising Australia, the only inhabitants were the aborigines, a primitive black race who lived as nomads. The way of life of some of them today has hardly changed from what it was centuries ago. The picture shows a typical aboriginal camp at night.**

Below **When a country acquires territory by exploration or conquest, planting its flag in the new colony is a very dramatic moment. In this picture, the British Navy is hoisting the Union Jack in Australia for the first time.**

Above **Captain Scott who died in Antarctica in 1912. Right Scott's ship 'Discovery', used on his first Antarctic expedition, 1901–4.**

Below **When Scott reached the South Pole in 1912, he found a party from Norway had got there first. Here is their leader, Amundsen, planting the Norwegian flag at the pole.**

hardship and exposure and was awarded a pension by the first parliament to rule in South Australia. The first man to explore the interior fully and live to tell the tale was John McDouall Stuart, who hoisted the British flag at Van Diemen's land in 1862 after a trans-continental journey from Adelaide.

Although explorers seeking trade routes through northern seas had visited the Arctic some 400 years ago it was not until the 20th century that the two polar extremes of the earth were actually reached by man. The first person to stand at the north pole was Robert Peary in 1909. In the Antarctic continent the race to the south pole was won by Roald Amundsen who arrived there before Captain Scott's party. Scott and his companions perished on their return journey from the pole, only a few miles from the warmth and safety of food and shelter.

Nowadays the Antarctic continent is a place where countries meet not to fight over boundaries but to co-operate in scientific research from permanent bases set in the icy wastes.

Far left **This picture shows Burke and Wills at Cooper's Creek last century when they explored the Australian bush.**

Left **At the time of Elizabeth II's coronation, Sir Edmund Hillary and Sherpa Tensing were climbing Everest, the highest mountain in the world. This is the dramatic moment when they reached the summit.**

Countries of the World

On these two pages is the familiar map of Europe from the British Isles to the Mediterranean. Geographically, of course, Britain has always been a part of Europe but her ties have been with the Empire and later with the Commonwealth. In recent years, Britain has been strengthening her links with Europe and she is now a full member of the 'Common Market' — an everyday name for the European Economic Community which was founded in 1958 to stimulate commerce between all its member nations.

Europe

The continent of Europe is part of the great area of land in the northern hemisphere formed by Europe and Asia. This land mass is sometimes referred to as Eurasia, and Europe itself can be thought of as the western peninsula of Asia.

There is no strict geographical or political boundary between Europe and Asia, and since Russia and Turkey have territories in both continents, the eastern boundary is somewhat blurred: it is generally taken to be the natural barriers formed by the Ural Mountains which run from north to south across Russia, and the Caucasus Mountains between the Caspian and the Black Seas.

Continental Europe stretches westwards to the lands which face towards the Atlantic Ocean and is bounded in the north by the Arctic Ocean and in the south by the Mediterranean Sea. Europe also includes many islands, the most important being Iceland, the British Isles, Sicily, Corsica, Sardinia, Crete and Cyprus.

The principal countries of Europe are listed below, with their capital cities, estimated populations and approximate areas in square miles and square kilometres.

Albania, Tirana, pop. 2,200,000, area 11,000 sq. m., 28,000 sq. k.

Austria, Vienna, pop. 7,500,000, area 32,000 sq. m., 83,000 sq. k.

Belgium, Brussels, pop. 9,800,000, area 12,000 sq. m., 30,500 sq. k.

Bulgaria, Sofia, pop. 8,600,000, area 43,000 sq. m., 110,000 sq. k.

Czechoslovakia, Prague, pop. 15,400,000 area 49,000 sq. m., 127,000 sq. k.

Denmark, Copenhagen, pop. 5,000,000, area 17,000 sq. m., 44,000 sq. k.

Finland, Helsinki, pop. 4,800,000, area 130,000 sq. m., 336,000 sq. k.

France, Paris, pop. 51,800,000, area 212,000 sq. m., 549,000 sq. k.

Germany (West) Bonn, pop. 60,000,000, area 96,000 sq. m., 248,000 sq. k.

Germany (East) East Berlin, pop. 15,900,000, area 42,000 sq. m., 109,000 sq. k.

Great Britain and Northern Ireland, London, pop. 56,200,000, area 94,000 sq. m., 243,000 sq. k.

Greece, Athens, pop. 8,900,000, area 51,000 sq. m., 132,000 sq. k.

Above **Aerial view of Paris from the Place de la Concorde.**

Left **Rome, showing Trajan's column (foreground) and the monument to Victor Emmanuel, known affectionately as the 'Christmas Cake'.**

Below left **Map of Europe.**

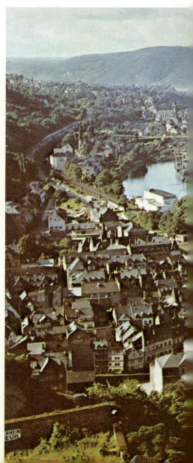

Hungary, Budapest, pop. 10,300,000, area 36,000 sq. m., 93,000 sq. k.

Iceland, Reykjavik, pop. 210,000, area 40,000 sq. m., 103,000 sq. k.

Ireland, Dublin, pop. 2,900,000, area 27,000 sq. m., 70,000 sq. k.

Italy, Rome, pop, 54,000,000, area 116,000 sq. m., 300,000 sq. k.

Luxemburg, Luxemburg, pop. 345,000, area 1,000 sq. m., 2,600 sq. k.

Netherlands, The Hague/Amsterdam, pop. 13,200,000, area 13,000 sq. m., 33,600 sq. k.

Norway, Oslo, pop. 3,900,000, area 125,000 sq. m., 324,000 sq. k.

Poland, Warsaw, pop. 33,200,000, area 120,000 sq. m., 310,000 sq. k.

Portugal, Lisbon, pop. 9,800,000, area 35,000 sq. m., 90,000 sq. k.

Romania, Bucharest, pop. 19,700,000, area 92,000 sq. m., 238,000 sq. k.

Spain, Madrid, pop. 33,000,000, area 195,000 sq. m., 504,000 sq. k.

Sweden, Stockholm, pop. 8,100,000, area 174,000 sq. m., 450,000 sq. k.

Switzerland, Berne, pop. 6,300,000, area 15,000 sq. m., 39,000 sq. k.

Turkey, Ankara, pop. 36,100,000, area 301,000 sq. m., 779,000 sq. k.

U.S.S.R., Moscow, pop. 247,000,000, area 8,650,000 sq. m., 22,403,000 sq. k.

Yugoslavia, Belgrade, pop. 20,700,000, area 99,000 sq. m., 256,000 sq. k.

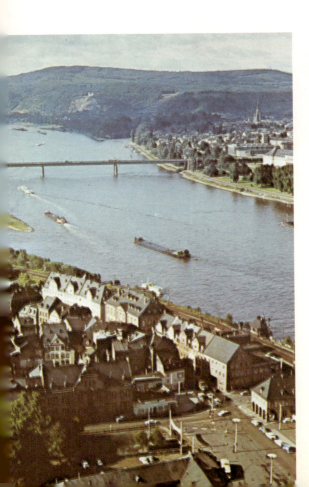

Top **Roofs of the Old Town of Prague. Prague castle is on the skyline.**

Above **Stockholm, showing the royal palace (centre) and the Town Hall.**

Right **Westminster Abbey.**

Left **A view of the Rhine, one of the main waterways of Europe.**

Asia is a continent of vast contrasts. Its land mass stretches from within the Arctic Circle almost to the Equator and this gives it a variety of climates. It has a population of about 2,000 million and contains over half of the human race. Two-thirds of the people live in India and China which are densely populated. Large populations are also found in Japan, Java and Sri Lanka. In contrast, Northern Siberia and Central Asia have thousands of square miles with very few inhabitants.

Asia

Asia is the largest of all the continents and occupies about one-third of the total land area of the world. It also contains the most heavily populated countries on earth. It is made up chiefly of the eastern half of the U.S.S.R., the Chinese and Mongolian Republics, and the sub-continent formed by India and Pakistan.

The principal countries of Asia are listed below, with their capital cities, estimated populations, and approximate areas in square miles and square kilometres.

Afghanistan, Kabul, pop. 17,100,000, area 253,000 sq. m., 658,000 sq. k.

Bahrain, Manama, pop. 220,000, area 210 sq. m., 545 sq. k.

Bangladesh, Dacca, pop, 51,000,000, area, 55,000 sq. m., 143,000 sq. k.

Bhutan, Thimbu, pop. 800,000, area 18,000 sq. m., 47,000 sq. k.

Brunei, Brunei, pop. 123,000, area 2,200 sq. m., 5,700 sq. k.

Burma, Rangoon, pop. 28,000,000, area 262,000 sq. m., 679,000 sq. k.

China, Peking, pop. 760,000,000, area 4,300,000 sq. m., 11,100,000 sq. k.

Cyprus, Nicosia, pop. 640,000, area 3,600 sq. m., 9,300 sq. k.

Hong Kong, Victoria, pop. 4,200,000, area 400 sq. m., 1,036 sq. k.

India, Delhi, pop. 560,000,000, area 1,260,000 sq. m., 3,264,000 sq. k.

Indonesia, Djakarta, pop. 120,000,000, area 735,000 sq. m., 1,903,000 sq. k.

Iran, Tehran, pop. 29,000,000, area 630,000 sq. m., 1,631,000 sq. k.

Iraq, Baghdad, pop. 9,400,000, area 170,000 sq. m., 440,000 sq. k.

Israel, Jerusalem, pop. 2,000,000, area 8,000 sq. m., 20,800 sq. k.

Above Tokyo, capital of Japan. It was originally the site of a small feudal castle and became the capital of the Tokugawa Shoguns in 1590. It has grown into a city which today has more than 11 million inhabitants. Tokyo today is an important industrial and business centre and although it is situated in the Orient, its appearance and many of its customs are Western. The name 'Tokyo' means 'east capital' and the town was first called this in 1868.

Left Gypsies are an ancient nomadic people found in a number of countries. Their origins are obscure but it is generally believed that they came in the first place from India. About AD 1000, they are thought to have migrated in two parties – one to North Africa and the other through Central Europe. Here they are seen at a gypsy fair at Jaisalmer in India.

USSR
Mongolia
Iran
Afghanistan
Pakistan
Nepal
Bangladesh
India
Burma
Laos
Thailand
Vietnam
Malaysia
Sri Lanka
Sumatra
Borneo
Indonesia
Java
China
North Korea
South Korea
Japan
Formosa
Philippines

Above Here is a map of Asia, one-third of the world's land. Asia's main crops are rice – in the monsoon countries of the south east – and wheat in Siberia and China. India is first in the world output of sugar cane, most of which is consumed at home. And India and Sri Lanka provide four-fifths of the world's tea supply. Other exports are copra from the Philippines and Indonesia, jute from India and rubber from Malaya and Indonesia. There are vast oil fields in the Middle East, especially in Saudi Arabia and Kuwait. Japan has the most advanced industry and produces iron and steel goods and textiles as well as building ships. India, China and Russia are also important cotton producing areas in Asia.

Below Here are some islanders fishing in the warm tropical waters off Sri Lanka in the Indian Ocean. The whole of Sri Lanka became a British Crown Colony in 1815 and remained so until 1948 when it became a self-governing dominion. The soil is very fertile and the country's economy depends largely upon the three main agricultural crops – rubber, tea and coconuts. A great deal of rice is also grown for home consumption. Of its minerals, graphite has the most commercial value. Rubies and sapphires are also found in considerable quantities. One of the highest mountains in Sri Lanka is Adam's Peak. It is regarded with great veneration by people of the Buddhist, Mohammedan and Hindu religions.

Japan, Tokyo, pop. 104,000,000, area 143,000 sq. m., 370,000 sq. k.

Jordan, Amman, pop. 2,300,000, area 35,000 sq. m., 90,000 sq. k.

Khmer, Republic (Cambodia), Phnom-Penh, pop. 7,000,000, area 70,000 sq. m., 181,000 sq. k.

Korea (South), Seoul, pop. 32,500,000, area 38,000 sq. m., 98,000 sq. k.

Korea (North), Pyongyang, pop. 14,000,000, area 46,000 sq. m., 119,000 sq. k.

Kuwait, Kuwait, pop. 700,000, area 6,000 sq. m., 15,600 sq. k.

Laos, Vientiane, pop. 3,000,000, area 90,000 sq. m., 233,000 sq. k.

Lebanon, Beirut, pop, 2,720,000, area 4,300 sq. m., 11,100 sq. k.

Malaysia, Kuala Lumpur, pop. 11,600,000, area 128,000 sq. m., 331,000 sq. k.

Mongolia, Ulan Bator, pop. 1,290,000, area 604,000 sq. m., 1,564,000 sq. k.

Nepal, Katmandu, pop. 11,300,000, area, 54,000 sq. m., 140,000 sq. k.

Oman, Muscat, pop. 570,000, area 82,000 sq. m., 212,000 sq. k.

Pakistan, Islamabad, pop. 42,978,000, area 310,000 sq. m., 801,000 sq. k.

Philippines, Manila, pop. 38,000,000, area 115,000 sq. m., 298,000 sq.k.

Saudi Arabia, Riyadh, pop. 7,350,000, area 870,000 sq. m., 2,253,000 sq. k.

Sikkim, Gangtok, pop. 197,000, area 2,700 sq. m., 7,000 sq. k.

Singapore, Singapore, pop. 2,100,000, area 224 sq. m., 581 sq. k.

Southern Yemen People's Republic, Madinet al-Shaab, pop. 1,300,000, area 112,000 sq. m., 290,000 sq. k.

Sri Lanka, Colombo, pop. 12,900,000, area 25,000 sq. m., 65,000 sq. k.

Taiwan (Formosa), Taipei, pop. 14,500,000, area 13,900 sq. m., 36,000 sq. k.

Thailand, Bangkok, pop. 36,000,000, area 198,000 sq. m., 513,000 sq. k.

United Arab Emirates, Abu Dhabi, pop. 85,000 area 32,000 sq. m., 83,000 sq. k.

Vietnam (South), Saigon, pop. 18,000,000, area 66,000 sq. m., 171,000 sq. k.

Vietnam (North), Hanoi, pop. 22,000,000, area 63,000 sq. m., 163,000 sq. k.

Yemen, Sana, pop, 5,300,000, area 75,000 sq. m., 194,000 sq. k.

The continent of North America (including Central America) extends almost from the north pole to the equator. Its most northerly point is the coast of Greenland, a country which is geographically part of North America although it belongs to Denmark; and its boundary in the south is the narrow neck of land around Panama. These two points are roughly an equal distance from, respectively, the north pole and the equator.

The principal countries of North and Central America are listed below, with their capital cities, estimated populations and approximate areas in square miles and square kilometres.

Canada, Ottawa, pop. 21,500,000, area 3,852,000 sq. m., 9,976,000 sq. k.

Mexico, Mexico City, pop. 52,400,000, area 760,000 sq. m., 1,968,000 sq. k.

United States of America, Washington DC, pop. 209,800,000, area 3,600,000 sq. m., 9,300,000 sq. k.

Greenland, Godthaab, pop. 50,000, area 840,000 sq. m., 2,170,000 sq. k.

Bahamas, Nassau, pop, 164,000, area 4,400 sq. m., 11,400 sq. k.

Bermuda, Hamilton, pop. 54,000, area 21 sq. m., 54 sq. k.

British Honduras, Belize, pop. 127,000, area 8,700 sq. m., 22,500 sq. k.

Costa Rica, San José, pop, 1,800,000, area 20,000 sq. m., 52,000 sq. k.

Cuba, Havana, pop. 8,600,000, area 44,000 sq. m., 114,000 sq. k.

Dominican Republic, Santo Domingo, pop. 4,400,000, area 19,000 sq. m., 49,000 sq. k.

Guatemala, Guatemala City, pop. 5,300,000, area 42,000 sq. m., 109,000 sq. k.

Haiti, Port-au-Prince, pop. 4,960,000, area 11,000 sq. m., 28,000 sq. k.

Honduras, Tegucigalpa, pop. 2,800,000, area 43,000 sq. m., 111,000 sq. k.

Jamaica, Kingston, pop. 2,000,000, area 4,400 sq. m., 11,400 sq. k.

Nicaragua, Managua, pop. 2,000,000, area 57,000 sq. m., 147,000 sq. k.

Panama, Panama City, pop. 1,510,000, area 29,000 sq. m., 75,000 sq. k.

Puerto Rico, San Juan, pop. 2,860,000, area 3,400 sq. m., 8,800 sq. k.

Salvador, San Salvador, pop. 3,600,000, area 8,200 sq. m., 21,200 sq. k.

Left In this aerial picture, the famous skyline of New York City can be clearly seen. The city, which is the metropolis and principal sea port of the United States of America, is made up of five boroughs – Bronx, Richmond, Manhattan, Brooklyn and Queens. New York is built within a relatively confined area and this explains why so many of its buildings have had to be built so tall. These include the Empire State Building, until recently the tallest skyscraper in the world. Broadway is the city's main thoroughfare and Wall Street is the centre of banking.

Above This is San Francisco, the chief city in the west. Many American cities have complex systems of flyovers and underpasses like this.

Below Football is a popular game in America. The players wear padded clothing and crash helmets and it is more like rugby than soccer.

113

Below **Lake Titicaca lies 12,600 feet** *3,840 metres* **up in the mountains in South America, partly in Peru and partly in Bolivia. It is 130 miles** *209 kilometres* **long and is very deep – about 1200 feet** *365 metres.* **Some interesting archaeological finds around the lake have proved that there was a civilisation there before the time of Christ. The local Indians are the direct descendants of those who were conquered by the Incas and yet managed to retain their own language. The picture shows them on 'rafts' of rushes on the lake. Some people believe that the potato was first cultivated for domestic use by the shores of Lake Titicaca.**

The most notable geographical feature of the South American continent is the longest continuous chain of mountains in the world, called the Andes, which stretch from north to south down the entire length of the Pacific coast. The other dominant part of the landscape is the vast jungle wilderness of Brazil, where few people live save for isolated groups of primitive Indian tribes. The whole country of Brazil is actually larger than the continental area of the United States. In the equatorial regions the climate is hot and humid, some of the most unpleasant areas being along the mighty River Amazon, where temperatures average over 27°C. and where it generally rains for about 250 days in the year.

The principal countries of South America are listed below, with their capital cities, estimated populations and approximate areas in square miles and square kilometres.

Argentina, Buenos Aires, pop. 24,700,000, area 1,072,000 sq. m., 2,776,000 sq. k.
Bolivia, La Paz, pop. 4,600,000, area 424,000 sq. m., 1,098,000 sq. k.
Brazil, Brasilia, pop. 96,000,000, area 3,280,000 sq. m., 8,496,000 sq. k.
Chile, Santiago, pop. 9,900,000, area 290,000 sq. m., 750,000 sq. k.
Colombia, Bogata, pop. 21,700,000, area 450,000 sq. m., 1,160,000 sq. k.
Ecuador, Quito, pop. 6,200,000, area 105,000 sq. m., 272,000 sq. k.
French Guiana, Cayenne, pop. 41,000, area 35,000 sq. m., 90,000 sq. k.
Guyana, Georgetown, pop. 750,000, area 83,000 sq. m., 215,000 sq. k.
Paraguay, Asuncion, pop. 2,400,000, area 157,000 sq. m., 406,000 sq. k.
Peru, Lima, pop. 13,900,000, area 496,000 sq. m., 1,284,000 sq. k.
Surinam, Paramaribo, pop. 420,000, area 62,000 sq. m., 160,000 sq. k.
Uruguay, Montevideo, pop. 2,920,000, area 72,000 sq. m., 186,000 sq. k.
Venezuela, Caracas, pop. 10,700,000, area 352,000 sq. m., 911,000 sq. k.

Below left **This is Rio de Janeiro, Brazil's main port and the country's former capital (it is now Brasilia). Overlooking Rio Bay at the foot of some mountains, the town boasts some striking 20th-century architecture.**

Below **Argentina has vast cattle ranches and is the world's largest exporter of meat. Here is a cattle market in Buenos Aires, the capital of Argentina.**

Many of the countries of Africa, the second largest continent in the world, have gained their independence during the present century. The principal countries of Africa are listed below, with their capital cities, estimated populations and approximate areas in square miles and square kilometres.

Algeria, Algiers, pop. 13,980,000, area 950,000 sq. m., 2,460,000 sq. k.

Angola, Luanda, pop. 5,700,000, area 481,000 sq. m., 1,245,000 sq. k.

Cameroon, Yaoundé, pop. 5,900,000, area 183,000 sq. m., 474,000 sq. k.

Congo, Brazzaville, pop. 950,000, area 130,000 sq. m., 340,000 sq. k.

Egypt, Cairo, pop. 34,000,000, area 380,000 sq. m., 980,000 sq. k.

Ethiopia, Addis Ababa, pop. 25,000,000, area 398,000 sq. m., 1,031,000 sq. k.

Ghana, Accra, pop. 9,000,000, area 92,000 sq. m., 238,000 sq. k.

Kenya, Nairobi, pop, 11,100,000, area 225,000 sq. m., 584,000 sq. k.

Liberia, Monrovia, pop. 1,200,000, area 43,000 sq. m., 111,000 sq. k.

Libya, Tripoli, pop. 1,900,000, area 679,400 sq. m., 1,759,500 sq. k.

Madagascar, Tananarive, pop. 7,000,000, area 229,000 sq. m., 594,000 sq. k.

Malawi, Zomba, pop. 4,600,000, area 36,000 sq. m., 119,000 sq. k.

Morocco, Rabat, pop. 15,800,000, area 170,000 sq. m., 500,000 sq. k.

Mozambique, Lourenço Marques, pop. 7,500,000, area 300,000 sq. m., 777,000 sq. k.

Nigeria, Lagos, pop. 65,000,000, area 356,000 sq. m., 922,000 sq. k.

Rhodesia, Salisbury, pop. 5,100,000, area 150,000 sq. m., 390,000 sq. k.

Senegal, Dakar, pop. 4,000,000, area 77,000 sq. m., 199,000 sq. k.

Sierra Leone, Freetown, pop. 2,600,000, area 27,600 sq. m., 71,000 sq. k.

South Africa, Pretoria, pop. 20,600,000, area 472,000 sq. m., 1,222,000 sq. k.

Sudan, Khartoum, pop. 15,900,000, area 970,000 sq. m., 2,510,000 sq. k.

Tanzania, Dar-es-Salaam, pop. 13,700,000, area 363,000 sq. m., 940,000

Tunisia, Tunis, pop. 5,000,000, area 63,000 sq. m., 163,000 sq. k.

Uganda, Kampala, pop. 9,500,000, area 93,000 sq. m., 241,000 sq. k.

Zaire, Kinshasa, pop. 21,640,000, area 900,000 sq. m., 2,400,000 sq. k.

Zambia, Lusaka, pop. 4,400,000, area 290,000 sq. m., 750,000 sq. k.

Below One of the world's most beautiful domes – the Bab Zuwela mosque, Cairo.

Below A view of the docks in Cape Town. The docks are built on land reclaimed from the sea.

Oceania and polar lands

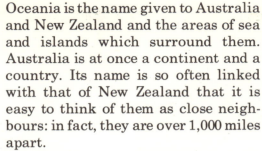

Left **Antarctica, an uninhabited area except for scientific bases. It has almost no plant or animal life.**

Oceania is the name given to Australia and New Zealand and the areas of sea and islands which surround them. Australia is at once a continent and a country. Its name is so often linked with that of New Zealand that it is easy to think of them as close neighbours: in fact, they are over 1,000 miles apart.

Australia is a vast country, about three-quarters of the size of Europe, but it supports less than one-fiftieth of that continent's people. It has six great mainland states and the island state of Tasmania. New Zealand is made up of two main islands, North Island and South Island.

Antarctica, the ice-covered continent surrounding the south pole, is larger than either Europe or Australia, yet it was not discovered until 1819. The Arctic area is centred around the north pole but contains no recognised mass of land.

The principal countries of Oceania and the polar lands are listed below, with their capital cities, estimated populations and approximate areas in square miles and square kilometres.

Australia, Canberra, pop. 12,700,000, area 2,968,000 sq. m., 7,695,000 sq. k.
Fiji, Suva, pop. 550,000, area 7,060 sq. m., 18,280 sq. k.
French Polynesia, Papeete, pop. 100,000, area 1,500 sq. m., 3,900 sq. k.
Gilbert & Ellice Islands, Tarawa, pop. 61,000, area 375 sq.m., 971 sq. k.
Mariana, Caroline and Marshall Islands, Saipan, pop. 100,000, area 690 sq. m., 1,790 sq. k.
Nauru, Nauru, pop. 7,000, area 8 sq. m., 21 sq. k.
New Caledonia, Noumea, pop. 100,000, area 7,300 sq. m., 18,900 sq. k.
New Hebrides, Vila, pop. 80,000, area 6,000 sq. m., 15,540 sq. k.
New Zealand, Wellington, pop. 2,900,000, area 104,000 sq. m., 269,000 sq. k.
Papua and New Guinea, Port Moresby, pop. 2,300,000, area 180,000 sq. m., 466,000 sq. k.
Solomon Islands, Honiara, pop. 158,000, area 11,500 sq. m., 29,800 sq. k.
Tonga, Nukualofa, pop. 90,000, area 270 sq. m., 700 sq. k.
Western Samoa, Apia, pop. 148,000, area 1,100 sq. m., 2,800 sq. k.

Left **Sydney, the largest and oldest city in Australia. It was here that the first white settlers came in 1788 and founded what was to become an important manufacturing area. The picture shows Sydney's harbour and bridge. At nearby Bondi Beach, the favourite pastime is surf-riding.**

Below **Wellington, founded in 1840, is the capital of New Zealand. An important industrial centre and port, its chief industries include wool, tobacco and engineering.**

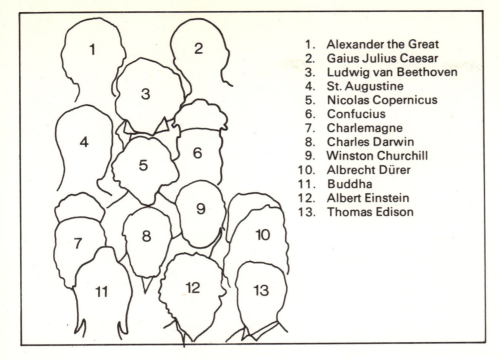

1. Alexander the Great
2. Gaius Julius Caesar
3. Ludwig van Beethoven
4. St. Augustine
5. Nicolas Copernicus
6. Confucius
7. Charlemagne
8. Charles Darwin
9. Winston Churchill
10. Albrecht Dürer
11. Buddha
12. Albert Einstein
13. Thomas Edison

Famous Lives

Alexander the Great (356–323 BC) King of Macedonia. One of the greatest generals in history, he united the Greek states and led them to victory against the Persians. His empire extended as far east as India and included all the Mediterranean lands.

Alfred the Great (849–901) King of Wessex. During his 30 years' reign he fought continually against the Danes. He founded a navy, reformed the laws and set up education schemes for the people.

Aquinas, St. Thomas (1226–1274) An Italian from a noble family who decided to become a monk. His writing is recognised as the basis of Roman Catholic doctrine to this day.

Aristotle (384–322 BC) Greek philosopher and scientist. Studied at Plato's Academy for 17 years. Was tutor to Alexander. Founded his own school at Athens called the Lyceum. Was also an accomplished scientific writer.

Augustine, St. (354–430) Bishop of Hippo and the greatest of the Latin fathers. Wrote his celebrated *Confessions* in 397. Was a great influence on the early Christian church.

Bach, Johann Sebastian (1685–1750) German composer. Appointed to the court of Weimar for nine years he spent the rest of his life as a church organist and choirmaster. His preludes and fugues are a major landmark in the history of music.

Beethoven, Ludwig van (1770–1827) German composer. Was taught music from the age of four. When he was young he started to go deaf and many of his greatest works were composed after he had entirely lost his hearing.

Buddha (6th century BC) This title means 'enlightened one' and was given to this Indian prince whose family name was Gautama. He gave up a life of luxury to spend his time teaching and preaching. He was the founder of Buddhism, the religion of the Far East.

Caesar, Julius Gaius (100–44 BC) Roman general and statesman. Led successful conquests in Gaul. After defeat of Pompey became dictator of Rome and extended Roman Empire. Was murdered in the Senate by a band of conspirators led by Brutus and Cassius.

Charlemagne (742–814) Roman emperor and King of the Franks. Known as Charles the Great. Was crowned as first Holy Roman Emperor by the Pope in 800. A champion of the Christian faith.

Chaucer, Geoffrey (1345?–1400) English poet. After various translations of French poetry he wrote his *Canterbury Tales,* one of the most famous poems in the English language.

Chekhov, Anton (1860–1904) Russian novelist and playwright. His plays are comedies but are full of the sadness in people's lives. They became very popular in the western world.

Churchill, Winston (1874–1965) British statesman. Had a distinguished military career. Entered parliament in 1900. Became prime minister of Britain in 1940 and was a leading figure in the victory of the Allies in the Second World War.

Confucius (551–479 BC) Chinese philosopher whose real name was Kung-Fu-tsze. Spent early years teaching and in politics. Wrote many books on history and religion. The Chinese religion of Confucianism is based upon his sayings.

Constantine (274?–337) First Christian emperor of Rome. Christianity became a state religion in 324, though paganism was not persecuted. Moved capital of the empire from Rome to Byzantium because of the threat from the invading Barbarians, and renamed it Constantinople.

Copernicus, Nicolas (1473–1543) Polish astronomer. Is often thought of as the founder of modern astronomy. He stated that the sun was the centre of our solar system. Was trained in medicine.

Cromwell, Oliver (1599–1658) Was a member of parliament during the Civil War against Charles I. Led the parliamentary armies. Became Lord Protector of England in 1653. He refused the crown of England.

Cyrus the Great (6th century BC) Founder of the Persian Empire. Was a great leader and conqueror. King of Persia in 548 BC. He controlled a vast empire which stretched from the Mediterranean to India.

Dante Alighieri (1265–1321) Italian poet. The first writer to use the Italian language for his work. His greatest work was *The Divine Comedy* and he is generally acknowledged to be the first great classical poet of the modern world.

Darwin, Charles (1809–1882) English naturalist and scientist. Wrote a journal of his voyage in *HMS Beagle* which made him famous. He wrote *The Origin of Species,* in which he advanced his theories on evolution.

Dürer, Albrecht (1471–1528) German painter and engraver. He was a great painter but was even more renowned for his woodcuts and engravings. He commanded respect for artists and gave them a new place in society.

Edison, Thomas Alva (1847–1931) American inventor. He patented over a thousand inventions including the phonograph and the electric light bulb. He began life as a newsboy and published the first newspaper to be printed on a train.

Einstein, Albert (1879–1955) German-born mathematician and physicist. Became a naturalised Swiss in 1901. One of the greatest intellects in the history of science. Is best known for his theories about Relativity.

Elizabeth I (1533–1603) Queen of England. Daughter of Henry VIII and Anne Boleyn. She was one of the most powerful monarchs in English history and throughout her life defied the might of Spain. The Elizabethan Age was a period of great glory for England.

Erasmus, Desiderius (1466?–1536) Dutch scholar. He spent much of his time in England where he was an important influence on men of learning. He was a great humanist and challenged the church on reform.

Franklin, Benjamin (1706–1790) American statesman. He was a printer and newspaper editor. Also interested in science and discovered electrical nature of lightning. Played a prominent part in drawing up the Declaration of Independence.

Galileo Galilei (1564–1642) Italian astronomer. He discovered the principles of the pendulum and perfected the refracting telescope. He was charged before the Italian Inquisition because his scientific theories were said to be against the teaching of the church.

Gandhi, Mohandas (1869–1948) Indian patriot and statesman. He was often called Mahatma which means 'great man'. He fought for independence for India, using non-violent means. While still trying to unite his country he was assassinated.

Genghis Khan (1162–1227) Mongol conqueror. Born in central India, he began to lead his tribe in battle at the age of thirteen. A great warrior and administrator, Genghis built up a mighty empire which stretched from the Volga to Mongolia.

Goethe, Johann Wolfgang von (1749–1832) German poet and dramatist. He studied painting and engaged in scientific research. He was talented in all branches of knowledge but his fame today rests on his writing.

Hadrian (76–138) Roman emperor. Proclaimed emperor in 117 after death of Trajan. He was a man of peace and a lover of art and literature. About 121 he began a famous journey through Europe and Asia.

Henry VIII (1491–1547) King of England. Son of Henry VII, from whom he inherited the kingdom and great wealth. Because of his wish to marry Anne Boleyn he broke with the church in Rome and made himself head of the church in England.

Herodotus (485?–425 BC) Greek historian. Cicero called him the 'father of history'. He wrote a great history of the Greek and Persian wars and travelled widely in all the lands of the Mediterranean.

Homer (about 9th century BC) Greek epic poet. Little is known about him historically but his name is linked traditionally with the *Iliad* and the *Odyssey*, the great tales of the Trojan Wars and the travels of Odysseus.

Ibsen, Henrik (1828–1906) Norwegian playwright who had an enormous influence on dramatists of other countries. His plays show him to have been an outstanding social dramatist.

Jesus Christ, the founder of Christianity, was born probably about 4 BC. Little is known of his childhood. He received a conviction that he was called by God for a special task. The Jewish leaders caused Jesus to be crucified on the hill of Calvary in Jerusalem.

Joan of Arc (1412–31) French patriot. She was a country girl who was inspired to lead the French armies against the English and caused the dauphin to be crowned as Charles VII. She was tried for heresy and burned at the stake.

Kant, Immanuel (1724–1804) German philosopher. He lived all his life in Konigsberg, where he became a 'living legend' to the students who followed his

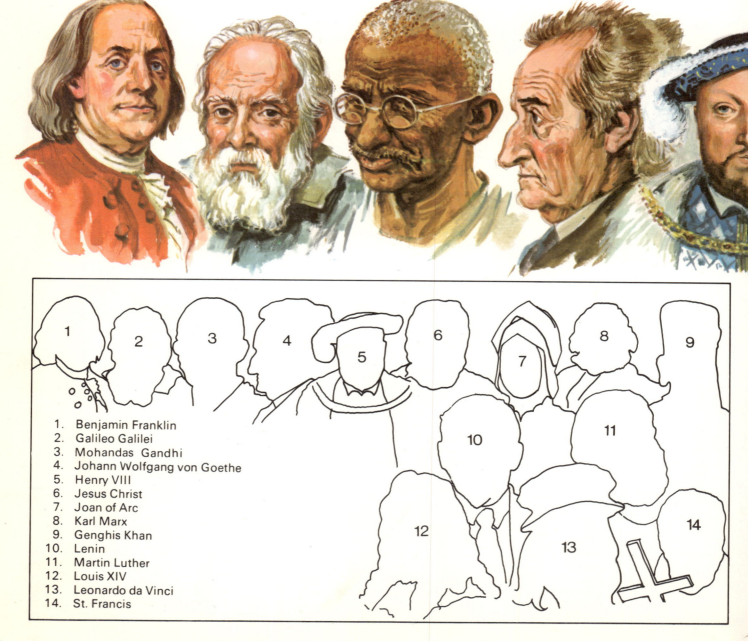

1. Benjamin Franklin
2. Galileo Galilei
3. Mohandas Gandhi
4. Johann Wolfgang von Goethe
5. Henry VIII
6. Jesus Christ
7. Joan of Arc
8. Karl Marx
9. Genghis Khan
10. Lenin
11. Martin Luther
12. Louis XIV
13. Leonardo da Vinci
14. St. Francis

teachings. His writings began a new era in philosophy.

Lenin (1870–1924) Russian revolutionary. He was formerly Vladimir Ulyanov. Was secretary of the Communist Party and led the Russian workers in their successful revolt. He became head of the new Russian state.

Leonardo da Vinci (1452–1519) Italian painter, sculptor, architect, engineer and musician. He has been called the universal man of the Renaissance, so great was his genius in every creative field. His scientific thought was far beyond the understanding of his age.

Lincoln, Abraham (1809–1865) American statesman and 16th president of the United States. He opposed slavery. Lincoln is looked upon as the saviour of his country yet he was assassinated soon after the American Civil War ended.

Louis XIV (1638–1715) King of France. He reigned over France for 72 years and became an absolute monarch. He was the most powerful figure in Europe and was known as *Le Roi Soleil*—the Sun King.

Luther, Martin (1483–1546) German religious reformer. Entered a monastery when he was a young man. Attacked the Roman Catholic Church on the sale of indulgences and began the movement called the Reformation.

Marx, Karl (1818–1863) German politician and philosopher. He was expelled from his own country and settled in London. Here he wrote his great work *Das Kapital* and founded the modern political philosophy of Communism.

Michelangelo (1475–1564) Italian artist. One of the greatest figures of the Italian Renaissance. Believed by many to be the greatest artist of all time. His most famous work was to decorate the ceiling of the Sistine Chapel in Rome. He was also a poet and military engineer.

Mohammed (571?–632) Founder of the Mohammedan religion. Born at Mecca, which later became a sacred city to the Moslems. He had a vision as the prophet of God, whom he called Allah. The Koran is a sacred book of his sayings.

Mozart, Wolfgang Amadeus (1756–91) Austrian composer. A musician of genius. Made his debut as a performer at the age of six. Wrote an enormous variety of great music. Suffered many hardships in his life and died in poverty.

Napoleon Bonaparte (1769–1821) French general. Became emperor of France in 1804 and was master of continental Europe. Planned to invade England but was beaten by Nelson at Trafalgar. Wellington and Blücher defeated him on land in 1815 at Waterloo and Napoleon spent his last days in exile.

Newton, Isaac (1642–1727) English mathematician and scientist. He is most famous for his study of the laws of gravity. He also worked in astronomy, invented a reflecting telescope and studied the nature of light.

Pascal, Blaise (1623–62) French mathematician, physicist and religious philosopher. A child prodigy, he was

1. Napoleon Bonaparte
2. Isaac Newton
3. Peter the Great
4. Rembrandt van Rijn
5. Maximilien Robespierre
6. Franklin Roosevelt
7. Joseph Stalin
8. St. Peter
9. St. Paul
10. William Shakespeare
11. Michelangelo
12. George Washington
13. Richard Wagner
14. Giuseppe Verdi
15. Saladin
16. Leo Tolstoy
17. Voltaire

concerned with numerous inventions. He also wrote the *Pensées*, a book of Christian thoughts and sayings.

Paul, St. (1st century AD) Known as the Apostle of the Gentiles. At first he joined in the persecution of the Christians but was later converted and became their champion. Was put to death by Nero.

Peter, St. (1st century AD) He lived at the time of Jesus and was one of the twelve apostles. He was a fisherman. The popes of Rome claim to be descended in direct line from St. Peter.

Peter the Great (1672–1725) Emperor of Russia. He was a strong and powerful ruler who studied the methods of European countries and did much to develop his own country's industry and bring it up to date.

Plato (427?–347? BC) Greek philosopher. He was a pupil of Socrates. Plato recorded many of his thoughts. Among his best-known books is *The Republic*, which contains a plan for an ideal state.

Polo, Marco (1254–1324) Venetian traveller. Went with his father and uncle to the court of Kublai Khan. He travelled all over Asia and spent 20 years in the service of Kublai as a special envoy.

Rembrandt van Rijn (1606–69) Dutch painter. One of the great masters of painting, he was self-taught. He was a genius who was not popular in his lifetime because of the honesty of his painting.

Robespierre, Maximilien (1758–94) French revolutionary. He was raised to supreme power after the Revolution and established the 'Reign of Terror'. He himself met his death on the guillotine.

Roosevelt, Franklin Delano (1882–1945) American statesman and president of the United States for four separate terms. He was one of the Allied leaders in the Second World War.

Saladin (1137-1193) Sultan of Egypt and Syria. Recognised by his opponents as a great man, he captured Jerusalem from the Christians in 1187. For centuries, traces of his wise administration were found in citadels, roads and canals.

Shakespeare, William (1564–1616) English dramatist and poet. One of the greatest figures in the history of literature. He was also an actor and theatre manager. 38 plays are attributed to him and most are still performed all over the world.

Socrates (469–399 BC) Greek philosopher. He sought for truth all his life and made many enemies. His method was to ask questions wherever he went. He was condemned to die by taking poison for supposedly corrupting the minds of the young.

Stalin, Joseph (1879–1953) Russian statesman. He was exiled to Siberia as a young man. After the death of Lenin was elected head of the Soviet state and is looked upon as one of the founders of modern Russia.

Tchaikovsky, Peter Ilyich (1840–1893) Russian composer. His symphonies, symphonic poems and ballet music have made him one of the most popular classical composers of all time.

Tolstoy, Leo (1828–1910) Russian novelist. One of the world's greatest writers. His epic novel was *War and Peace*, which deals with the Napoleonic invasion of Russia and its effect on the people.

Verdi, Giuseppe (1813–1901) Italian composer. Most of his work was in the field of opera. He had an astonishingly long musical life and was active for over 50 years.

Virgil (70–19 BC) Latin poet. Studied philosophy and then became a court poet in Rome. His great epic was the *Aenid*, the story of Aeneas the Trojan, the legendary founder of the Roman nation.

Voltaire (1694–1778) Pen-name of one of the greatest of French writers and philosophers. His attacks on organised religion and civil repression influenced movement which led to the French Revolution.

Wagner, Richard (1813–1883) German composer. Like Verdi, Wagner chiefly composed operas. These usually had very grand themes and were based on German myths about legendary heroes and heroines.

Washington, George (1732–1799) American statesman. One of the founders of the United States and its first president. He was a general in the Wars of Independence against the British.

William I (the Conqueror 1027–1087) Duke of Normandy and later King of England. He led the Norman invasion of England in 1066 and defeated King Harold at the Battle of Hastings.

Thinking and Believing

Below **The gods of ancient Rome were the counterparts of the Greek gods. The head is that of Minerva, who was identified with Athena.**

In ancient times, man knew little of the world apart from the area where he lived. He believed that spirits, who lived in rivers, trees or rocks, controlled things like darkness, sun, thunder, rain, life and death. The people thought that they must please the spirits so that the spirits would help them, and they prayed to them and offered sacrifices.

Right **Zeus, the great god of the Greek family, or pantheon. The gods are remembered today by myths and legends and it is sometimes forgotten how real they were to the Greeks, whose religion was based on a passionate belief in the existence of the gods.**

Below **Reconstruction of the inner shrine of the Parthenon which contained the mighty statue of Athena, goddess of wisdom, made of ivory and pure gold.**

Many early tribes thought that some animal, plant or other object was sacred to their tribe and had to be especially cared for. They also felt that other objects or actions had to be avoided for the safety of the tribe. These beliefs are still held in certain parts of the world, though they are now dying out.

When people began to live in villages and towns, their religions became more advanced. The people of the settlements in the river valleys of Egypt and Mesopotamia, nearly 5,000 years ago, all had their own gods, most of which they feared. These people believed that if they worshipped their gods and made sacrifices to them the gods would bring them good weather and good crops.

At this time also man began to attach a religious significance to the changing seasons and celebrate these changes. The people had priests, men

Below **Jupiter, the supreme Roman god.**

trained to understand the gods, who told everyone how to behave and how to worship. Shrines and temples were built to the gods.

The ancient Egyptians believed that life on earth would continue after death, so long as the dead person was helped into the next life. The bodies of their kings were mummified – spread with oil and wrapped in bandages to keep them lifelike – and put in royal tombs, or pyramids, after a long ceremony had been performed.

About 4,000 years ago, in ancient Greece, the people worshipped many gods, believed to be all-powerful beings which never died. The Greeks believed the gods to be like men and women, only taller, stronger and more beautiful. They thought of them as a

family, or pantheon, with Zeus, the king of the gods, at the head of the family. Hera was his wife, Poseidon the god of the sea, Ares the god of war and Aphrodite the god of love.

The gods were supposed to eat special food, called ambrosia, and a special drink called nectar. The Greeks thought that if a human being could eat some of this special food he would never die. The Greeks believed they had a duty to worship the gods, and they offered them prayers and sacrifices. For the sacrifices, meat, cakes or grain were used. Some was burned on the altar, while the rest was eaten by the congregation.

The Romans, who first settled around Rome in the 8th century BC, believed in similar gods to the Greeks, but they thought that they must worship them in the right way and at the right times. If they did so, the gods would give them all they wanted. Jupiter was the king of the gods, Juno his wife, Neptune the god of the sea, Mars the god of war and Venus the god of love.

In the 14th century AD, the Aztec empire ruled in Mexico. Their religion was very cruel. They believed that to make the gods strong and powerful they must offer them human sacrifices. So the Aztecs made war with their neighbours and captured prisoners in order to kill them at religious ceremonies.

Above **When a pharaoh of ancient Egypt died his body was preserved and placed in an elaborate coffin. This is one of the splendid golden coffins in which the body of Tutankhamen was found.**

Below **A statue of a worshipper from the ancient state of Sumer.**

Above **The Celtic peoples in Britain cut several of these white chalk figures in hillsides. Their purpose is not known but probably they were religious in character. This white horse can still be seen at Uffington in Berkshire. The turf of the hillside is removed to reveal the chalk.**

An Aztec ceremonial knife from Mexico.

Living religions

The Hebrews were the first people to believe in a supreme God, who had created the world and now controlled it. They lived in Palestine in the 19th century BC. Later they were known as Jews and their religion Judaism. The story of their early sufferings is given in the first five books of the Old Testament of the Bible. Jews believe they are the chosen people of God and that a Messiah is coming to save them. When Jesus was born, a few Jews believed he was the Messiah. After the Jews lost Jerusalem, in AD 70, they did not have their own country again until 1948 when the state of Israel was formed. There are about 10 million Jews today.

Jesus Christ was the founder of the Christian religion. His life and teachings, and the teachings of his disciples, are told in the New Testament of the Bible. When Jesus died he had few followers, but now about one-third of the human race is Christian. This is the only great religion which claims that its founder is more than a prophet. Christians believe much of the Jewish teachings, but also that Jesus is the Son of God who by his crucifixion paid for the sins of mankind, and that their present life is a preparation for life after death.

Moslems also believe in one all-powerful God, whom they call Allah. Their religion, Islam, was founded in Arabia in the 7th century AD by

Below left **Buddhist monks in their traditional robes.**

Below right **A reading from the sacred book of the Moslem faith, the Koran.**

Bottom **A street in Damascus, almost unchanged for 2,000 years.**

Mohammed. According to tradition, Mohammed received messages from God telling him to go out and teach the people that there was only one God and that he, Mohammed, was his prophet. Mohammed's sayings are written down in a book called the Koran. The Arabs conquered other countries and so the Islamic religion spread. Today there are about 200 million Moslems. Their beliefs come largely from Jewish and Christian teachings, but Allah is the only God and they must obey his will.

The Hindu religion is very complicated and has no one founder. It is thought to have started in India in 1500 BC. Hindus believe that when someone dies he may be reborn, and each person has a series of lives. They believe that their actions in this life

determine the sort of life they have in the next, but they seek to escape from the cycle. There are about 250 million Hindus in the world today.

Buddhism was formed in the 6th century BC in India by Gautama. Nothing of his life was written until 200 years after he died, but there are legends about him. He thought men suffered because they were full of selfish desires, and they could only escape and achieve *nirvana* (blessed peace) by training themselves not to have desires. He was called Buddha (enlightened one) by his followers. Buddism has now almost disappeared in India, but there are about 150 million Buddhists in other countries.

China and Japan have both been influenced by Buddhism, but have their own religions: Confucianism and Taoism in China, and Shinto in Japan. Confucius lived in the 6th century BC. He was concerned with the way men treat their fellows and taught ancestor-worship.

Lao Tzu, who lived 50 years before Confucius, is thought of as the founder of Taoism. He taught that men should do nothing and live in harmony with nature. Shinto followers believe the Japanese emperors are descended from the gods, and they too worship nature.

Above **A 9th-century figure of the Shinto goddess Nakatsu-Hime. She is dressed in Japanese Court dress.**

Top **8th-century temple from Mamallapurum, India.**

Above **Two Jewish boys studying the bible.**

Below **Jesus as a boy, working in his father's carpenter's shop. A painting by Millais.**

Above **The Dome of the Rock, Jerusalem. Built in 691, it is the first monumental building erected by the Moslems to have survived intact.**

Above **Socrates, the earliest of the three great Greek philosophers, fought with the army in three campaigns, in which he showed bravery and a total indifference to pain and hardship. Although he was called by his friends 'the wisest man in the world' he wrote no books. It was his custom to teach and talk to the people in the Agora, or market place, of the ancient city of Athens.**

Philosophers and their beliefs

A philosopher is a man who thinks deeply about the meaning of life, the nature of the world and the people in it. The earliest philosophers lived in ancient Greece. Socrates, in the 5th century BC, is the first man to profoundly affect human thinking. He believed that wisdom is based on recognising one's own ignorance. He enjoyed walking about Athens, asking people what certain words meant to them, words such as 'good' and 'right'. He was condemned to death by the state, which accused him of teaching wrong ideas and was sentenced to die by drinking a poison called hemlock.

Socrates did not write any of his ideas down, but Plato, who was one of his pupils, wrote about him and developed his ideas. Plato opened a school of philosophy called the Academy which lasted in different forms for 800 years. He taught about the importance of ideas, deep thought and beauty, and had a great influence on later philosophers.

Aristotle studied in Plato's Academy for twenty years and then became a teacher. Later he founded a rival school to the Academy called the Lyceum. He left Athens when he was accused of ungodliness and died a year later. Aristotle wrote a great many books on different subjects, including natural history, astronomy, politics and logic. He was one of the greatest thinkers to have lived.

Aristotle's ideas were followed during the Middle Ages through the influence of Thomas Aquinas. Modern philosophy is often said to have started with René Descartes, who was born in France in 1596. Descartes was a rationalist. Rationalists believe they can find out about the real world by thinking carefully about it. Descartes found that the one thing he was certain existed was himself. Because he was thinking, he knew he existed. Two other famous rationalists in the 17th century were Spinoza in Holland and Leibniz in Germany. In his book *The Ethics* Spinoza developed Descartes' ideas into a complete philosophy.

Philosophers who do not agree with this rationalist way of thinking are called empiricists. They believe that knowledge of the world is gained from experience. Three British empiricists in the 17th and 18th centuries were John Locke, George Berkeley and David Hume. Locke proved that know-

Below **This drawing of the two other great philosophers Plato** (left), **a disciple of Socrates, and Aristotle, in his turn a pupil of Plato, is based on the famous painting by Raphael called** *School of Athens*.

Above **Karl Marx** at a desk in the British Museum reading room, where he spent much of his time during the period when he lived in London. Marx was a German and the founder of international Communism.

Right **In this picture are seen the philosophers (1) Descartes; (2) Kant; (3) Rousseau; (4) Locke; (5) Voltaire; (6) Hume; (7) Hegel.**

ledge is not consciously innate in man but must be a gradual growth that depends on his experience.

Immanuel Kant is often said to be the greatest modern philosopher. He lived in Konigsberg (now known as Kaliningrad), a town which once belonged to Germany, all his life. He lectured at the university for fifty years. He challenged the empiricists in his book *Critique of Pure Reason* one of the greatest works of philosophy ever written. His theories profoundly influenced 19th century thought.

The most influential philosopher of the 19th century was a German, Friedrich Hegel. Hegel believed in the fusion of opposites in a universe of perpetual self-creation. Sören Kierkegaard and Friedrich Nietzsche did not agree with him. These two men started one of the modern movements in philosophy, later developed by Jean-Paul Sartre, called existentialism. Kierkegaard believed that each man is free to do what he wants and is not just part of the world as Hegel believed.

Two famous 20th-century philosophers are Ludwig Wittgenstein, and the English mathematician and logician, Bertrand Russell.

Below **The English philosopher Bertrand Russell is remembered as a great logician and mathematician. He was also deeply involved in the campaign for nuclear disarmament.**

Left **Jean-Paul Sartre, leading modern French philosopher and accomplished novelist and playwright. Above his portrait is a scene from one of his existentialist plays.**

Myths and Legends

Long before there were any books, and even before people knew how to read and write, men wandered about the countryside of Greece telling stories of the gods and great heroes to the music of the lyre. The stories were remembered and passed on for hundreds of years before the first poets began to write them down. One of these poets was the blind Homer who retold many of them in the *Iliad* and the *Odyssey*.

Many of the stories were the first attempts by the Greeks to explain the world around them, and they were alone in this until the great thinkers, or philosophers, came along. Other stories, such as that of Troy, were partly true, but they are now called myths and legends to show that they are different from stories based on known historical events.

The ancient Greeks, who lived centuries before Christ was born, had

Right **During Jason's search for the Golden Fleece of a ram, which lay in a sacred wood guarded by a serpent, he had many adventures. In one of them he battled with a sea-monster. In this vase painting Jason is shown being ejected from the sea-monster's mouth while his protectress, Athena, looks on.**

Below **The most popular story of Orpheus concerns his journey to the Underworld to find his dead wife Eurydice. He charms the gods of the Underworld with the sound of his lyre.**

their own forms of religion. They began by worshipping the spirits in stones, trees, groves and animals. There are many myths and legends about these spirits. There were also gods of fire, water, sun, sea and sky, and many more. Zeus became ruler of them all.

The twelve great gods and goddesses (with the names of their Roman equivalents in brackets) were Zeus (Jupiter) and his wife Hera (Juno), the goddess of marriage; Athena (Minerva), a warrior goddess and protectress of cities; Apollo (Apollo), a god of prophecy and healing, sometimes a sun god; Artemis (Diana), goddess of the chase and of the forest; Hermes (Mercury), god of travellers; Ares (Mars), god of war; Hephaestus (Vulcan), god of fire; Aphrodite

Above **The Olympians were the twelve great gods in Greek mythology. They are, reading from left to right: Hestia, Hephaestus, Aphrodite, Ares, Demeter, Hermes, Hera, Poseidon, Athena, Zeus, Artemis and Apollo.**

(Venus), goddess of love; Poseidon (Neptune), god of the sea; Demeter (Ceres), goddess of the earth; and Hestia (Vesta), goddess of the hearth.

The gods assembled on Mount Olympus in Greece and made their own laws. There were other lesser gods on Olympus too, and all of them spent their days in merrymaking and dining on ambrosia and nectar. Although the gods had the bodies of mortals, they were bigger, stronger and more handsome, and never grew old. They could be wounded and suffer pain but their bodies always healed and they could change themselves at will into animals or objects.

Like mortals, the gods had their troubles. The Titans, who were jealous of the new gods on Olympus, rebelled, and it took Zeus ten years to defeat them. After this long and terrible battle, the War of the Giants was fought.

As well as gods, heroes figure very largely in Greek myths and legends. A hero was regarded as a half-god, being able to speak to the great gods on Olympus on behalf of mortals. Perhaps the best-known hero is Heracles (Hercules) who was a half-god of great physical strength. He was also a tremendous athlete and the foundation of the Olympic Games has been attributed to him. The most popular legend about Heracles concerns his twelve labours, which includes his journey to the Underworld.

Another hero of great strength was the warrior Jason, who set out with the Argonauts to recapture the Golden Fleece. To help him in his task he took some of the other heroes with him, among them Heracles, Peleus and Theseus.

Before the birth of Christ, the Romans conquered a great part of the world and adopted many of the Greek gods and heroes, which is why they are often better known today by their Roman names.

Below **One of Heracles's lesser known exploits is his fight with the Cecropes, two thieves who attacked Heracles while he slept. He overcame them, then trussed them up and tied them to opposite ends of a pole which he carried on his shoulders.**

Above **Mount Olympus in Greece was the traditional home of the gods. The Olympians were named after it and were said to live in a palace on the mountain's summit.**

Myths and legends of other lands

The Greeks were not the only nation to have myths and legends. People in every corner of the world have their own traditional tales, which have been passed on from one generation to another. As with the Greek legends the stories tell of such things as the birth of the world, and the relationships between the gods and man.

The Teutons and Vikings, of Germany and Scandinavia told many wonderful tales of their chief god Woden, or Odin, and from him we get our word Wednesday (Woden's day). Another great Viking god was Thor, god of thunder, from whom we get our word Thursday (Thor's day). The Teutons believed that if a great hero died in battle the Valkyries or warrior-maidens would ride down from the sky and carry him to Valhalla to feast with the gods.

Egypt had myths about many gods and pictures of them can be seen on wall paintings and carvings in their temples. Apart from their names little is known of the myths which surround them, and only the story of Osiris has been passed on to us in detail. The Babylonians have a famous legend about a hero, Gilgamesh, who seems

Above **A lion being held in the arms of Gilgamesh, a hero about whom the ancient Semites composed a long epic poem. Although some of his exploits were legendary, it is possible that he was a real king of Sumer as many of the episodes in the poem already existed in Sumerian folklore. Sumer was in Babylonia.**

Below **Subrahmanya was one of the names of a Hindu god of war. He is usually depicted with six heads and six pairs of arms.**

to have been a real person and was most probably a king of the land of Sumer. A favourite Roman myth concerns Romulus and Remus, the sons of Mars, who were set adrift on the Tiber in a basket, suckled by a she-wolf and brought up by a family of shepherds. They are traditionally the founders of the city of Rome.

Chinese myths have come from a mixture of three different religions in China and the most popular character of these myths is the God of Wealth, Ts'ai-shen. People today still offer up a sacrifice to him on his birthday. The door gods are depicted on the outer doors of some Chinese houses in the form of two armed soldiers. One has a red or black face and the other a white face. These gods prevent the spirits of the dead from escaping out of hell to disturb the living.

Japanese myths tell of the Kami. Kami does not have quite the same meaning as the word god, but means 'beings more highly placed', and could refer to tall trees, high mountains and great rivers, as well as to some men.

Right **The Valkyries who were the messengers of Woden, the Scandinavians' chief god. In war, they would ride into the fray mingling with all the soldiers in combat. Legend says that when a soldier saw a Valkyrie it was a sign that he would be slain. The Valkyrie would carry his soul away to feast with the gods.**

The Eskimos in Arctic lands are constantly having to battle with fierce weather conditions and it is not surprising that their myths and legends should be so savage. The totem pole plays an important part in the myths of Alaska, where it is regarded as a force of nature. The totem poles of the Red Indians are meant to show the fame and importance of a family.

One of the most familiar legends in English-speaking countries is that surrounding King Arthur, Sir Lancelot, Guinevere, Merlin the magician, and the magic sword Excalibur. Arthur was probably a real leader who fought against the Saxons after the Romans left Britain in the 5th century AD. The legends about Arthur became popular in France and England during the Middle Ages, when the knights of the Round Table and the court at Camelot were introduced to illustrate the code of chivalry. Later, in 1477, Sir Thomas Malory collected the stories together and put them in a book called *Morte d'Arthur* (The Death of Arthur) and this was printed by William Caxton, the first English printer.

Another character who has stirred the imagination almost as much as Arthur is Robin Hood, and there are many old tales about his adventures.

Right **In medieval legend, King Arthur was a king of England. He presided over the Round Table and his knights, such as Sir Lancelot, set out in search of adventure and to perform good deeds. The story is told in Malory's book, 'Morte d'Arthur' which was printed by Caxton.**

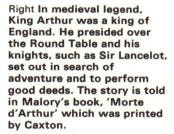

Left **Kama, god of love. The Indians, like the Greeks and other ancient peoples, had a god for each aspect of their lives. In Hindu mythology, Kama was destroyed but reborn again as Pradyumna or Cupid.**

Below **An African rainmaker.**

Customs and ceremonies

Some customs and ceremonies, whether religious, military or social, have survived the passing of time and are re-enacted today as carefully as they were in olden times. Others have been changed almost out of recognition so that their original purpose has been forgotten.

The oldest customs are connected with the religious festivals of Easter and Christmas. Practically all Christian countries have their own particular Christmas ceremony, although Christmas has not always been celebrated as the birth of Christ. Centuries before, ceremonies used to be held in honour of the Sun-boar, at a time when the sun was farthest from the equator, and people used to worship fire.

In Sweden today the nation pays homage to the patron saint of light, St. Lucia, on 13th December. In every home St. Lucia is portrayed by a young female member of the family who is dressed in white and wears a crown of lighted candles on her head. Every town, too, has its own St. Lucia and the biggest ceremony of all is held in Stockholm.

Great Britain has the pomp and ceremony of tradition very deeply rooted in her life and ceremonial events occur frequently. One of the more lighthearted customs is the pancake race held at Olney in Buckinghamshire on Shrove Tuesday. The race dates back to a time more than 500 years ago when eggs and butter could not be eaten during Lent, which began on the next day, Ash Wednesday. Any supplies of these foods left over were used up in the making of pancakes.

Germany has special wedding customs and some can be traced back for hundreds of years, such as the choice of Tuesdays and Thursdays for weddings. These two days were devoted to the old German gods. Screaming during the bride's wedding reception is meant to scare away demons and witches, while the feeding of cats by the bride dates back to the times of Freya, the Nordic goddess of love, whose favourite animal was the cat. In Germany, also, the story of the Pied Piper of Hamelin is re-enacted every Sunday during the summer.

Across the border in France some of the most colourful ceremonies are held. One is the Nice Flower Carnival,

Far left **Some music, like that of the snake charmers of the East, has a hypnotic effect upon wild creatures. Legend tells us that in 1284, Hamelin, a small German town, called upon a rat catcher to charm away the rats with his music. He did so but the townspeople refused to pay him. The rat catcher played his pipes again and this time the children of the town followed him and were not seen again.**

which is a survival of the ancient ceremony of welcoming the return of spring. This beautiful festival lasts for the twelve days before Shrove Tuesday and ends with a tremendous firework display.

The Icelandic people are not without their own special customs and on the first weekend in August the people of the Westman Islands gather in the valley of Herjolfsdalur to watch a young man swing on a rope from the top of a crag rising from the floor of the valley. For centuries this has been the method used for gathering the eggs of seafowl from the cliffs.

In Italy the Race of the Candles takes place in Gubbio in the middle of May. This is a unique custom which probably began in pre-Christian days, for the date corresponds with the Ides of March in the pagan calendar. The huge candles, which are now made of wood reinforced with iron bands, weigh nearly a quarter of a ton each. The teams of bearers carry them at a run from the Piazza dei Consoli to the top of Monte Igino.

The male citizens of Frederikssund in Denmark celebrate the Viking Festival of late June or early July by growing beards especially for the occasion and wearing Viking costumes. They revive some of Denmark's ancient history in the form of a special Viking play.

Above left **In a great many religious observances, light has a special symbolic significance. Especially is this true of Christianity which regards Christ as the Light of the World. In Sweden today, the patron saint of light, St. Lucia, has a special festival shortly before Christmas. The saint is portrayed by the youngest girl in the family wearing white with candles on her head. Each town, too, has its own St. Lucia ceremony.**

Right **The different countries of the world have many customs and ceremonies. This individuality is reflected in these national costumes from all over the world.**

Left **Just as light has a religious significance, so have flowers. They often represent the bounty of nature and are used, for example, at harvest festivals. In Jersey, in the Channel Isles, a Battle of Flowers is held every August.**

Artists and Craftsmen

Primitive art

The art of early man was an expression of his feelings about life; most of all, his need to survive. The vital thing was to be successful in the search for food and, later, when man became a farmer, to grow good crops. The earliest forms of art, such as the magnificent cave paintings discovered in France and Spain, were probably a means of capturing an animal's spirit, so that it could be overcome in the hunt.

Primitive art has much to do with primitive religion. Man's fears of the natural world and his desire to control nature caused him to make such images as he thought would please the gods and spirits. In the making of these things he painted or modelled directly from his own feelings – no one taught him how to create his images. In this sense primitive art does not belong to any one period for it has always existed in men's lives and is still practised today in various parts of the world.

Above **A North American ritual mask. Most primitive people believe that the head of a person contained his spirit. Partly for this reason, masks were often used in religious ritual and magic. Some masks represented spirits of gods.**

Right **In various parts of the world, there are to be found paintings on the walls of caves and many of them date back thousands of years. They often depict wild animals like this boar.**

Below **This is a bark painting of a kangaroo hunt. Some early artists drew the animal's internal organs like this.**

Below **Because heads, and therefore masks, contained spirits, they were often used to drive away evil spirits, as in healing and fertility rites. This picture shows a dance mask from the Ivory Coast in West Africa.**

Left **Part of an embroidered mantle border from Peru dated about AD 400.**

Below **A Pueblo Indian clay vessel of the 19th century.**

Above **Aboriginal paintings found in a cave in Australia.**

Left **This Chinese sacred vessel belongs to the Shang period (14th–12th centuries BC). The man is not being devoured by the tiger. Instead, he is clinging to his 'tiger-spirit' for protection.**

Right **This strange looking object is in fact an Eskimo mask. It is made of painted wood and feathers and belongs to the 19th century.**

Below **Here is a turquoise mosaic ornament which came from Mexico and is of the 14th or 15th century.**

Art in the ancient world

The art of the ancient civilisations was already very highly developed when, on the evidence of archaeological finds, we first became aware of it. An interesting fact about the style of art, in ancient Egypt in particular, is that it changed hardly at all for hundreds of years, unlike art today.

We know about the art of the early Egyptians from the pyramids and tombs they built. Into the tomb of a dead person was put a likeness of his head, carved out of granite. On the walls of the tomb were paintings of scenes of everyday life. This was done to help the dead person travel into the next life.

Artists in those days did not look at a subject and draw what they saw. They wanted to show everything as clearly as possible and show it from the best view, even if this meant painting or carving in a stylised, formal way. It was quite usual for a drawing of a side view of the head to have on it a front view of an eye. The

Above **Ur of the Chaldees was an ancient Sumerian city believed to be the birthplace of Abraham. Here we see two sides of a casket which is known as the 'Royal Standard' of Ur.**

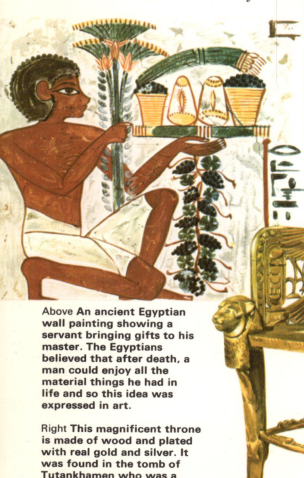

Above **An ancient Egyptian wall painting showing a servant bringing gifts to his master. The Egyptians believed that after death, a man could enjoy all the material things he had in life and so this idea was expressed in art.**

Right **This magnificent throne is made of wood and plated with real gold and silver. It was found in the tomb of Tutankhamen who was a relatively unimportant pharaoh of the mid-14th century BC.**

Above **This bronze Greek statue of a young man was found in fragments in the sea and then carefully reconstructed.**

Egyptians also had strict rules about style. For instance, if a sculptor made a statue of a seated figure, the figure had to have his hands on his knees.

Art in ancient Mesopotamia is less well-known to us today. One reason is that the people made no stone buildings, but used baked bricks which eventually crumbled away. Stone sculpture, too, was rare. The Mesopotamian kings built monuments to celebrate victory in war. At first these were sculptures showing the conquered king surrendering, but later they told the whole story of the war in pictures. Art in Mesopotamia is similar in style to Egyptian art, but not as formal and neat. Some of the pictures look very convincing.

On the island of Crete there were artists who worked in a much more free and graceful style than the artists either in Egypt or Mesopotamia. Their art was copied on the mainland of Greece.

Art in Greece in about 1000 BC was rather primitive. Pottery was decorated with plain geometric patterns. Buildings, probably made of wood,

Left This is a ritual vessel carved in the shape of a bull's head. Dated about 1500 BC, it was found in the Little Palace at Knossos in Crete. The bull played a very important part in Cretan mythology as it was the emblem of 'The Great God'.

were constructed in a simple style. But during the following centuries in Greece there was a great change in the world of art. Buildings, often beautiful temples to the gods, were built of stone, with stone columns instead of wooden props.

The Greeks found new ways of picturing the human body, drawing it in a more lifelike way. Feet had been drawn by the Egyptians as seen from the side, but the Greeks began to draw them as seen from the front. Materials changed, too, some statues being made in bronze and buildings in marble.

Greek artists had a style which was very graceful, simple and clear. People became interested in painting and sculpture because of their beauty, not just because of their religious or political meaning. Eventually Greek artists learned to draw moving people, and give faces expressions. When Alexander the Great founded the Hellenistic Empire, in the 4th century BC, art became less refined and more dramatic.

This Hellenistic style was copied by most artists until the Romans had established their huge empire by about AD 200. The Romans introduced new types of buildings, including aqueducts (which carried water across the land) and public baths. The Romans were fond of portraits, and artists made these more lifelike than ever before. Picture stories were popular, too, and the Romans liked them to be accurate – accuracy was more important to them than beauty or dramatic effect. And Roman artists learned to draw landscape pictures.

Above This sculpture of a ram in a thicket was found at Ur.

Left A statue of a winged human-headed bull found at the palace of Sargon II, king of Assyria, 722–705 BC.

Art in the western world

As the Roman Empire broke up and the Christian church became established, art began to change once again. The early Christian artists wanted their work to be as simple and clear as possible, as the Greeks had, rather than completely accurate. No statues were allowed in Christian churches, but the church in the West allowed paintings. These were simple illustrations which told stories for those who could not read. Sometimes these pictures would be mosaics of pieces of coloured glass or stone.

The city of Constantinople, at the heart of the Byzantine Empire, was relatively unaffected by the barbarian invasions of the Dark Ages. It produced some of the most nearly perfect buildings and works of art ever made. These include the church of St. Sophia in Constantinople and the mosaics of Justinian and Theodora in the Church of San Vitale, Ravenna.

The Dark Ages (between AD 500 and 1000) was a time of many wars and upheavals. Various tribes invaded Europe bringing with them their traditional crafts of wood carving and metal work. They were very skilled and made complicated patterns, sometimes of twisted bodies of dragons. In England this had an influence on Christian art, where manuscripts were illustrated with intricate patterns. Most art at this time was religious, but the Bayeux tapestry tells the story of the Norman conquest of England in 1066 in simple, clear pictures.

Above **A Byzantine mosaic in the oratory of Galla Placidia, built during the 5th century at Ravenna in Italy. It shows the Good Shepherd with His lambs.**

Above **The Book of Kells, an 8th-century illuminated manuscript of the Gospels written in Latin. This great treasure is kept in Trinity College, Dublin.**

Above **A section of the Bayeux Tapestry, a long strip of linen embroidered in wool. It depicts the conquest of England in 1066 and is now in the Bishop's palace at Bayeux in Normandy.**

Right **One of the rose windows of medieval stained glass in the Cathedral of Notre Dame in Chartres, France. The building dates from about 1194 and is often regarded as the best example of Gothic architecture in the whole of Europe.**

142

At the beginning of the 11th century the most powerful influence on the development of art was still the church. Stone carving and metal work decorated the massive churches of the Romanesque period. Wall paintings, called murals, were painted, often in panels. They looked like enlarged pages from a Bible picture-book. In the monasteries manuscripts continued to be illustrated with brilliantly coloured borders and initial letters.

A hundred years later a new architectural style, called Gothic, appeared. It was light and graceful, and sculpture and painting had a Gothic style as well. Artists tried to make figures look convincing and tell a story movingly. Figures in manuscript drawings showed feelings, though the illustrations did not look lifelike, as they had to be fitted into a pattern. France was the leader of the Gothic style, which was soon copied by other countries. It was some time before its influence was felt in Italy, where artists were still influenced by the old Byzantine style.

One Italian painter however, Giotto di Bondone (1267–1337), brought a great change to art. His individual style broke away from Byzantine influence and his paintings had life— the scenes in them looked as if they were really happening. His work influenced artists in northern Europe, as Gothic art began to spread south into Italy. Among the most interesting

Above **A carved head from a cart found in a Viking Ship dating from AD 850. It was unearthed in 1904 at Oseberg, in Norway.**

Below **A beautiful bird shaped brooch dating from the 6th century. It was found in Saragossa, Spain.**

Above **The sun-chariot from Trundholm in Denmark. It was found in fragments in 1902 by a farmer when he was ploughing a field, and has since been re-assembled. It illustrates the belief of many Bronze Age people that the sun was drawn across the heavens in a chariot.**

Left **Ever since the Christian Church was founded nearly 2,000 years ago, painters and sculptors have depicted scenes from the Gospels. One of the most beautiful of the Nativity paintings is 'The Adoration of the Magi' shown here. Painted by the Limbourg brothers in the early 15th century, it shows the wise men bringing their gifts.**

works of art during the 14th century were small objects made in metal or ivory. These were full of delicate detail. At this time, too, portraits began to be painted again.

The next century saw the great period of the Renaissance in Italy, although other important developments took place in northern Europe as well. Jan van Eyck, who lived in Flanders, improved the paint artists used by adding oil to it. He was the first successful oil painter. He studied nature and made exact copies with great care and patience. He also painted many portraits, which were more realistic than ever before.

143

The greatest period of Italian art was in the late 15th and early 16th centuries. This was the time of the Renaissance, when there was a rebirth of interest in the arts and sciences of ancient Greece and Rome. It was also a time when artists escaped from the dark mood of the Middle Ages and found new glory in their power to create beautiful things. Leonardo da Vinci, Michelangelo, Raphael, Titian, Durer – each man a genius – and all of them lived within the space of little more than a hundred years. And they were only the men of genius: there were hundreds of lesser but still great artists working alongside them all over Europe.

Leonardo da Vinci was the 'ideal man' of the Renaissance – artist, scientist, engineer, scholar, musician – there seemed to be no skill that he did not possess. Although we have few works of his, each one is a masterpiece. His painting of a Florentine lady known as Mona Lisa is probably the best-known picture in the world. Leonardo left many notebooks containing his drawings and thoughts on a vast number of subjects. One curious thing about them is the 'mirror-

Above **Michelangelo's heroic statue of David is one of his masterpieces. Carved out of a single block of marble it stands over 16 feet high. It was commissioned by the city of Florence, where it now stands.**

Right **Some 5,000 pages of Leonardo da Vinci's notebooks have been preserved. This drawing shows his model for a kind of helicopter, and the curious mirror-image writing he used can be seen.**

Below **Two miniatures by Isaac Oliver, an English painter who lived from 1560 to 1617. He was the pupil of Nicholas Hilliard, who founded the English school of miniature painting.**

Above **A detail from one of Albrecht Durer's engravings** *Knight, Death and the Devil.*

Below **Many tapestries were made from drawings by Raphael which were called cartoons.**

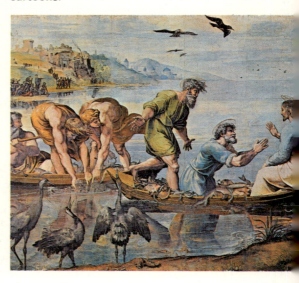

writing' which Leonardo used to make his notes. He was left-handed and wrote backwards from right to left so that his words can only be read when reflected in a mirror.

Michelangelo was another great figure of the Renaissance. He lived until he was nearly 90 and in his unusually long life saw tremendous changes in the world and in the position of the artist. As a boy Michelangelo was trained in the workshop of a master painter, learning all the tricks of the trade and how to paint a pleasing picture. But Michelangelo was interested in greater things. He devoted his life to paintings and statues of the human figure. Michelangelo tried to give the feeling that within every block of marble he carved, there lay already a human figure, and that when he chipped away at the stone it was simply to reveal the form which lay hidden within. His most famous work was to paint scenes from the Bible on the ceiling of the Sistine Chapel in Rome.

Raphael admired the work of Michelangelo and Leonardo and learned a lot from it. Although he did not have their majestic power his paintings look as if the paint flowed from his brush without effort. He painted many beautiful frescoes (a method of painting on wet plaster) on the walls of palaces and villas. His other great

Right **Adoration of the Magi**, by the great Spanish portrait painter, Diego Velasquez (1599–1660). In 1624 he entered the court of Philip IV of Spain and painted over 100 portraits of the royal family and their courtiers.

Below **Peter Bruegel (1520–69)** painted many country scenes of peasants. This one is called **Harvesters**.

achievement was to arrange large groups of people in his paintings in a flowing way which was pleasing to the eye.

Titian was handsome and rich, and lived in great style. He became the official painter to the court at Venice and was a great portrait painter. Even so, colour remained more important to him than the subject of his paintings. He was also one of the first artists to paint natural human figures in religious paintings. Durer is famed not only for his paintings but for his illustrations in the pages of religious books. These usually took the form of woodcuts and engravings on metal.

After the Renaissance there are many great artists and many styles in the story of art. Two artists who followed a dramatic style called Mannerism in the 16th century were Tintoretto in Italy and El Greco in Spain. The best-known painter of the Baroque style in the 17th century was Rubens, who lived in Flanders but spent many years in Italy.

In England at the beginning of the 18th century William Hogarth set out to create a new kind of painting. He planned several series of story paintings. Though he earned fame and money, it was Joshua Reynolds whose style really pleased English tastes. He borrowed from the Italian masters and painted many dignified portraits.

Towards the end of the century, ideas about art were changing. A Spaniard, Francisco Goya, painted many fine portraits which won him a position at the Spanish court. But if we look closely at his stately portraits we see that Goya revealed the bad points in the characters of his subjects as well as the good.

The English poet William Blake

Above **Another artist who gave his attention to light and colour was J. M. W. Turner (1775–1851). His 'Snowstorm' illustrated here shows how he made nature more dramatic than it was in reality.**

Below **John Constable (1776–1837) was an English painter who wanted nothing to do with 'airy visions' but only to paint nature faithfully. Here is his picture of Salisbury Cathedral in England.**

Above **This is a magnificent bronze work called 'Head of Sorrow', sculpted in 1882 by Auguste Rodin, a Frenchman.**

Left **'Nypheas' by Claude Monet (1840–1926), a French artist who helped to found the Impressionist school. He loved to experiment with light and colour as this picture shows. The Impressionists tended to concentrate on one feature in their pictures, leaving the background out of focus.**

was a religious man who lived in a world of his own. He refused to draw from real life and concentrated on drawing his personal visions. Few people believed in Blake and it was much later before he was appreciated. Two other English painters became famous for their landscapes – J. M. W. Turner and John Constable. They had very different styles. Turner's world was full of life and he made his pictures very dramatic. Constable's aim was to paint the countryside as it really was, in the true colours of nature.

In the 19th century some artists became dissatisfied with art as it was. The great academies of art claimed to follow the tradition of the early 16th-century painter, Raphael. A group in England called themselves the pre-Raphaelites because they thought they must follow an earlier tradition, but their movement was not very successful and did not last long.

At the end of the century in France a group of artists looked at art with completely new eyes. These artists painted to give a general effect without elaborate detail. It was a long time before the Impressionists, as they became known, were accepted. Edouard Manet led the way in this movement, which included the painters Monet, Renoir and Pissarro.

One painter who was interested in the Impressionists, although he did not paint like them, was Vincent van Gogh. He was a Dutchman who went to live in the south of France in order to spend all his time painting. His pictures were full of sun and brilliant colour even when the intensity of his feelings had driven him mad. One man influenced by van Gogh in a group working in Paris at the beginning of this century was Henri Matisse. He used bright colours and his paintings were often like decorative patterns.

The 20th century has had many styles: Cubist, Abstract, Expression-

ist, Surrealist, and never before has the style of artistic expression changed so rapidly. Two famous artists of modern times are the painter Pablo Picasso, and the sculptor Henry Moore. Picasso, born in Spain, had his first exhibition when he was sixteen. At nineteen he went to Paris and studied primitive art. He led the Cubist movement but has always varied his methods, using many different and exciting styles. Henry Moore was born in Britain and is famous for his stone sculptures of human figures.

Above 'The Card Players' by Paul Cézanne (1839–1906). He was an Impressionist but his work had a more 'solid' look than that of Monet or Manet.

Below left 'The Chair' by Vincent Van Gogh, a 19th-century Dutch painter of The French Expressionist school.

Below Pablo Picasso is one of the greatest modern painters belonging to the Cubist school. He often uses vivid colours and unusual outlines. The picture shown here is his 'The Three Dancers'.

Above Henry Moore, the British sculptor, has had a great influence in modern times, as his work is always an interesting study in shapes. This picture shows his 'Mother and Child'.

Far Left Lichtenstein's 'Wham', one of the most famous examples of Pop-art,

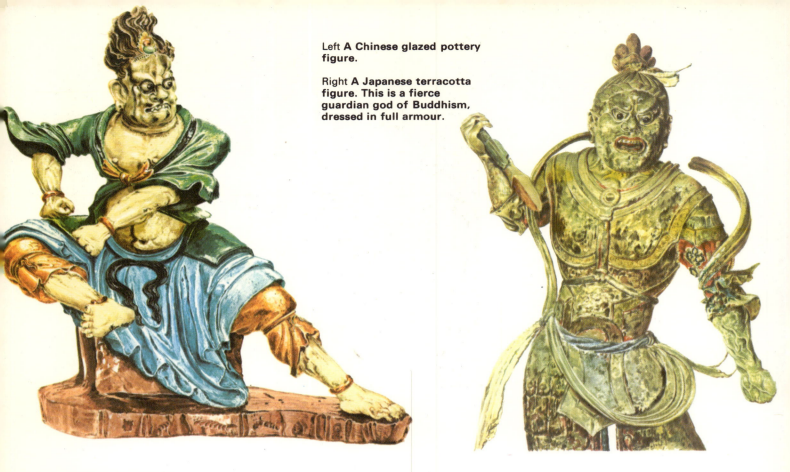

Left **A Chinese glazed pottery figure.**

Right **A Japanese terracotta figure. This is a fierce guardian god of Buddhism, dressed in full armour.**

Art in other lands

Some of the earliest Oriental art belongs to a period about 5,000 years ago when there was a civilisation in the Indus Valley in the north-west of India. Images of bulls, sacred animals in those days, and bronze figures, have survived from this time.

Until the conquests of Alexander, no Indian artist had presumed to portray Buddha. Then, inspired by statues brought from Greece, the first statues of Buddha were created in the image of Apollo. Large figures of the Buddha were built and the Roman way of telling a story in pictures was copied by artists depicting the story of Buddha.

Eventually, Buddhism disappeared in India because of Hindu persecution. Many carvings decorated the tall towers of Hindu temples. By the 16th century India had been conquered by the Moslem Moguls, whose emperors built beautiful palaces and tombs.

We do not know much about early Chinese art, but the Chinese had certainly mastered the craft of making bronze vessels several thousand years ago. Chinese artists and sculptors liked curves and rounded shapes and

Above **Mixtec gold breastplate depicting the god of death.**

Below **A traditional Japanese Noh Mask.**

they were soon able to represent the movement of the human figure. When Buddhism reached China in about AD 1000, lifelike statues were made of Buddha and Buddhist monks. People began to appreciate artists and China was one of the first places where artists were considered important members of society.

Art in China was not for story-telling but existed as an aid to meditation (deep thought), which was an important part of Chinese religions. People kept pictures of water, mountains or landscapes on silk scrolls and brought them out in quiet moments to help them meditate. An artist learned to draw from the old masters. He then went out to study nature and capture its mood. He would already be able to handle his brush and ink well, and could make his drawing while he still felt inspired. The paintings of the masters were so admired, that the style of Chinese art changed little.

Japanese art developed out of Chinese art and carried along the same lines for about 1,000 years. In the 18th century some Japanese artists made colour woodcuts, choosing scenes of daily life as their subjects. Two of these artists were Hokusai and Utamaro. Many people in Japan did not like the woodcuts, but prints of them reached Europe, where the Impressionists and other artists were influenced by their simplicity.

In the 7th and 8th centuries AD the Islamic religion spread from Arabia to Persia, North Africa and Spain. The new religion allowed no images of any sort, but craftsmen created lacework patterns which decorated the mosques. Later, figures and illustrations were allowed as long as they had no connection with religion. Book illustrations of the period do not look very real but make lovely fairytale patterns.

In the 16th century AD the Aztecs in Mexico and the Incas in Peru ruled mighty empires. Though their art has links with primitive art, they were not a primitive people. They could draw the human face in a very lifelike manner, and certain vessels in Peru were shaped in the form of human heads. If some of their art seems primitive it is because of the ideas behind them. Rain was important to these people and images of the rain god were made in the shape of a rattlesnake, because they considered it a sacred being.

Above **An example of Incan art. A gold funeral mask with emerald pendants.**

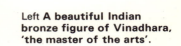

Left **A beautiful Indian bronze figure of Vinadhara, 'the master of the arts'.**

Below **A Mogul miniature from India.**

Left **A Japanese actor, taken from an 18th-century woodcut.**

Building Through the Ages

When man first lived in caves he wore no clothes and spoke no language. His life was concerned with finding food. But the climate of the world was changing and man was developing in intelligence and culture. In time, he began to set about making homes to shelter himself. Man became a builder, using wood and other natural materials. He made homes of grass and leaves, skins and logs. Even today, the Bantu tribes of Africa have houses which are very cleverly made of gras , reeds and branches.

The Bedouin, a people from the desert regions of Africa, live in tents made from cloth and animal hair. These homes are portable and are carried by the Bedouin to wherever they can find water. Other tent dwellers were the Red Indians of North America who lived in tents called tepees made of buffalo skins. Similar to the tepees of the Red Indians are the tents of the people called Samoyeds, who live in the cold lands that fringe the Arctic Ocean. These are made of reindeer skins and birch bark and are easily carried when the people roam the tundra in spring with their herds of reindeer.

Like the tent, the hut has been used since the early days of home-making. Some Eskimos today still live in snow huts called igloos. In almost every part of the world wood plays an important part in house building and the lumberjacks of Canada live in houses made of logs. The people of Alpine countries live in beautiful wooden chalets, and in Burma the elephant helps man to transport the teak from which he will make homes. Bamboo huts built on stilts can still be seen in the flood regions of Thailand.

The first really great building works were produced by the ancient civilisations of Egypt and Mesopotamia, and later of Greece and Rome. These people took their art to many countries and some of their work still exists today, although most of it is in ruins.

In the Middle Ages there were many periods, or styles, in architecture, most of which began on the continent of Europe and spread to other areas.

Above In most arctic lands there are no trees or plants to provide building materials so the Eskimos who live there have to build their homes, called igloos, out of solid blocks of snow. The Eskimos are a hardy race and find in these igloos enough protection from the winds.

Above Nomads, being people who have no settled home and are always on the move, live in tents because they can be packed up easily when the time comes to move on. The tents in this picture are tepees and were once used by some tribes of American Red Indians.

Above A magnificent example of a 17th Century interior, the Heaven Room by Antonio Verrio c.1696 at Burghley House, England.

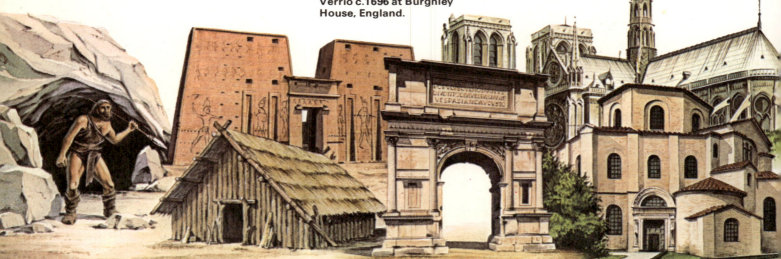

The Renaissance style of the 15th century began in Italy and soon became fashionable in other countries where it was adapted to their individual tastes. The Tuscan city-state of Florence took the lead in the Renaissance, there being plenty of fine stone and marble in Tuscany. A typical princely mansion of this time is the Medici-Riccardi Palace in Florence.

A fine example of 16th-century English architecture is Little Moreton Hall in Cheshire, which shows how well timber could be combined with other materials. Then, early in the 17th century, architects began to be more interested in designing houses and public buildings within the overall plan of a town.

One of the reasons why we can still see examples of people's houses and other buildings from centuries past is the nature of the material used in their construction. Man discovered long ago that stone was the most durable of all building materials, for it did not decay and was completely weatherproof.

Soon he began to look for something to take the place of stone, which was often difficult to work, so he made bricks and roof tiles from clay and built his houses from these. Then he discovered cement, which was mixed with sand and water to make concrete. By using steel as a framework for the concrete he was able to build very tall buildings in areas where land was scarce. Today, builders are experimenting with all kinds of new materials, including plastics, prefabricated units and even houses which are inflated like balloons.

Above **People who live by lakes and swamps often build their homes over the water like this one.**

Below **The pictures at the bottom of the page show the evolution of architecture from the primitive cave to the skyscraper on the right.**

Left The palace of Versailles in France was built for Louis XIV as a place for him to live, as he hated Paris. It was begun in 1669 and in 1683 it became the chief royal residence of the kings of France. No expense was spared to make this the most magnificent royal palace in the world. After the First World War the Treaty of Versailles was signed there in 1919 between the Allied powers and Germany. Today it is used as a museum.

Castles and palaces

The earliest types of castles were little more than ditches and earthworks. The outlines of prehistoric hill forts can sometimes still be traced on the land. They were built on hill tops and had a series of roughly circular or oval defensive walls, usually of wood, leading to a central stockade on the highest point. All the people of a village and their animals would shelter in this if there was danger of attack from an enemy.

In the Middle Ages in Europe, princes and barons had their own private armies and were always fighting each other. For the same reason that primitive people needed a place of safety to which they could turn, so the medieval lord had to provide a refuge for himself, his family and his servants. In this way his home became a fortified castle.

The earliest castles had only a single tower called a keep. As time went on, defensive walls and new buildings were added until the structure could contain a whole community within its walls. A good example of this type of development and possibly the most famous castle in the world is the Tower of London. Its stone keep was built by William the Conqueror, and the mass of walls, towers and battlements were added at various times until, by the 16th century, it had taken on the appearance of today's castle.

Many fine castles were built in the East during the period of the Crusades. The 12th-century Krak des Chevaliers in Syria can still be seen today.

Above On a height of the Dorset downs in England can be seen the remains of a fortress known as Maiden Castle. The earthworks date from the Iron Age, about 400 BC, but the hilltop has been used as a defensive position since about 2000 BC. On the right is a simple Iron Age pot found at Maiden Castle.

Above The Alcazar at Segovia in Spain. "Alcazar" is a Moorish word for a palace or fortress and this castle was built in medieval times on the western end of a long spur of rock upon which the city of Segovia itself was built.

Above This castle with its fairy-tale towers and romantic setting is the Schloss Neuschwanstein in Bavaria, built in 1869–81.

Below The Doge's Palace in Venice, which was for years the residence of the head of the State. The present building dates from the 14th/15th centuries.

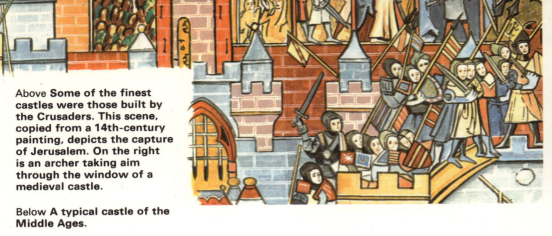

Above **Some of the finest castles were those built by the Crusaders. This scene, copied from a 14th-century painting, depicts the capture of Jerusalem. On the right is an archer taking aim through the window of a medieval castle.**

Below **A typical castle of the Middle Ages.**

Below **Troy was the ancient city in Asia Minor which Homer writes about in the** *Iliad.* **The archaeologist Heinrich Schliemann dug up the site in modern times and found traces of nine different cities buried one under the other, the earliest going back over 3,000 years.**

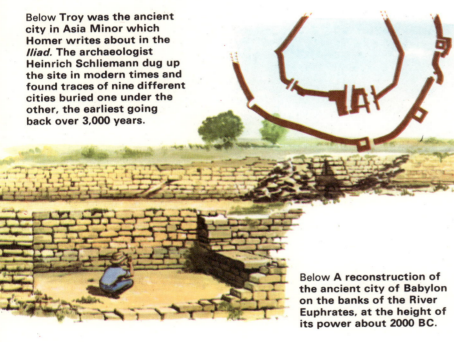

Below **A reconstruction of the ancient city of Babylon on the banks of the River Euphrates, at the height of its power about 2000 BC.**

During the 1st century AD the Roman emperor Augustus built a magnificent home and from its site on the Palatine Hill in Rome comes our word 'palace'. Kings and emperors in the ancient world were all-powerful. They built large palaces to live in, not only to please themselves but to impress ordinary people with their wealth. Today, the ruins of some of these palaces in Egypt, Babylon and Crete are enough to suggest to us what beautiful places they were.

The emperors of old China built palaces within the walls of 'forbidden' cities, which the common people were not allowed into. Both in China and Japan the emperors hid themselves away behind these walled cities and their palaces were full of mystery and not built for show. The Japanese built their palaces like their houses, with blank outside walls, looking into a central courtyard.

Palaces in the modern world, which are still in use as homes, museums or show places, date mostly from the 16th–18th centuries. They were built by the rulers of European kingdoms for just the same reasons as those in the ancient world. The monarch had to make a splendid show of his royal power, and nowhere was this more true than in France, where the palace of Versailles was built for Louis XIV. It took over a hundred years to complete this enormous collection of buildings with their surrounding parks, avenues and gardens. The most splendid palace in England, at Blenheim, near Oxford, was built by the nation as a present to its great military leader, the first Duke of Marlborough, who led his country to victory in many battles against the French in the 18th century.

Churches, temples and monuments

The houses that people have built over the centuries tell us something of the way they lived, but their churches, temples and monuments tell us even more. They tell us a little of what people thought.

In prehistoric times, centuries before Christ was born, people had many different gods. Early man did not build churches but something of his religious beliefs do show in the monuments, wall paintings and other art-forms of his time. The monument at Stonehenge on Salisbury Plain in England was probably begun about 1900 BC. It is clear that Stonehenge was a very important religious centre, and served as a temple of the sun for hundreds of years. It is the largest and most impressive monument of its period in northern Europe.

The first true temples appeared much later than this with the ancient civilisations of India, China and the Near East. Because people feared the gods the temples were lavishly built so as to please them. Both private worship and public rituals took place in the temples and they were often very large. The Temple of Ammon at Karnak in Egypt, built about 1200 BC, had an inner and an outer temple, and only the king and the priests were allowed in the inner chamber.

As a place of worship this form contrasts sharply with the pyramid-shaped temples called ziggurats in Mesopotamia. Pyramids were also part of the landscape in Egypt, where

Above **Stonehenge on Salisbury Plain, England, believed to be the finest Bronze Age monument in Europe. It consists of enormous blocks of stone standing in concentric circles, although some of the stones have disappeared. Its actual function is not known but it is generally supposed to have been connected with sun worship.**

Right **The picture shows part of the magnificent temple of Rameses III who was a pharaoh of ancient Egypt. The statue is of the pharaoh himself and he is depicted as wearing the double crown of Upper and Lower Egypt. The statues in the inner court have been badly damaged since it was first built about 1200 BC.**

Below **The pyramids of ancient Egypt have inspired explorers and archaeologists for many hundreds of years because of the strange air of mystery and legend which surround them. Excavations in modern times have shown that they were built as vast tombs for the pharaohs. As the Egyptians believed in life after death, they filled the tombs with all kinds of articles which had been used and enjoyed in life.**

the oldest pyramid is the Step Pyramid at Sakkara, which is the tomb of King Zoser. The Aztec people of Mexico also built pyramids on top of which human sacrifices to the gods took place.

The Greeks developed a style of architecture which we refer to as 'classical'. It reached its highest peak of perfection in the 5th century BC at the time of Pericles and Phidias, the Greek sculptor. The Romans inherited the Greek forms and both races were masters of the art of building temples and the remains of many can still be seen today. The most perfect of them was the Parthenon, a temple to Athena on the Acropolis at Athens. A great masterpiece of Roman architecture is the Pantheon in Rome, which was begun in 27 BC, rebuilt by the emperor Hadrian, and is still used as a church.

Left **St. Basil's Cathedral, Moscow. The Orthodox Church, of which it is a part, is found chiefly in Russia, Greece and Eastern Europe.**

Below **This modern building which is in Tel Aviv, Israel, offers a striking contrast in architectural style when compared with the others on this page.**

Left **The Taj Mahal built in 1650 at Agra in India by a Mogul emperor, Shah Jehan, as a tomb for his wife. It has a brilliant white exterior and its decorations are very rich in style.**
Below **St. Peter's Rome. As there has been a church on this site since the early days of Christianity, it is of great historic interest and houses priceless works of art.**

When Christianity came it spread quickly through the civilised world, although not many churches were built in the early years. Then the Roman Empire split up and a second capital was founded at Byzantium, a town which was renamed Constantinople and which is known nowadays as Istanbul. The style of the Byzantine church, on which domes were a prominent feature, changed little during the next 1,000 years. Probably the finest and most famous example is the church of St. Sophia in Istanbul, which is now used for worship by the Moslems and known as the Great Mosque.

During the 11th century a new way of building churches developed, called Romanesque. These churches had round arches supported by large pillars. In France in particular the churches were decorated with impressive solemn sculpture.

During the Gothic period an enormous amount of energy and money went into the building of churches. Gothic buildings had graceful pointed arches and large windows instead of thick walls. Stained glass was used in the windows for the first time.

There are many beautiful temples in the Orient, such as the Taj Mahal in India, and the exotic golden temples to Buddha in the Far East.

Writing and Printing

Writing is a tool of a developed society and is one of the things which separates civilised man from the savage. In the old worlds of Egypt and Mesopotamia writing was a rare art, practised mostly by scribes. It was only with the successful use of printing in the 15th century that knowledge became more readily available. Very gradually, writing began to be thought of as an accomplishment for the majority of people. But even today this is still only true of western society. There are many backward and underprivileged people for whom education in the basic skills is still lacking.

Some of the earliest systems for recording events were what are called mnemonic, which means something used as an aid to memory in recalling and recording facts. The Peruvian *quippu* or knotted string is an example, as is the familiar knotted handkerchief which is supposed to remind us of some fact to be recorded or action to be performed. Notched sticks served a similar purpose in keeping records of sums of money and weights of goods.

Later systems of writing were pictorial, that is they consisted of actual picture-drawings of the event to be recorded. Ideographic systems use conventional symbols to suggest a particular idea. The numbers 1, 2, 3, 4, 5, 6, 7, 8, 9 are called ideograms and exist without being dependent on language. The ideogram '2' is interpreted as two, or *deux*, or *due*, according to the language one speaks, but in what it suggests the ideogram is international.

Phonetic systems can be verbal, in which images are used directly to suggest particular words, or syllabic, when images are used to suggest each separate sound of a word, such as 'bee' and 'leaf' = belief. Alphabetical systems break a word up into individual elements and a conventional symbol is used to signify each one.

Above **These pictures show wampum beads which were small tubular shells used by North American Indians instead of money and for record purposes. The quippu (1) was used by the ancient Peruvians as a recording device. The wampum circle (2) and belt (3) were to record events, like minutes of a council meeting.**

Below **Tally sticks, used to record numbers and as a method of keeping accounts.**

Above **This tablet, showing Ashurbanipal, the emperor of Assyria, commemorated his founding of a temple. In his palace at Nineveh, Ashurbanipal had a 'library' of such tablets, most of them telling stories of the history of the time.**

Below **This stone, found at Rosetta near the Nile, is important because it led to the deciphering of Egyptian hieroglyphics. A magnifying glass will show that it is written in various languages.**

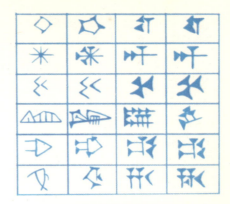

Above **Here we have an example of cuneiform writing which was in use in the Near East for a long period from about 3000 BC onwards. During its long life, it underwent some changes and was used for more than one language. True cuneiform is as shown in this picture and was written with a pointed stylus which made little wedges in the stone tablet. Today, though, the name is often used loosely for other old forms of writing.**

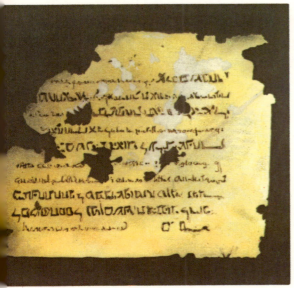

Above **Pictures like these are to be found painted on the walls of many ancient Egyptian tombs. The strange looking creatures are gods and behind them can be seen characters written in hieroglyphic, one of the most important ancient systems of writing. This writing consisted of various picture symbols instead of words.**

Left **This is a fragment of the Dead Sea Scrolls discovered in jars hidden in a cave in 1947. Written in Aramaic, they are an early copy of some books of the Bible. Aramaic was a Semitic language close to Hebrew and was the language spoken in New Testament times by Jesus Christ and His apostles.**

Below **Some writing instruments.**

Left **These symbols show how the Roman letter 'A' may have evolved from a picture sign for an ox** (Aleph in Phoenician which became the Greek Alpha).

Below **The Greeks sometimes wrote in both directions. This style of writing is called boustrophedon, which means 'ploughing like an ox'.**

IFYOUREADTHISWRI
TINGFIRSTFROMLEF
TTORIGHTTHENFROM
RIGHTTOLEFTDOWNT
HELINESYOUWILLTH
ENUNDERSTANDWHAT
BOUSTREPHEDONWRI
TINGREALLYISALL
ABOUT

Printing and making books

Printed books, magazines and newspapers are so much a part of our everyday life that it is difficult to imagine what it must have been like in the days before the invention of printing. When talking about the invention of printing it is necessary to know what is meant by the term 'printing'.

People in the ancient world, particularly in Mesopotamia and Egypt, were able to transfer images by the impression of seals, which worked rather like rubber stamps do today.

Left **An 18th-century printing press. The printer is taking an impression from the type.**

These were made of wood or clay, and were used as signatures or personal marks by traders. But this crude form of printing never developed into the more complicated craft which records the written word by some mechanical means.

The first real printers were probably the Chinese. In the library of the British Museum in London is an ancient Chinese manuscript called the Diamond Sutra, which was printed from wood blocks in AD 868. The date is known since it is inscribed on the manuscript, which is generally reckoned to be the earliest surviving printed 'book'. It is also believed that the Chinese may have begun printing as early as the 7th century AD.

The process used in these early days is called block printing, a method which continued to be employed in Europe right up to the 15th century. As a method it was costly and took a long time. In block printing, letters were written in ink, in reverse, on a

Above left **The Letterpress process. This is a method of printing from a raised surface.**

Above centre **Offset Lithography. A method of printing from a flat surface. The image on the bottom cylinder is transferred to the rubber surface of the centre cylinder. The image is finally printed on paper.**

Right **Photogravure. This is a method of printing from an incised surface. The cylinder is immersed in ink and then wiped clean. Ink remains in the incised surface of the cylinder and when pressure is applied, the paper lifts the ink out of the recesses.**

smooth block of wood. Then the surface of the wood around the letters was cut away until they appeared standing out in relief. The raised letters were then inked and an impression taken.

The one idea which really speeded up printing and made possible the production of a number of copies of a single book was the invention of movable type. As it happened it was also the Chinese who thought of this first. A man named Pi-Sheng did make some wooden movable type in the 11th century, but as the Chinese language is not an alphabetical one and uses many characters, the idea was never developed.

In Germany, about 1440, Johann Gutenberg, working in Strasburg and afterwards in Mainz, invented metal moulds into which hot liquid was poured to produce separate letters. The first books printed from this movable type were published in the 1450s. The famous 42-line Bible (the

name refers to the number of lines on a page) attributed to Gutenberg appeared in 1455. After this, printing spread rapidly to other countries in Europe.

The hand printing press remained in general use for over 400 years, with few variations in its essential features. Power was first applied to printing when steam rotary machines were used to print *The Times* newspaper in London in 1814. Such machines as the Linotype and Monotype made the job of composing type easier and quicker. Rotary machines were built which could print hundreds of thousands of copies of newspapers and magazines in a few hours.

Since then the development of printing has been concerned with cheaper, faster and better methods of producing the enormous mass of printed material which the modern world demands. Automation is now the key word in printing, as it is in so many other sectors of industry.

Left **The four stages of putting a book together. Books are generally bound in 16 or 32-pages signatures. Several signatures make up the complete text. The books are then cased and bound.**

Right **Colour printing. Most modern colour reproduction is printed in four colours — yellow, cyan (blue), magenta (red) and black.**

Above **Potato printing. The simplest method of relief printing.**

Right **A modern Monotype composing keyboard.**

Writers and their books

One of the earliest writers we know about is the Greek poet Homer, who lived about 700 BC. He wrote two epic poems, the *Iliad* and the *Odyssey*. The *Iliad* tells of the siege of Troy and the story of Achilles. In the *Odyssey* Homer tells of the return of Odysseus after twenty years away from his home. Other famous Greek writers were Plato and Aristotle.

Among Roman writers around the 1st century BC were Cicero, who was a famous public speaker and wrote books on oratory, and Julius Caesar, one of the greatest generals in history, whose best-known work is his history of the Roman wars in Gaul. Three Latin poets were Virgil, Horace and Ovid. The hero of Virgil's *Aeneid* is Aeneas, a Trojan prince who tried to found a new Trojan empire in Italy. Virgil did not finish this book before he died and left instructions for it to be destroyed, but this did not happen.

The *Fables* of Aesop are a collection of Greek fables which were first brought together in the 2nd century AD and made into a book by a monk in the 14th century. Aesop is said to have been a slave on the island of Samos in the 6th century BC.

The stories in the *Arabian Nights* – stories of Aladdin, Ali Baba and others – in fact come from India, but they were put into Arabic in the 11th century. The names of the characters are Persian and it is thought that the stories travelled from India to Persia and then to Arabia. The stories are the work of several writers.

The Latin language was used in Europe until the Middle Ages. One of the first great works in Italian was Dante's long poem, *The Divine Comedy*, written in the 14th century. In the same century in England Geoffrey Chaucer wrote *The Canterbury Tales*. This is a story of pilgrims travelling to Canterbury. Each pilgrim tells a story on the way. Chaucer had intended to have 120 tales in all, but the work was not finished.

In France in the 16th century lived the writer François Rabelais. His book, *Gargantua*, tells the story of a giant and is full of humorous satire.

Above **The legendary Greek poet, Homer, who is thought to have lived between the 11th and 7th centuries BC. Tradition says he was blind and he might have been a court minstrel.**
Below **In one of his books, the *Iliad*, Homer tells of the siege of Troy, but it is in the *Odyssey* that the story of the wooden horse is told. At one stage, the besieging Greeks built a wooden horse, making out it was a religious offering to Athena. The horse actually concealed some of the Greeks' best soldiers. Then the attackers pretended they had lost the war and went away leaving the horse behind. By a series of ruses, the horse was let into the city, the soldiers inside were released and the rest of the Greek army returned to overthrow the city and end the siege.**

Don Quixote written by Miguel de Cervantes in 1605 was the first real adventure novel and satirical romance. The hero of the book, Don Quixote, was an eccentric who had read so many tales of noble knights that he wanted to copy their deeds. So accompanied by his servant, he rode out to do battle with the world. He regarded all kinds of everyday things as fearsome objects which he had to overcome. But, in the end, all his adventures ended up with his getting a beating. Here is the famous episode from the book in which he is tilting at windmills because he thinks they are giants.

Left **A scene from *Treasure Island*, one of the greatest adventure stories of all time, beloved by boys and girls and adults too. The picture shows Long John Silver and Jim Hawkins in trouble.**

Below **Robert Louis Stevenson, the author of *Treasure Island*, who lived from 1850–94. He qualified as a barrister but ill health forced him to travel in Europe and the USA. He settled in Samoa in the South Seas where he died.**

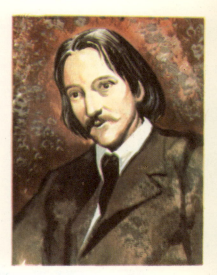

It was in Spain in 1605 that the first adventure novel, *Don Quixote*, was written. Miguel de Cervantes is said to have started it when he was in prison. It describes the adventures of Don Quixote, who leaves his home with a servant, Sancho Panza.

The greatest poem of John Milton, who was born in 1608, was *Paradise Lost*. This tells of the rebellion of Satan and the fall of man. When the poem was published it was a great success. *Pilgrim's Progress*, written by another Englishman, John Bunyan, is called a moral fable. It was written in two parts, the first in 1674 and the second in 1684.

Daniel Defoe was a government agent, a traveller and journalist. He was nearly sixty when he wrote *Robinson Crusoe*, but he went on to write many more books. *Robinson Crusoe* became popular at once and has remained so. Jonathan Swift's most famous book is *Gulliver's Travels*, published in 1726. On the surface this is a charming fable, but underneath is a sharp attack on society. Man is shown as a small creature, with his many faults magnified.

Below **Aesop was famous for many wonderful fables. One of these told how the sun and the wind had an argument as to who would be the first to get a man's coat off. The wind blew hard but failed in this. Then the sun was so hot that the man took off his coat. Here we see the sun winning the strange contest.**

Above left **Gulliver meets one of the Lilliputians in *Gulliver's Travels*, a tale of fantasy.**

Above **Jonathan Swift, the author of *Gulliver's Travels*.**

Papers were published in 1836 and were a great success. Dickens's books include *David Copperfield* and *Oliver Twist*. There were many other novelists in England. Thackeray's books include *Vanity Fair* and Trollope's *Barchester Towers*. Charlotte Brontë wrote *Jane Eyre* and her sister Emily, *Wuthering Heights*. George Eliot was a pen name for Mary Ann Evans, who wrote *Middlemarch*. Thomas Hardy wrote novels set in Dorset, such as *Tess of the D'Urbervilles*.

Minor novelists included Captain Marryat, who wrote *The Children of the New Forest* and many sea stories; and Charles Kingsley, who wrote a fairy tale, *The Water Babies*, and historical novels like *Westward Ho!* Robert Louis Stevenson was a highly successful writer. He wrote *Treasure Island* and *Kidnapped* and many other books. Rudyard Kipling was born in India and wrote about the country

One of the first great English novelists was Henry Fielding. His masterpiece was *Tom Jones*, written in 1749. Also in the 18th century, Samuel Johnson spent eight years compiling his *Dictionary of the English Language*. Boswell, a friend of Johnson, wrote a famous biography of him, and Edward Gibbon wrote a great history, *The Decline and Fall of the Roman Empire*, during the same period. Two French writers at this time were Voltaire and Rousseau. Both of them were philosophers, but they also wrote novels.

At the beginning of the 19th century in England Jane Austen wrote her six novels, the best known being *Pride and Prejudice*. Sir Walter Scott was a romantic writer, who often wrote about Scotland, as in *Rob Roy*.

One of the major novelists of the 19th century was Charles Dickens. After an unhappy childhood he be-became a journalist. The *Pickwick*

Above left **This is the scene in *Oliver Twist* by Charles Dickens, in which Oliver asks for a second helping of gruel.**

Above **Here is a picture of Charles Dickens, the great English novelist who lived from 1812–70. A former newspaper journalist, he turned to writing novels. In these he brought to light the dreadful conditions in which the poor in general and children in particular had to live during the 19th century. It was through his works that many social reforms were begun.**

Right **A scene from *The Hobbits* – a marvellous tale by J. R. R. Tolkien.**

in books like *Kim* and his two *Jungle Books*.

On the continent of Europe there were many great writers. The first major Russian novelist was Nikolai Gogol who wrote an amusing book, *Dead Souls*. Another Russian was the short story writer, Ivan Turgenev. Leo Tolstoy's great work was *War and Peace*, a novel which tells the history of Russia's part in the Napoleonic Wars. Dostoevsky, one of the most brilliant Russian writers, wrote *Crime and Punishment*.

Mark Twain (1835–1910) was a very great American humourist. One of his most famous characters, Huckleberry Finn, is seen here watching a paddle steamer sailing down the Mississippi River.

Left A thrilling moment in *The Three Musketeers* – D'Artagnan and his musketeers fight a duel with their sworn enemies, Cardinal Richelieu's men.

Below This is a scene from *War and Peace*, a massive work by the 19th-century Russian novelist, Tolstoy. In it, he tells the story of Napoleon's retreat from Moscow in 1812.

Cabin, the famous anti-slavery novel, was written by Harriet Beecher Stowe. Henry James's many books included *Portrait of a Lady*.

American 20th-century writers include Ernest Hemingway, who wrote *For Whom the Bell Tolls*, and John Steinbeck, one of whose best-known books is, *The Grapes of Wrath*. In Europe, among the vast number of famous writers we find James Joyce, D. H. Lawrence, Franz Kafka, Thomas Mann, Marcel Proust and André Gide.

In France in the 19th century Honoré de Balzac wrote ninety works in twenty years. *The Human Comedy* is a series of novels giving a complete picture of life at that time. Three other French writers were Stendhal, who wrote *The Red and the Black*, Zola, who wrote *Thérèse Raquin*, and Gustave Flaubert, whose best-known book is *Madame Bovary*.

The first truly American writers appeared in the 19th century. One was Fenimore Cooper who wrote *The Last of the Mohicans*. Another, Herman Melville, wrote tales of the sea, such as *Moby Dick*. Samuel Clemens, writing under the name of Mark Twain, wrote *Tom Sawyer*. *Uncle Tom's*

Below Can you identify Fagin, Pinnochio, Cinderella, Oliver Twist and Whittington's cat?

Left crowns worn by kings and gods in ancient Egypt had a special meaning. They were considered to be magic symbols of power.

Featured in this pageant of costume through the ages are (1) Primitive man dressed in animal skins; (2) Queen from ancient Egypt; (3) Assyrian nobleman; (4) Minoan man from Crete; (5) Roman woman, 4th century AD; (6) Byzantine emperor, 10th/11th century; (7) Teutonic woman and child, c. 400–800; (8) Norman soldier at the time of the Battle of Hastings; (9) 12th-century princess; (10) Crusading knight, 12th century; (11) A king in the early 13th century; (12) Boy and girl in late 13th-century dress; (13) A lady of the 14th century; (14) Various costumes from the late Middle Ages, about 1400.

Costumes

For thousands of years clothes have been designed to suit the fashion conscious and for most of that time men's clothes have been as colourful and elaborate as women's – and, in some periods, more so. Perhaps man took a leaf out of nature's book when he discovered that male animals possessed the gayest colours and shapes.

In the days of the ancient Greeks and Romans, costumes were simple. The Greeks were great athletes who believed in the sun and air reaching their bodies, so their clothing was mostly loose robes. Women rarely wore hats except to protect them from the sun, but they did wear a great deal of jewellery. The Romans wore flowing, dignified clothes which reached to the floor, while their soldiers wore short, functional tunics.

Men rarely wore more than a ring as adornment, but women decked themselves with necklaces, bracelets, ear-rings and other elaborate jewellery. Trousers for men were not worn by civilised races until the barbarians from the East, who swooped over the Roman empire, introduced them. These trousers were similar to the ones the Cossacks wear today.

Right In the days of the Empire in ancient Rome hair-styles were elaborate, and it was not unusual for patrician ladies to keep several slaves solely for the purpose of hair-dressing. Many of the aids and devices used by women then to adorn their hair are very similar to those in use today.

In the days of the Saxons, costumes were made from linen, wool and silk and were often fur-lined. With the Saxons, as with all civilisations up to the 20th century, the dress of the nobles differed from that of the peasants in as much as their clothes were made from better materials and were generally more elaborately designed. Like the Norsemen, a Saxon noble wore trousers which were gartered from ankle to knee, a knee-length over-tunic and a cloak.

His lady wore a full-length long-sleeved kirtle over which was worn a short-sleeved tunic. The women of the time were skilful at embroidery and they used their art to decorate the tunics they wore. Saxon peasants wore clothes that were simply cut, as did the Saxon war leaders, the only addition to a warrior's costume being a chain mail shirt.

There was little change in costume in Europe until the 12th century, when new materials were brought back from the East by returning armies. These beautiful fabrics resulted in far more luxurious fashions than had been seen before. Armour had been invented and because this rusted so

quickly the surcoat was devised to cover the metal. The surcoat then became a common feature of fashion for many years. It was at this time, too, that the hood became popular. Today the hood can still be seen in the costumes of monks and friars.

Gowns and mantles were the vogue in Italy and their fashion spread north to the colder countries, where they were fur-lined to protect the wearer from the poorly heated and draughty rooms. An attractive addition to the costume of the men were gauntlets, some of which were jewelled.

The age of colour began in the 14th century and the art of blending colours became much more important in costumes. Velvets from the East were being worn and rich brocades and gleaming satins were popular. The men wore costumes which fitted their bodies more closely and, instead of the gartered or baggy trousers, tights were fashionable. Women

Above **In the 15th century a hat for women called the hennin was introduced. It consisted of a high cone made of stiff paper or linen, covered with silk. It had a long veil attached to it.**

Right **Ornaments have been worn by men and women since primitive times. The first personal decoration in this sense was the painting of the body, which is still practised by certain tribes. This had a religious or social meaning, as did the first jewellery to be made.
This consisted of everyday objects which lay to hand, but man soon began to use precious metals and gems. The jewellery shown here all belongs to the Middle Ages, when very beautiful work was done.**

Above **These soldiers are wearing helmets and body armour belonging to the late 16th century.**

Below **Elaborate starched neck-dresses were popular with court ladies during the late 16th century.**

in the 14th century still tended to wear the fashions of their predecessors, although hair, which had usually been kept hidden, was now displayed. In England in 1363 a law was passed in an attempt to control personal spending. Common folk were permitted to wear only woollens, and if they were ever seen wearing the richer clothes reserved for knights and their ladies, the garments were confiscated.

In the 15th century women were once again wearing hats, but now these were very ornate constructions, sometimes copying the architectural features of buildings, such as the steeple of a church. Fighting men continued to wear suits of armour but the invention of the gun during the 14th century meant that armour

no longer protected the wearer and gradually its use died out.

During the 16th century men's costumes became more and more complicated and colourful, while women's dresses were more and more uncomfortable. For centuries they had endured awkward skirts, and by this time they were wearing vast, hooped skirts, often supported by a wooden frame.

In the 17th century the ladies of Venice were wearing enormously high heels, while women in China had their feet bound to prevent them growing. By the 18th century corsets were part of a woman's apparel. Waists became smaller and smaller as the corsets were laced ever tighter. In the 18th century, too, soldiers were wearing very showy uniforms with high-cut boots and tall hats, quite unsuitable for fighting in.

Early in the 19th century there was a marked change in European fashion and very simple designs became popular. As these tended to suit only the youngest figures, the crinoline, and later, the bustle, appealed to many more women. Men's clothes showed

On these pages are seen costumes dating from the 16th century until the 1890s. (1) 16th-century boy of noble family; (2) 16th-century peasants; (3) Man in a short open gown, and a woman, both 1540; (4) Child in mid-17th century; (5) 17th-century lady; (6) 17th-century cavalier; (7) Puritan man and woman about 1640; (8) 18th-century night watchman; (9) 18th-century nursemaid with two children; (10) Lady's walking costume; (11) Hussar and a guardsman of the 19th century; (12) Lady's evening gown, 1875; (13) Man's casual dress, 1880s; (14) Man in a frock coat and woman in walking dress of the 1890s.

Right The man is wearing a cravat and top hat of the late 18th century. Also shown are a fan (c. 1900), and a 17th-century shoe and a handbag of about 1870.

little of their former glory and became very plain.

In the 20th century women began to revolt against awkward and uncomfortable fashion, helped by such people as the American dancer, Isadora Duncan, who believed in loose, flowing clothes which allowed her dancers to move freely. For years, men's clothing has been very sober and the only fashion changes have been small alterations to such things as the width of lapels on jackets, or whether or not trousers should have turn-ups. But recently there has been a revival of interest in men's fashion and it is beginning to show signs of recapturing its variety and colour.

The beauty of past fashions can still be seen in traditional costumes, such as the elegant kimonos of Japan and the graceful saris of India. Sometimes, traditional costume reveals something of the character of its people, such as the practical national dress of the Dutch, or the dramatic frills and flounces of Spanish flamenco dancers.

Music, Dance and Theatre

Musicians and their music

Music was one of the first things in human life. Every primitive people possessed a form of music-making, however simple or crude. The human voice was the first musical instrument and man has always expressed his feelings with his voice as a matter of instinct. Often it was used in ceremonies to please the gods so that the hunt for food or the growing of crops would be successful.

It is not possible to say when music became an art, that is the moment when a conscious effort was first made to reproduce sounds which had previously come naturally. We know from the pictures drawn by artists in the ancient worlds of Egypt and Assyria that music played an important part in their lives. For the Egyptians in particular music performed a religious function and had a very serious purpose.

The Greeks used music in their drama, and in fact the plays of the early Greek dramatists, such as Aeschylus and Sophocles, were more like operas. The voice was used as an instrument, particularly in chorus, for declaiming the lines of a play. Although no complete piece of Greek music survives to this day, many books were written as long ago as 300

BC on subjects like harmony and musical notation (that is, the way the notes are written down).

In the Middle Ages, music, in common with most forms of art and knowledge, developed within the church, particularly the form of chanting known as Gregorian, which is still used in services today. In the 11th century an effort was made to improve on the system of notation inherited from the Greeks, and about this time Guido of Arezzo first made use of the lines and spaces which were to become the modern stave. Part singing was introduced, so that instead of always singing in unison men were able to sing different parts within one song. One of the greatest names in the history of early music is Giovanni Palestrina (1515–94) who composed music for the Mass which is still used as a model of church music today.

The first secular music, that is music which was not composed for religious ceremonies, grew up in the Middle Ages with the minstrels. These wandering vagabonds earned their living by singing and playing for the amusement of anyone who would give them a supper in return for a song. After the minstrels came the troubadours, who were often men of noble birth and were treated with honour and respect.

Above **A lute.** This stringed instrument, popular in Europe in the 16th and 17th centuries, came originally from the Arab world.

Below **Here are a rebec, a lute and a psaltery.** Psalteries are a medieval kind of zither played with a plectrum.

Bottom **This Bolivian Indian** is blowing into a conch shell. Since earliest times man has used this type of shell as an instrument and it produces a loud sound rather like a trumpet.

Left **Ancient Egypt was a highly cultured civilisation** with a great love of music. Many of their wall paintings like these show they used stringed instruments.

Here are some musical instruments from other lands. The sitar (1) is an Indian stringed instrument. Harps of various kinds and shapes (2) are to be found in most parts of the world. Figure (3) shows ceremonial trumpeters in Uganda. The peasant musician (4) from Ecuador is playing the pan pipes. The Japanese woman (5) plucks the koto. Drums and flutes are usually used to accompany it.

Left **Ludwig van Beethoven**, was a great German composer. Born in 1770, with Haydn and Mozart, he represents the Viennese classical school of composing. When he was 30, he had ear trouble and became totally deaf. This dreadful handicap did not stop him from composing many masterpieces.

Below A scene from *Les Sylphides*, a romantic ballet.

Opera, which combines acting and singing, began in the 16th century. Some Italian poets and musicians had the idea of setting certain Greek stories to music and performing them on a stage. At first, the dramatic action was much more important than the singing. Monteverdi's operas, composed in the first half of the 17th century, in which the music came first, were the first true operas. Monteverdi was also one of the first composers to employ an orchestra.

The man who did more than any other to establish the shape of the modern orchestra and to develop the symphony as the chief form of musical expression was Haydn. He lived in Vienna in the 18th century when that city was the centre of the musical world. Mozart, Beethoven and Schubert all lived in Vienna during a period when the greatest classical music was written. The romantic music of Brahms, Schumann and Chopin, and the grand operas of Wagner and Verdi, led to the new musical sounds of the 20th century.

Although modern musical instruments have become complex and often difficult to play, each of the three great classes into which they fall – percussion, wind and stringed – could be found readily to hand by primitive man.

Percussion instruments, such as the drum or triangle, produce sounds by being struck, and almost any hard substance will make some kind of sound if struck with a stone or stick. Wind instruments, such as the trumpet or clarinet, are, at heart, hollow tubes through which the player blows. Reed pipes or animals' horns, even

Left **Pop groups rely mainly upon electronic guitars and the percussion section.**

Right **Brass and military bands use wind and percussion.**

Below **This is an orchestra that has been assembled for a recording session. It brings together the 'classical' and 'pop' elements which are so popular in music today.**

without keys and mouthpieces, will produce a 'wind' sound. Stringed instruments work on the principle that any tightly stretched cord can be made to produce sound if it is vibrated; in the case of a violin, for instance, by a bow being drawn across it. The bow and arrow, one of man's first mechanical weapons, would have introduced him to such a sound.

The piano and the guitar are examples of instruments which make use of the principles of both percussion and strings.

Right Wind, string and percussion are the chief types of instruments used today.

Dancing round the world

People have always danced to express their feelings and different races have their own special dances which show something of their character. When primitive peoples danced, they often imitated animals or went through the actions of their work. By doing this they thought they were pleasing their gods. When these pagan beliefs died out, people carried on dancing for pleasure although they may have forgotten the original purpose of it. With the passing of time, some of these simple dances have undergone great changes and now need much more skill in performance.

Almost every country has its own national dances and these are performed on special or ceremonial occasions. In Finland dancers still imitate bears and seals, and in the forest

Below **The American dancer, Isadora Duncan, who died in 1927. She wore flowing draperies and danced in her bare feet. Everywhere she went she was a sensation and she had a very great effect upon the Russian ballet.**

regions many wood-cutting dances survive. In Italy and Portugal dances can illustrate the gathering of grapes for wine-making. The people of India, Japan and China perform dances with little body movement and instead use mainly the hands and arms. Even the smallest gesture has some meaning and although most of the dances are religious in origin, there are also charming dances which tell stories of birds, bees and flowers.

Countries with strong warlike traditions have dances which reflect their warriors' deeds. Yugoslavia has its own special sword dance, and the same kind of dances performed by Highlanders in Scotland are almost certainly war dances from that country's past. The Red Indians of North America have their own tribal dances, as do the many tribes of Africa.

With the increasing attractions of town life and more varied forms of entertainment, folk dancing lost a lot of its appeal but did not die out completely. People in towns adapted the dances so they could be performed in

Above **A scene from the popular classical ballet, *The Sleeping Beauty,* first produced in 1890 with music by Tchaikovsky.**

Below **Classical Indian dance is very graceful and once had close connections with Indian mythology and religion.**

ballrooms and so fit in with the new, more formal, way of life. The waltzes, quick-steps, rumbas, tangoes and fox-trots of the modern ballroom all come from the many folk dances of Europe, America and Africa.

Ballet is a form of dancing that knows no language barriers. It expresses feelings which can be understood by all who watch it. It began in the royal courts of Italy and then moved to France, where Louis XIV was himself a fine dancer. Louis founded a school of dancing in 1661, the Royal Academy of the Dance, which is still the most famous ballet

Below **When the Moors were settling in Spain up to the 16th century, they brought their traditional dances with them. These form the basis of flamenco dancing which we know in Spain today. However, the jumping, beating of the feet and the use of castanets are European in origin and were added to the Moorish dance.**

Above **Primitive African dances were once used in war or religion or in healing. Many of them have now been adapted into an exciting stage spectacle presented by the West African Ballet.**

Left **Two male dancers of the Russian Kirov Ballet. One demonstrates a classical pose in the Blue Bird solo from** *The Sleeping Beauty* **and the other is performing a Polovtsian dance from** *Prince Igor.*

school in France. Here, Beauchamps, the king's dancing master, laid down the rules of classical ballet and that is why ballet terms today are always written in French.

At the end of the 17th century ballet moved into the theatre and new schools sprang up in all the major European cities. Most of the difficult and brilliant dance steps were done by men, for women were restricted by the fashions of the time. La Camargo, a famous ballerina in the early 18th century changed women's role in ballet. She shocked Paris in 1724 by shortening her skirt and showing her ankles in order to execute more ambitious jumps and movements.

Ballet moved to Russia and it was a Russian, Sergei Diaghilev, who gave us ballet as we know it today, by deciding that music, scenery and dancing must be made to fit the story. His ballet company caused a sensation in Paris in 1909 and set the standard for all modern ballet.

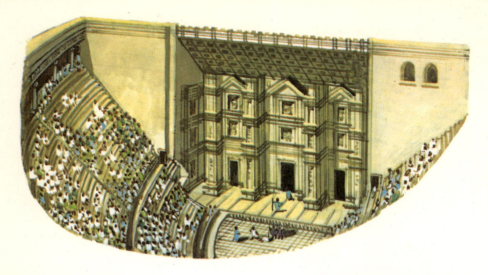

Left A view of a Roman theatre about 100 BC. By this time raised stages with permanent scenery were in use. The picture shows the stage and the auditorium. The Greek theatre did not have a raised stage.

The Theatre

Drama grew out of religious festivals and dances. The Greeks of nearly 3,000 years ago were the first to make these dramatic and the first to write plays and build theatres in which to act them. At first dances were performed on a dance floor on a hillside, so people could see. Then the Greeks built amphitheatres with seats cut into the hill in a semicircle. Gradually theatres developed from this.

A 'skene' or small building was built behind the central floor for the actors to wait in, then the stage was raised off the ground and a 'proskene' was built between the 'skene' and the stage. The 'proskene' consisted of columns and doors for the actors to enter and exit through.

Eventually Sophocles, one of the three great Greek writers of tragedies, that is, moving plays with unhappy endings, introduced stage scenery. He wrote at least 120 plays but we have only seven of them today. His three plays about Oedipus are probably the best known. The other two tragic writers were Aeschylus and Euripides. Another Greek playwright, Aristophanes, is famous for writing comedies – plays with happy endings. These four playwrights lived around the 4th and 5th centuries BC.

When the Romans built their theatres they did not use open hillsides but arranged the seats in tiers inside buildings. They built the first covered theatres. The Romans liked plays of action, farces and pantomimes. Roman actors wore masks, and classical actors wore shoes with very high heels.

After the fall of Rome, during the period of the Dark Ages in Europe, which lasted from about the 5th to the 11th centuries AD, theatres were pulled down and the stones used for building. The only drama was provided by troupes of minstrels, jugglers and acrobats who travelled to castles giving performances to the feudal lords. In France troubadours travelled round the country singing love songs and telling legends.

Above By the end of the 16th century, commedia dell'arte comedies were played all over Europe. The characters, like Harlequin and Columbine, had to dance, sing and play the fool. They often wore masks.

Right The traditional theatre of Japan was the Noh drama and it has not changed since the 17th century.

Far right An actor in Kabuki costume. This traditional form of popular theatre evolved from the Noh drama.

Above and right In Noh drama, the actors wear masks symbolizing the type of character they are playing.

174

The first theatres to be built in Europe after Roman times were in Italy in the 15th century. At this time in Italy there was a form of drama called *commedia dell' arte*, which later became popular all over Europe. The actors played characters like Harlequin and Columbine, who in turn played the parts in a story.

In 1564 England's greatest playwright, William Shakespeare, was born in Stratford-upon-Avon. The first English theatre was built around 1576 and about ten years after this Shakespeare went to London where he joined a company of actors. With them he not only acted but directed and wrote the series of over thirty

In the East, however, drama was growing. In China during the 13th and 14th centuries plays telling a simple story were popular. In India there was the Indian Classical Theatre which consisted mainly of dancing. Between the 13th and 17th centuries in Japan the Noh theatre developed. The plays had no scenery and very little action, and actors had to perform in a certain way.

The theatre grew again in Europe from the ceremonies of the church, which became more and more dramatic. The story of Easter, for instance, was acted out in the Easter celebrations. By the 14th century religious plays were allowed in England and this was the start of the mystery, miracle and morality plays.

The mystery plays dealt with the creation of the world, the day of judgement and the story of Adam and Eve. The miracle plays were about the miracles of Jesus Christ and the early saints, and the morality plays were about vices, or evil actions.

The best-known morality play is called *Everyman*, and it was written about the end of the 15th century. Stages were erected in market places in towns and villages and the plays were performed by guild members.

In some cities in England a non-religious play, called an interlude, was performed in between two religious plays. Later, troupes of men travelled with a cart which they pulled into the yard of an inn and used as a stage for their interlude plays.

Above **The famous Globe Theatre which was opened in 1589 on the south bank of the Thames in London. The Globe's first play was Shakespeare's *Henry V* performed by his own company. Within a few years, the Globe was burnt to the ground.**

Right **The 18th-century actor David Garrick, as Richard the Third.**

great plays, most of which are still acted regularly all over the world.

Another famous English dramatist of the period was Ben Jonson, a great scholar whose plays did not enjoy the popular success of those of his friend Shakespeare. One of the most famous writers in France in the 17th century was Molière. He wrote comedies and usually acted the main part in them, amazing the audience with his realistic and forceful acting.

Theatres now had a proscenium arch separating the audience from the stage, and curtains, which could be drawn across the proscenium opening, were introduced. For the first time, performances took place at night. Theatres began to look as they do today: the auditorium was horseshoe shaped and the stage platform was generally built out into the audience. The first 'modern' theatre of which there are complete plans is

Above **Actors learning their lines. At first they read through the play. Then they have to learn all their movements. Finally, they run through the dress rehearsal in full costume shortly before the first public performance.**

Above **Sometimes an actor must play the part of a character older or younger than himself. To achieve this, he has to use make-up. This is either grease paint or 'pancake' which is put on with a damp sponge.**

Right **The same actor after he has made himself up as a much older man. All the wrinkles, highlights and shadows have been painted on to the face with grease paint or pancake.**

Left **A sectional view of a stage with a play in progress. At the far left, an actress is making up while her dresser fetches a costume. The call boy knocks to say it is almost time for her to go on stage. While some actors are performing, others are waiting in the wings for their cue. On the right by the proscenium is the prompter following the play. If an actor 'dries up', he will read out the lines.**

Below **Most young children love dressing up and giving plays at school and for their friends at home. The Nativity story is always a favourite.**

the famous Schouwburg Theatre in Amsterdam, built in 1637.

The 18th century in England was a period of famous actors and, usually, rather bad plays. One of the most popular actors was David Garrick, who was also a theatre manager and dramatist. The only major playwrights at the time were Richard Sheridan and Oliver Goldsmith, who wrote witty comedies.

In Germany two famous writers of plays were Lessing, who introduced melodrama, and Schiller. The greatest German writer, Goethe, was also a playwright. He was concerned with the practical side of the theatre, for he ran the Court Theatre in Weimar for over forty years.

Throughout the 19th century the theatre in Europe was very popular with ordinary people. They demanded great spectacles and strong melodramas. It was also an age of great 'star' actors and actresses. These included the Englishmen, Edmund Kean and Henry Irving, and the celebrated women actresses, Sarah Bernhardt from France and Eleonora Duse from Italy.

The outstanding playwright towards the end of the 19th century was the Norwegian, Henrik Ibsen. His plays changed the whole course of dramatic writing in Europe.

Two important companies founded at this time were the Abbey Theatre in Dublin, which produced the plays of J. M. Synge and Sean O'Casey. Another was Stanislavsky's Moscow Arts Theatre, where the plays of the great Russian writer Chekhov were first seen.

The modern 'revolution' in the theatre was begun in the 1950s with John Osborne's *Look Back in Anger*.

Popular Entertainment

Below **Guglielmo Marconi (1874-1937)** was the first man to win the race to send wireless messages through space. His first broadcast was a morse code message from Wales across the Bristol Channel in 1897. Four years later, he broadcast across the Atlantic to Newfoundland.

Above **Thomas Edison (1847–1931)** invented the phonograph – the first gramophone among many other inventions.

Radio and television

Among the early pioneers of radio were Hertz of Germany, Branly of France, and Lodge and Fleming of England. But it was the young Marconi from Italy who took radio out of the laboratory and made it speak to the world.

In 1925 the Scot, John Logie Baird, was the first to transmit a picture by television, but it was an American, Vladimir Zworykin, who perfected electronic television. It was called 'high definition' because it built up pictures from 405 tiny lines instead of the 30-line system used by Baird.

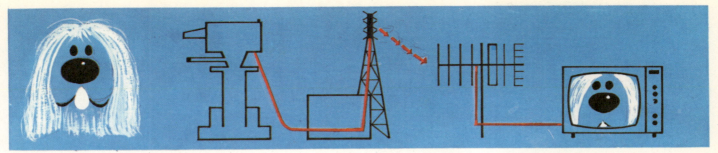

Above **The sequence of TV broadcasting. Cameras in the studio take different pictures shown on the monitor screens. The producer selects one. This is converted into radio waves, transmitted through the ether and converted back again to a picture on the TV set at home.**

Above left **Portable radios use transistors instead of valves.**

Above **Tape recorders, unlike gramophones, use magnetic tape.**

Above **In 1926, John Logie Baird, a Scottish scientist, first demonstrated television.**

Above **The zoetrope was a device invented in the 19th century in which a series of stationary figures was given the impression of movement when the viewer looked through the slits of a revolving drum.**

Cinema

Men have always tried to communicate with each other by the use of pictures, but only in the last century have there been serious attempts to make them move. In 1824 an English doctor, Peter Roget, discovered by chance the scientific fact that a picture remains on the retina for slightly longer than it takes the eye to record it. In other words, each successive picture we see lingers a little so that one overlaps the next.

Dr. Roget's thoughts and those of a Belgian professor called Plateau, did result in the invention of toys which demonstrated this 'persistence of vision'. A typical example is the thaumatrope, which is a simple device made from a circular piece of card, on one side of which may be shown a bird and on the other its cage. By rotating the card quickly by means of pieces of string attached to its sides, the two images appear to merge and the bird is 'seen' sitting in its cage.

There were many pioneers in the early days of cinema and no one man can be credited with the major part in the invention of moving pictures. In Britain it was Robert Paul, an amateur inventor, and William Friese-Greene, a professional photographer, who led the way. In France it was

Jules Marey who studied the science of cinematography, and the Lumière brothers who developed the film as a commercial entertainment. In America Thomas Edison and his assistant W. K. L. Dickson built a motion-picture camera for roll film. All these men worked independently of each other until finally in each of their countries public performances were held.

These first moving pictures were silent and very short and there was no great public enthusiasm for them at first. It was not until pictures began to tell a story that people really became interested. In 1903 an American, Edwin S. Porter completely broke away from the old style and made *The Great Train Robbery*, the first American story film and, incidentally, the first western.

Film-making was just getting under way in Europe when the First World War broke out. This meant that the United States, who did not enter the war until 1917, were able to take the lead in supplying films to a now eager world market. The great English comedian Charlie Chaplin made his name as a 'star' in America, and directors like D. W. Griffith and Cecil B. de Mille made films which pleased the public and were the first big box-

Left **The names of some of the great stars and films are illustrated in these drawings. (1) A scene from** *The Great Train Robbery,* **the first western; (2) Charlie Chaplin; (3) Greta Garbo; (4) Humphrey Bogart; (5) Mickey Mouse; (6) Clark Gable; (7) A scene from** *Gone with the Wind;* **(8) Elizabeth Taylor; (9) Marlon Brando; (10) John Wayne; (11) Paul Newman; (12) Julie Christie; (13) A scene from** *2001, A Space Odyssey.*

5

7

Above **Filming on location for a big epic picture is an expensive business and involves hundreds of people.**

9

11

13

office 'hits'. The great heroes and heroines of the silver screen at that time were led by such names as Rudolph Valentino, Douglas Fairbanks and Mary Pickford.

The coming of sound made a big difference to films. After long years of experiment Al Jolson's two films *The Jazz Singer* (1927) and *The Singing Fool* (1928) saw the arrival of talking pictures. Now that actors and actresses could talk the action of a story became more human, and people responded to the appeal of the movies by filling cinemas in their millions in the 20s and 30s.

Hollywood in the United States became the world centre of film-making. In 1926 the first successful colour film, *The Black Pirate*, starring Douglas Fairbanks, was made. Then in 1929 and 1930, many spectacular musical films like *The Vagabond King* and *The Desert Song* were made. Europe came firmly back into the movie business in the 1930s with directors like Hitchcock, Korda, Clair and Pabst.

Films today have developed from one-minute peep-shows into a splendid art form, and despite the advent of television continue to entertain us.

Right **A western 'ghost' town in the United States. A permanent set such as this serves as the background for many film and television westerns. In the centre of the page is seen a projection room in a modern cinema. As each reel of film is finished the picture is switched automatically from one projector to another.**

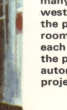

Fairs, circuses and puppets

The fairs of long ago were not like the fairs we know today. They began as markets where foreign goods could be purchased. Fairs were usually held once a year on special saints' days which were holidays for the local people. The word 'fair' comes from the Latin word *feria*, meaning a holiday. No prices were marked on the goods as it was the custom for the seller and buyer to barter until they had fixed a price between them.

During the Middle Ages people used to come to the fairs to be amused and there were many entertainers in the crowd. Jugglers and acrobats kept the people enthralled by their daring acts, while the minstrels' songs could be heard all around. There were other entertainers with dancing bears and performing monkeys.

As time went on the buying and selling of goods became less important and the fairs became chiefly places of entertainment. The most popular part of them was the travelling theatre.

In the early 1800s the first merry-go-rounds were seen, which led to the many mechanical fun-makers of today. Fairs are now so popular that permanent ones have been built in holiday resorts.

Left This is part of an eastern bazaar. Such bazaars date back thousands of years. Although they are so old they have changed very little over the centuries. In remote desert regions a system of barter is used — that is to say, things are exchanged for goods of the same value. In an eastern bazaar, you would be able to buy perfumes, spices, silks, meat, cooking pots and even drinking water.

Below Medieval fairs were not only places where people bought things but also where they could meet and enjoy themselves. Gradually, buying and selling became less and less important and fairs were more places of entertainment than anything else. At the fairs, the people could watch the jugglers, acrobats, dancers and minstrels.

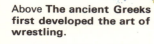

Above The ancient Greeks first developed the art of wrestling.

Below Fairs today have more mechanical diversions like switchbacks and dodgem cars.

THE GREATES SHOW ON E

There were circuses in Rome long before Jesus was born, in which gladiators either fought each other or wild beasts. Chariot races were another popular form of entertainment with the Roman public. Modern circuses are not really descended from these Roman spectacles, for they were different in both form and structure. The circuses of today probably evolved from the performing animal acts at fairs, such as the performing horse at Bartholomew Fair in London which the great diarist Samuel Pepys wrote about.

The founder of the modern circus was an Englishman called Philip Astley who, in 1780, opened his circus in Westminster Bridge Road in London. This was in a wooden building he had erected himself, in which there was a ring surrounded by seating accommodation. The building was without a roof.

The circus in America dates from 1785 and today the United States is the principal home of the 'big top'. This came about when P. T. Barnum went into partnership with Coup and Costello. Later, Barnum's circus came to be known as the 'greatest show on earth'. In 1873 Barnum opened the first two-ring circus in America and now there are two, three and four ring circuses. Barnum eventually formed the famous partnership of Barnum and Bailey.

Above **During the last century, circuses began to have sideshows like this one – 'The Fattest Woman on Earth'.**

Below **Familiar scenes from the circus ring.**

Below **A puppet theatre.**

Nobody knows what the first puppet in the world looked like or where it came from. China, India and Egypt can all claim to be the original home of the puppet. The shadow puppet was one of the earliest forms and the ancient Greeks and Romans make mention of string puppets. Glove puppets were used by travelling artists in the Middle Ages because they were easy to carry.

Before then, even before writing was invented, people learned of events through storytellers or by seeing plays acted by people or puppets. In 10th-century Asia the puppet stage hung from the performer's neck on a string.

Many of the puppet shows seen in the Far East today have been performed for centuries. Records of puppets in India go back nearly 2,000 years. When man started to travel, his puppets went with him and spread right across the world from the East.

Today more and more puppet theatres are being built and new methods of animation tried out. The coming of television has brought a whole new world of puppet favourites.

Below **Lawn tennis** is based on the very old game of 'royal' or 'real' tennis and began life as a country house pursuit in the 1870s. The game is now world-wide.

Above **The sport of falconry**, in which game is hunted by trained birds, is very old. It was particularly popular in the Middle Ages. Today it is kept alive by small groups of enthusiasts.

Above **Rugby football** began as an amateur game. The English Rugby Union was formed in 1871. Rugby League is a professional game which began when 20 clubs broke away from the Union.

Above **Cricket**, which is sometimes called the national game of England, began as early as the 16th century. In other countries, cricket is played seriously only in those places which have been influenced by Britain, such as Australia and India.

Left **Baseball** began in the United States. It was derived from the English games of cricket and rounders early in the 19th century.

Sports and Games

In a little over a hundred years soccer has become the most widely played international game in the world. Football was played centuries ago, but it was a very rough and tumble affair. By 1550 Italy had organised the game with rules, and in Britain in 1846 a set of rules was laid down governing rugby football. Later, in 1863, another set of rules appeared forbidding 'hacking and handling', and this is when football divided into the two separate games of rugby and soccer.

Tennis has been played since the 13th century in Europe and was a favourite game of Henry VIII. In 1870 the game known as lawn tennis was devised, and in 1877 the All England Lawn Tennis and Croquet Club at Wimbledon came into being. The Wimbledon championships are still regarded as the greatest event in the lawn tennis calendar.

References to cricket in England go back to about 1300, and although the game has altered a lot since then, it has always been popular in many parts of the world.

Above **Fishing** is a popular pastime. There is also competitive angling with championships and awards.

Above **Swimming** is a natural activity which became a competitive sport in the 19th century. The best swimmers come from Russia, the United States and Australia.

Below **Association football** is the most widely played game in the world and attracts more spectators than any other. It began in England and is now played in every part of the globe.

Above **Although competitive skiing** dates from the end of the 19th century, skis themselves are believed to be over 5,000 years old. In fact, there is evidence from carvings that skis were used in Stone Age times.

Below left **Golf** is a very old game played originally in Scotland. The Royal and Ancient Club at St. Andrews was founded in 1754.

Below **The Queensbury Rules** under which boxing is fought were drawn up in 1867. Before this bouts were fought for prize-money with bare knuckles and often with no limit to the number of rounds.

Above **The first motor race** took place in 1894 and was run from Paris to Rouen. Grand Prix racing is now a spectacular sport and motor rallying is a useful trial ground for the motor industry.

Above **Horse racing** goes back to the time of ancient Rome. The oldest racecourse still in use is the Roodee at Chester in England, which opened in 1540.

Above **The game of table tennis is comparatively new as it was invented only at the beginning of the present century.**

Above **Chess is a very ancient board game requiring thought and skill but many children can play it quite well.**

Above **Dominoes probably came from 18th-century Italy.**

Below **Playing cards may have originated in the East but many of the games are modern.**

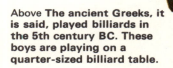

Above **The ancient Greeks, it is said, played billiards in the 5th century BC. These boys are playing on a quarter-sized billiard table.**

Below **This game of five stones is called by many names and has been played in one form or another throughout history.**

Games and recreations

Some indoor games have a long history and have been played for many years. Chess is perhaps the most important international game. It probably began in the East and spread into Europe during the time of the great Arab conquests in the 8th century. The modern game came into being in the 15th century, and one of the earliest known books about chess was printed in London by William Caxton.

Draughts have been known in Europe since the 16th century, although very similar games were played in the ancient world. Dominoes probably originated in Italy in the 18th century and the game has become very popular in cafés in France and Belgium.

Many other board games are very ancient and this type of game is probably the oldest of all. Very simple forms of them may have been played by primitive man on a 'board' scratched out on the surface of the earth or sand, with stones as counters. Some board games are played with dice, which were used in ancient times in exactly the same way as today.

Card games are endless in their variety. Some, like Bridge – which is thought to have begun in Russia – are very skilful, while others rely on pure chance, such as *Beggar My Neighbour* and many gambling games. It is believed that playing cards were invented in France in the 14th century, but it is more likely that they began much earlier in the East and, again, were brought to Europe at a time when people first made contact between East and West.

Some indoor games such as table tennis and billiards require a fair amount of space and equipment in order to be played properly. With such games it is often a good idea to join a club which provides this. Table tennis began around the beginning of the 20th century and was commonly called 'ping-pong' from the sound made by the celluloid ball as it bounced on the table. Billiards, too, is an ancient game. Some say it was played by the Greeks in the 5th century BC. Many famous people owned billiard tables, such as Mary, Queen of Scots and Louis XIV of France.

A lot of fun can be had from a hobby which can be enjoyed when you are alone. Of all hobbies, stamp collecting is probably the most popular and widespread over the world. Other everyday objects which lend themselves to the formation of a worthwhile collection are matchbox labels and cheese labels. For instance, there are over 500 Swiss cheese labels alone, and collections of them have been known to change hands for quite large sums of money. A person who collects cheese labels is called a 'fromologist'.

Postcard collecting is another interesting hobby, particularly if holiday postcards from friends abroad are made the basis of a collection. Keeping a scrapbook of newspaper and magazine cuttings on some particular subject of interest is another idea. It is surprising how much knowledge can be acquired in this way.

A great deal of satisfaction can be gained from building models, not only in the actual construction from kits but in the proper finishing and display of the models. Model aeroplanes can be hung from a ceiling, and ships placed in a dockyard setting.

Toy theatres provide a good opportunity for displaying acting talent, as well as the writing of plays and designing of scenery.

Above Hopscotch means hopping over the 'scotches' which were the lines drawn in the sand with a knife or stick.

Below left One of the most pleasant ways of spending our spare time, whatever our age, is by creative activities – like making and painting things such as masks and model trains and planes.

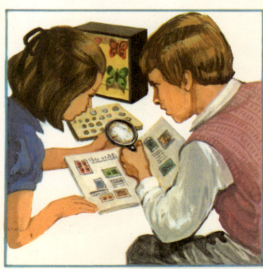

Below Stamp collecting is a very popular hobby that is entertaining and instructive.

Toys

The study of toys can tell us a great deal about the simple domestic life of people long ago. For toys reflect the larger adult world, and over the years the whole progress of man's social life is reproduced in miniature.

There have probably been toys since man first settled as a family unit in some primitive home. A kitten does not need instruction in how to chase a piece of paper for its amusement, and a primitive child played with whatever it could find as naturally as a child would today. Primitive toys have not survived simply because they

Right **These Victorian dolls' houses reflect an age of comfort when houses were much larger than they are today. The rocking horse (below) was another popular toy.**

were, most likely, natural objects and not manufactured as toys.

One of the first toys that a child plays with is a rattle, and rattles made from clay and earthenware have been found that date back to 1360 BC. In the ancient civilisations of Egypt and the Middle East there were dolls, some with movable arms and legs, although it is possible that these were sometimes made as religious effigies. There were certainly toy animals and some of these were jointed so that mouths could be made to open and shut, and tails to wag.

Many toys have survived from the classical world of ancient Greece and

Rome – dolls, balls, animals, tops – and wall paintings show the popularity of games played on a board with counters and such universal pastimes as knucklebones. It is probable that games of chance or skill were invented before toys but these were mainly for the amusement of adults. Nevertheless, it is from these games that such things as knucklebones, or five-stones, and draughts, and 'ducks and drakes' have evolved.

Very little is known of the playthings of children between the earliest civilisations and the Middle Ages. Girls played with dolls as they have continued to do ever since, and toy soldiers were made from glazed stoneware or clay and dressed in the costume of the times.

In the 16th century, hobby-horses, hoops, marbles, pop-guns, stilts and money boxes were all popular toys. The earliest-known dolls' houses date from the 17th century and originated in Germany. These dolls' houses were very large and elaborately equipped with furniture, replicas of the homes in which they were kept.

In the 18th century jigsaw puzzles were invented and the rocking horse galloped into popularity. Towards the end of the century, mechanical toys began to appear, powered by water, steam or quicksilver.

The 19th century was an era of learning and discovery and this was reflected in the toys. There were kaleidoscopes, stereoscopes and zoetropes, all toys which gave the illusion of depth and movement to flat images, and magic lanterns showing the wonders of nature. Magnetic toys were introduced early in the century, as were bubble pipes and, later on, inflatable and rubber toys.

These were days of luxury for dolls and their outfits ranged from corsets to kid gloves. Toy theatres, with 'penny plain, tuppence coloured' cut-out characters and scenery, were popular. The making of needlework samplers was a common occupation for girls.

Modern toys are often expensive, exact replicas of the real thing. Train sets, racing cars and washing machines – powered by electricity – have perhaps taken some of the fun out of make believe.

Above **Victorian dolls had very delicate china heads.**

Below right **Modern toys copy new things in just the same way. Here is the latest thing in toy cars – one which can travel at 15 miles, *24 kilometres*, an hour.**

Below **A collection of old toys which represent people, events and inventions of the time – (1) lead acrobats from America; (2) a model steam engine; (3) soldiers made of lead or tin and (4) a wickerwork doll's pram of the 19th century.**

These pictures show how we use levers in our everyday lives. Without them, many jobs, like rowing a boat, lifting heavy objects and removing nails, would be impossible.

Right A water well uses a device called a windlass or winch to raise the bucket. Would you say its principle is similar to or the same as the one employed in a pulley?

Science and Invention

When man first began to observe and consider the simple facts and workings of nature, he also began to study science. Some of the ways in which nature works are easily understood; some are more difficult to interpret and have taken hundreds of years to understand properly. Primitive man discovered certain scientific truths in the same way that he found out about the basic forces of nature – by observation and experiment.

Science in the modern world has become divided into different areas of study. These cover such things as geology, biology, astronomy, chemistry and physics. Geology is the study of the structure and history of the earth. Biology is the study of the origin and evolution of living things, and is itself usually divided into three parts, botany (the study of plants), zoology (the study of animals) and physiology (the study of the human body). Astronomy is the study of heavenly bodies in the universe. Chemistry is the study of changes in the formation of matter. Physics is the science of the fundamental relationship between matter and energy.

Science is a word which applies to all knowledge on any subject properly organised and classified. This knowledge may be obtained in three different ways: by reading about the discoveries and conclusions of other men; by seeing things for yourself; and by experiment to show how a theory works in practice.

Any device which uses energy to advantage and improves man's efficiency is a machine. One of the earliest was the bow and arrow, which converts muscular energy into energy to power the arrow.

There are six basic forms of simple machines in everyday use. They are the lever, the pulley, the inclined plane, the wedge, the screw, and the wheel and axle. All the complicated

Above When man first invented the bow and arrow, he made an important discovery in physics. As the string is pulled, force is applied to each end of the bow which, when released, springs back to its original position, thrusting the arrow into the air with equal force.

machinery of the modern world makes use of these essential forms in different combinations.

All levers have a fulcrum, or support, which is the point about which they move. They have two other points, one where the effort is applied and the other where there is resistance to the effort. According to the position of the fulcrum, effort and resistance, so levers are classed into three types called first, second and third order levers. A spanner, or a spade, or a pair of nutcrackers are all good examples of levers.

Pulleys are machines which use ropes and wheels to make it easier to lift heavy loads. According to the number of wheels used and the way in which the ropes are arranged, a large object can be moved through a greater distance with smaller effort. The inclined plane is simply a sloping surface up and down which it is possible to control the movement of heavy objects without the problem of having to lift them. The staircase is another example of the inclined plane which allows a person to climb a considerable height with little effort.

The wedge and screw are forms of the inclined plane. The wedge is used

Below A pulley is a means of lifting heavy loads with relatively little effort. The more wheels that are used, the easier the lifting becomes. Some pulleys have a number of wheels of different sizes.

to force things apart by being driven between them: examples are an axe or a carpenter's chisel. The screw has a spiral thread which can be turned round and round into wood as if a spiral staircase is moving around you. The wheel and axle, probably the most important invention of all, may have developed from the earlier idea of placing rollers beneath a heavy object in order to move it.

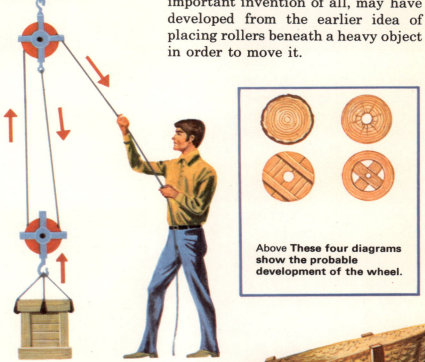

Above These four diagrams show the probable development of the wheel.

Above The first time that man devised a simple wheel, he had stumbled upon a very great invention. It enabled him to carry heavy loads over long distances and paved the way for the development of trade.

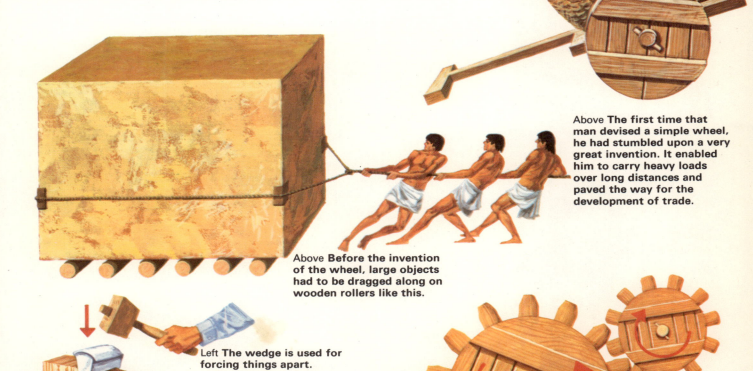

Above Before the invention of the wheel, large objects had to be dragged along on wooden rollers like this.

Left The wedge is used for forcing things apart.

Right Simple wooden gear wheels. If the larger of the two is the driving wheel the gear would be higher than if the drive were on the other.

Ancient science

In the ancient world of Egypt and Mesopotamia early scientific knowledge was to a great extent bound up with astronomy and mathematics. This is also true of what little we know of the early science of India and the Far East. There were simple systems for calculating with number symbols, and the Babylonians and Assyrians in particular made quite complicated predictions about the movements of planets and stars. There were also very early forms of calendars and primitive maps were drawn.

The real development of scientific thought began with the Greeks and it was they who transformed the scattered bits and pieces of knowledge inherited from their predecessors and gave them real meaning. Most early scientific discoveries were prompted by the practical needs of peoples' everyday lives, but the Greeks went beyond this and pursued knowledge for its own sake.

It is important to remember that the Greek love of science was based on a belief that a sense of order existed in the natural world. This meant that outside men's minds there were certain laws and rules which governed the

 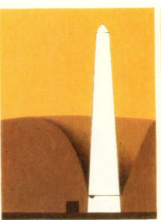 

Top For a long time, archaeologists were curious to know how the ancient Egyptians managed to build the pyramids before lifting gear had been invented. The most likely explanation is that objects were hauled into position up ramps by thousands of slaves. Primitive cranes, like the one in the picture were probably also used to lift small weights.

Centre These pictures show how obelisks were erected without a crane. It was effected simply by digging a hole in the ground first and then partly filling it with sand. The obelisk was then tilted into the top of the hole and lowered into position as the sand was removed from the bottom.

Left Archimedes, the Greek mathematician who lived during the 3rd century BC, made a great discovery when climbing into his bath. It was that an object placed in water will displace a volume of water, the weight of which is equal to its own weight.

universe. The aim of Greek philosophers, who were also the scientists of their day, was to discover how and why these laws worked. They wanted to know these things for no other reason than that they existed. The solution to every new problem was one further step to an understanding of the whole nature of the world in which man lived.

Today, although the scientist still seeks out knowledge for its own sake, the time, money and equipment are often made available to him by government and organisations which have positive ends in view. These may be to do with the improvement of an industrial process or the invention of a new weapon of war or a means of defence.

One of the earliest Greek men of science was Thales, who lived in Asia Minor at a place called Miletus in the 7th and 6th centuries BC. He is said to have made an accurate prediction of an eclipse of the sun in 585 BC which caused a stir. For here was a philosopher forecasting a mysterious event, which people had always seen as an act of the gods, as though it were the solution to a mathematical problem. Thales developed the Egyptians' knowledge of geometry and put his findings to practical use, such as measuring the height of a pyramid by comparing the length of its shadow with the length of the shadow cast by a pole of known height.

There were many theories about the way in which the universe was made up. These theories tried to reduce

Above **Democritus, a Greek philosopher who lived during the 5th century BC. He advanced a theory of atoms, believing – as we do today – that everything is made up of atoms. But he thought that the atom could not be divided.**

Top **These diagrams describe the way thinkers through the ages have explained the structure of matter. Democritus said that things consisted of atoms which looked like those in (1). Epicurus agreed with him but thought that the atoms in solids were all hooked together as in (2). The next theory of atoms was put forward by Newton in the 17th century. Figure (3) shows his pattern of atoms, kept together by magnetism or some other force. In (4) we see the theory advanced by Dalton who said that atoms were each surrounded by heat. Kelvin believed they were spirals of electricity (5). Figure (6) shows Thomson's theory of a ball of electricity completely encircled by a structure of electrons. In 1911, Rutherford claimed that the atom was a nucleus in a ball of electrons (7).**

everything to a formula, so that matter and all the things made from it, including man himself, was thought to be composed of certain basic elements, such as fire, water and air. Democritus, who lived from about 470 to 400 BC, formed an atomic theory (revived by modern scientists) which laid down that all things are made up of atoms and the space which divides them. He thought of atoms as the smallest particles of matter, and the Greek word *atomos* means indivisible.

Pythagoras and his followers made many discoveries to do with the 'harmony' of numbers. They tried to show that nature was based on certain numerical ratios and proportions. These were sometimes expressed as geometric principles, such as the famous one: that the square on the side opposite to the right-angle of a triangle is equal to the sum of the squares on the other two sides. But numerical harmony was also found to exist in such things as music, painting and architecture. Because Pythagoreans believed the number 10 to be perfect, and only nine heavenly bodies were visible in the sky at the time, they even invented a 'counter-earth' to make up this 'perfect' number.

Forces of nature

In the same way that man increased his efficiency by inventing simple machines, so he looked at the forces of nature about him and thought of ways to use their energies to work for him.

Probably some time during the Stone Age man discovered fire, one of the most important of these natural forces. He most likely came across it accidentally, for the friction caused by certain objects being rubbed together will produce a spark which will ignite dry substances. For instance, two sticks or stones rubbed together cause friction and heat. Another good example is to rub your hands together quickly and see how much heat is produced. Man may also have got the idea of fire from the action of lightning, or from the sun which can set grass alight by its own direct heat in dry areas.

Fire was a wonderful discovery for primitive man, for it changed his life in so many ways. Not only did it provide warmth and the means of boiling and baking food, but it also enabled certain solid metals to be converted into liquids by the application of its heat. It would not have taken man long to realise that before liquid metal cooled, its shape could be determined by the use of moulds into which the liquid was poured. In this way the first rude metal tools and weapons were fashioned. But the chemical nature of fire was not understood for a long time, and fire was worshipped and looked upon as a gift from the gods for hundreds of years.

Heat created by fire can reach us

Above (A) Hot air rises and cold air falls. (B) We experience radiation when warming our hands at a fire. (C) Heat can be conducted like this through the ground. Figure (D) shows evaporation of water.

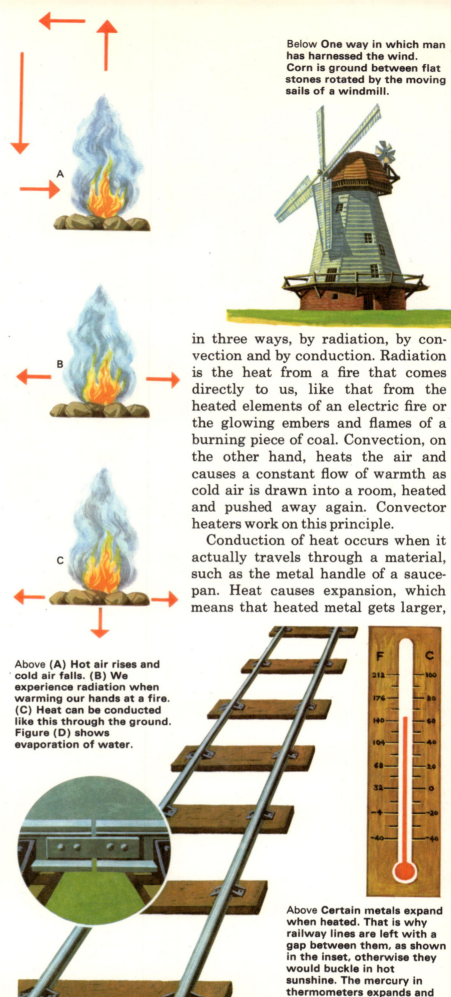

Below One way in which man has harnessed the wind. Corn is ground between flat stones rotated by the moving sails of a windmill.

in three ways, by radiation, by convection and by conduction. Radiation is the heat from a fire that comes directly to us, like that from the heated elements of an electric fire or the glowing embers and flames of a burning piece of coal. Convection, on the other hand, heats the air and causes a constant flow of warmth as cold air is drawn into a room, heated and pushed away again. Convector heaters work on this principle.

Conduction of heat occurs when it actually travels through a material, such as the metal handle of a saucepan. Heat causes expansion, which means that heated metal gets larger,

Above Certain metals expand when heated. That is why railway lines are left with a gap between them, as shown in the inset, otherwise they would buckle in hot sunshine. The mercury in thermometers expands and so is able to show the temperature on the scale.

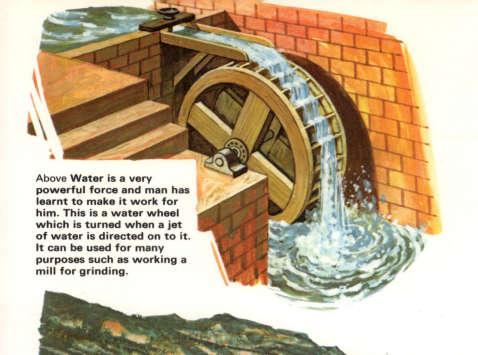

Above **Water is a very powerful force and man has learnt to make it work for him. This is a water wheel which is turned when a jet of water is directed on to it. It can be used for many purposes such as working a mill for grinding.**

Wind is another natural force used by man from earliest times. It helped to propel the first ships on the seas and was turned into a source of power in the form of windmills. The wind, however, is unreliable, since the strength with which it blows is inconsistent. Nevertheless, wind can also be used to turn the wheels of a water pump or to generate and store electricity in accumulators.

Below **Here is another example of how nature has been harnessed. The concrete dam (E) controls the water and directs it on to the turbines (F) which generate electricity. Compare the water wheel above.**

or expands. Heat also makes changes in substances and can turn solids into liquids or gases.

Ours is a world almost filled with water, for it is everywhere around us, although it is not always as obvious as the water that crashes upon sea shores or lies still in a lake. Our bodies contain large amounts of water and some fruit, such as apples, are made up almost entirely of water.

Water is a life force for all growing things – plants and animals – for without it nothing could live. It can also be used as a great source of power. The water mill is one of man's earliest, successful attempts to harness the energy of nature. Hydro-electric power stations make use of the falling and driving power of water by creating huge dams which conserve that power and release it through special outlets which turn turbines and so work electric generators.

Below **When man first discovered fire, it was a great advance for it gave him warmth and the means of cooking. Here is an aborigine making a fire by friction.**

Right **It was in 1666 that Sir Isaac Newton decided that the earth holds everything on it by the force of gravity. This picture shows how this force acts equally on every part of the globe.**

Above **The heater in a tropical fish tank causes the water to circulate because water, just like air, rises when heated and descends when cooled.**

195

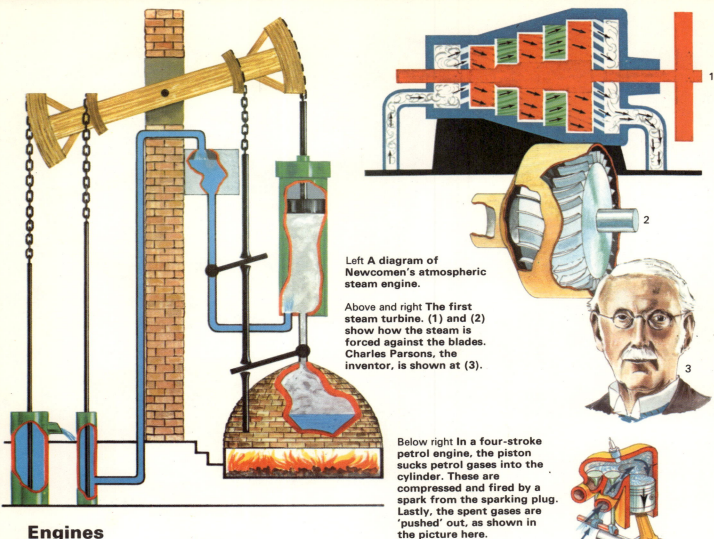

Left **A diagram of Newcomen's atmospheric steam engine.**

Above and right **The first steam turbine. (1) and (2) show how the steam is forced against the blades. Charles Parsons, the inventor, is shown at (3).**

Below right **In a four-stroke petrol engine, the piston sucks petrol gases into the cylinder. These are compressed and fired by a spark from the sparking plug. Lastly, the spent gases are 'pushed' out, as shown in the picture here.**

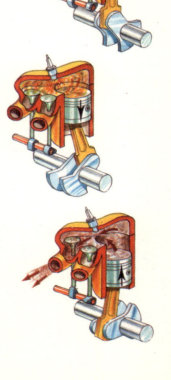

Engines

An engine is a device which can convert energy into mechanical work. Different types of engines use different means of achieving this end. The steam engine uses the energy of steam to move a piston, and the internal combustion engine burns fuel inside a cylinder to produce gases which also work a piston. Another type of engine is the hydraulic engine which uses the power of water to turn machinery. Whatever the type of engine, it works by transforming energy into motion.

A small steam turbine engine is said to have been invented about 2,000 years ago by a Greek called Hero, but the idea was not developed into something which could turn machinery. For centuries men relied on natural energy provided by wind and water and on the strength of their own bodies. The demand for a mechanical means of lifting, digging and hauling began in the mines. The first successful steam engine was built in 1712 by Thomas Newcomen. It was designed to pump water out of deep mine shafts

in Britain, and before long similar engines had been constructed all over Europe. Other engineers in Britain, such as Watt and Trevithick, were mainly responsible for modifying and improving these first crude machines.

In the original steam engines the to-and-fro motion of a piston was converted into rotary motion by means of a crank attaching the piston to a wheel. The steam turbine engine sought to use the power of steam to produce a direct rotary motion without pistons, but it was not until 1884 that Charles Parsons perfected the first successful turbine engine, which was to be used in power stations and on ships.

The idea of burning fuel directly in a cylinder gave rise to the invention of the internal combustion engine. In 1860 the Frenchman Lenoir built the first practical gas engine and by 1865 some 400 such engines were at work in Paris performing a variety of mechanical tasks. The four-stroke engine was worked out in principle by another

Frenchman, Beau de Rochas, but it was the German Nikolaus Otto who actually made the first working four-stroke gas engine. In 1864 Siegfried Marcus built a four-stroke engine using petrol instead of gas as a fuel, and in 1885 Gottlieb Daimler and Karl Benz both installed petrol-driven internal combustion engines in vehicles.

The diesel engine is a type of internal combustion engine used mostly for heavy-duty work in locomotives and large lorries. It was invented in 1893 by the German engineer Rudolf Diesel, during an experiment in which an explosion nearly killed him, and used in his first successful engine in 1897.

The rockets used by the Chinese in warfare over 700 years ago worked on the same principle as the rocket which sends an artificial satellite into space. The projectile is propelled through the air by a jet-exhaust of gas produced by burning a fuel. The jet engine was patented by Frank Whittle in England in 1930. The Germans developed a jet fighter aircraft at the end of the Second World War. This was the gas-turbine engine, and from it developed the turbo-jet engine. The ram-jet is a development of the turbo-jet and one form of it was used by the Germans in the Second World War in the V–1 or 'flying bomb'.

Below **One of the most important events in aeronautics was the invention of the jet engine which completely altered aircraft design in war and peace. Frank Whittle, an Englishman, took out his first patent in 1930 and the first successful jet engine was tested in 1937. Since then, there have been variations of this engine. One of these is the turbo-jet in which air is sucked in, compressed and then mixed with fuel. Our picture shows another version, the turbo-prop. Here, basically, the same principle is used to drive a conventional propeller.**

Below **(A) pictures a gas engine and (B) shows how a moving piston can open the inlet and exhaust pipes without valves.**

Above **A modern diesel train.**

Right **The cylinder of a diesel engine. Invented in 1897 by Rudolf Diesel. It is important because it needs no carburettor and works off cheap oil.**

Electricity

Electricity is a mysterious force which can flow from place to place rather like water. But it is invisible, except when it causes a spark or makes something light up. Electricity has existed in the world since the beginning of time. Although man has been aware of it for over 2,000 years, it is only recently that he has begun to understand what it is and how it works. Electricity is either static, that is still, or it is current, which is always on the move.

Static electricity was known to the Greeks. In the 6th century BC Thales demonstrated that dry leaves could be picked up by a piece of amber which had been rubbed vigorously. The Greek word for amber is *elektron*, and it is from this that the English word 'electricity' comes.

Most people have discovered for themselves what Thales found out about static electricity. On a dry day a comb passed through your hair will crackle. Rub the same comb on cloth and it will attract small pieces of paper like a magnet if it is held over them. In certain dry atmospheres in

Left **Benjamin Franklin** is seen here conducting an experiment which might have killed him. In a thunderstorm, he flew a kite connected by a metal thread to a battery called a Leyden jar. In the experiment, the battery became charged and proved that lightning is a form of static electricity.

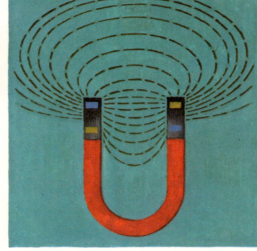

Right **A straight magnet tends to demagnetise itself. One way of preventing this is to make it in the shape of a horseshoe. The dotted lines in the picture show the forces around the two poles of a horseshoe magnet.**

Fixed wire
Rotating magnet
Salt Solution
Insulated Support
Rotating wire
Fixed Magnet Salt Solution
Battery

Above **Samuel Morse** discovered by chance that the electromagnet could be used in communications. But his most famous invention was the Morse Code in 1838. It is an 'alphabet' of dots and dashes and has been used ever since for worldwide telegraphic communications.

Above **Michael Faraday.** His greatest discovery was that electricity could be produced magnetically.

Top **This was the device which Faraday used in 1821 to demonstrate electro-magnetic rotation. It used a rotating wire on one side and a rotating magnet on the other.**

carpeted rooms a handshake between two people will produce a mild electric shock. All of these examples indicate the existence of static electricity and the fact that friction causes it to be seen or felt. Static electricity is important in many areas of science, particularly in radio and television.

Current electricity is used to produce light, heat and power. All matter is composed of atoms, and atoms consist of a nucleus around which tiny particles called electrons rotate. The movement of these electrons produces electricity. Electrons are always in movement and sometimes they even jump across a gap from one object to another: the result of this is a spark which can be seen. Electrons can be made to run along wire or metal and produce an electric 'current'. Metal is thus a conductor of electricity. This is why lightning conductors on high buildings are made of metal. If lightning were to strike, its current is carried to safety down the metal and into the ground.

Electrical current is created from chemical or mechanical energy. In 1800, an Italian physicist Alessandro

Hydro-electricity is the name given to generating electric power by using water. Huge dams control the water, letting it flow through channels to work the turbines.

Below This is a conventional electricity generating station fired by coal.

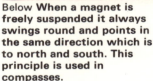

Below When a magnet is freely suspended it always swings round and points in the same direction which is to north and south. This principle is used in compasses.

Volta, invented the first device for producing continuous electric current. Another Italian, Galvani, had stated that electricity can be made from the chemical action of particular liquids on two different types of metal. Volta demonstrated this by placing alternate plates of zinc and copper on top of one another separated by pieces of cloth soaked in salt water. By fixing a piece of wire to the copper plate at the top of the 'pile' and connecting it to the bottom zinc plate, he found he could make an electric current flow along the wire.

Batteries and accumulators are made using a similar principle. They are capable of storing electricity, like the dry battery which lights a torch. Here the current flows from one end or pole of a battery to another. Along its length it is connected to a light bulb and the circuit is broken at a point where a switch is placed. Push the switch down and the flow is complete and the bulb lights up. In time the electrical energy in a dry battery is used up and another is needed. Similarly, the battery in a car which provides electricity to start it and power its electrically-operated features, needs to be recharged in order to work properly. In a car this happens automatically while the vehicle is in motion.

Light, colour and sound

In the ancient world, the question 'what is light' had long puzzled natural philosophers, or scientists. All sorts of theories were advanced, like that of Empedocles in the 5th century BC, who thought that something went out from the eye to meet something else sent out from the object it was looking at. Pythagoras believed that actual particles were sent out to the eye from the surface of objects, and in the 17th century the great Isaac Newton revived this theory, which is still held to be partly true in modern times. Scientists now believe that light is a kind of energy which, although made up of particles called *photons*, travels in waves at a tremendous speed – so fast that it can go nearly eight times round the world in a single second.

We see things because of the light reflected from them: if there is no light we can see nothing. Light travels in straight lines and cannot 'bend' round corners. It was Isaac Newton who first demonstrated that natural white light is a combination of all the colours. If light is passed through a glass prism it will be seen to consist

of violet, indigo, blue, green, yellow, orange and red – the colours of a rainbow in the sky. The reason why we see individual colours is that an object absorbs some colours and reflects others. A red door, for example, is covered with paint which is made to absorb all the rays in white light except the red ones; these it reflects back to our eyes so that we see only that colour.

Men have used artificial light in their homes since the days when a flaming torch first broke the darkness in the caves of primitive man. Electric light was invented at almost the same time about 1878–9 by two men working independently, Thomas Edison in America and Joseph Swan in Britain. The first public building to be lit entirely by electric lamps was the newly opened Savoy Theatre in London, home of the Gilbert and Sullivan operas. On the opening night in 1881 the manager, Rupert D'Oyly Carte wrapped an illuminated lamp

Above **Artificial light through the ages.** At the top are an ancient torch, an oil lamp and a wax candle. In the middle is a gas lamp bracket which was in use until a few years ago. At the bottom is a gas-filled electric lamp bulb.

Below **By placing two or more mirrors over a design and moving them, a variety of patterns can be obtained. This is the principle on which the kaleidoscope works.**

in a handkerchief and smashed it with a hammer to show how safe it was compared with the old gas lighting.

Sound, too, travels in waves. The air is full of sound waves which radiate in all directions rather like the expanding ripples which follow the dropping of a stone in a pool of water. These vibrations in the air reach our ears, where the complicated structure of the ear-drum converts them into sounds. The sounds we hear differ from each other because of their pitch, loudness and quality.

Left **A periscope works on the simple principle of reflecting mirrors which are placed parallel to one another, but at an angle of 45°, in some form of a tube. By looking at the lower mirror, the boy in the picture can watch the football match on the other side of the wall.**

Above right **When someone has his photograph taken, light is reflected from his body through the camera lens on to the film, the lighter parts of his body appearing dark and vice versa. Light is then shone through this negative on to photographic paper to reverse the tones.**

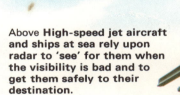

Above **High-speed jet aircraft and ships at sea rely upon radar to 'see' for them when the visibility is bad and to get them safely to their destination.**

Right **A revolving radar scanner as used at airports.**

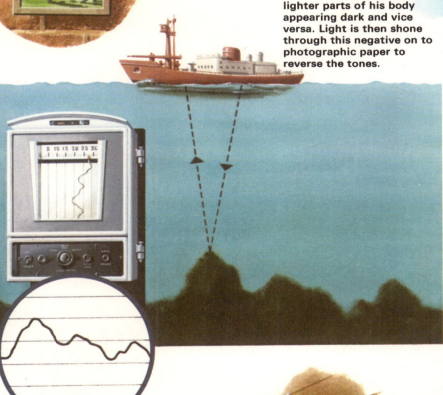

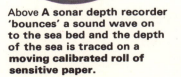

Above **A sonar depth recorder 'bounces' a sound wave on to the sea bed and the depth of the sea is traced on a moving calibrated roll of sensitive paper.**

Right **Sound waves are sent out when someone knocks on a door.**

Above **A radar operator sits at his cathode ray tube watching the pattern of circling lines. As soon as an object gets in the radar beam it is shown at once on the screen.**

Time, counting and measuring

Human beings can hear a wide range of sounds from the very high to the very low. At either end of the scale sound becomes inaudible to us, but many animals can hear sounds which do not reach human ears. The most common example is the bat which has a form of echo-location it gives off to enable it to find its way about in the dark. It sends out very high frequency sounds which bounce back from objects in its path. This echo-sounding is also used by ships at sea, which direct sounds towards the bottom of the ocean. According to the time it takes for the sound to bounce, or reflect, back to the ship so the depth of water can be calculated.

Thomas Edison was the first man to record sound successfully and his invention has been developed through all the stages of phonograph, gramophone and tape-recorder. The first effective telephone was made in 1876 by Alexander Graham Bell.

It was the ancient Egyptians who invented a way of registering the passing of time at night or when the sun was not visible. This was the water clock, in which the level of water in a vessel was gradually lowered over a marked time scale by the controlled leaking away of the liquid through a hole. The Greeks had a more complicated form of water

clock, called a clepsydra, and there were other 'clocks' in the ancient world based on the burning down of marked candles or knotted ropes.

In the Middle Ages there were sundials, and hour glasses in which sand slowly trickled from top to bottom of a glass vessel through a narrow neck.

Here are some ancient methods of telling the time. The hour-glass (1) works like an egg timer. A similar principle is used in the water bowl (2) which is emptied through a drip hole. The knotted string (3) is burnt like a fuse. Each time the smouldering end reaches a knot, it marks the passage of an hour. The sundial (4) shows the time by shadows cast by the sun. The lantern clock (5) is of the 18th century and (6) is a modern electric clock.

Below Before land can be developed for building or be excavated by archaeologists, it has to be surveyed by means of survey tapes, levels, a prismatic compass and a theodolite. The picture shows a surveyor using a theodolite.

These have survived in the old-fashioned egg-timers still used today. The first clocks were made in the 14th century, and there is one at Salisbury Cathedral in England, still in working order, which is said to be the oldest clock in the world.

Registering the passing of time is not only important in everyday life, it is also vital for such things as the navigation of ships. At first, sailors used the position of stars in the sky to help them decide their course and location at sea. But it was essential to know the time. This is why an especially accurate clock called a chronometer was invented. The first successful one was built by John Harrison in the 18th century. Accuracy in a clock has always been important, and today there are atomic clocks using the movement of electrons as a standard of time measurement which are estimated to lose or gain as little as one second in every 6,000 years.

Two of the first scientific inventions were a means of recording facts and the ability to make measurements.

Above **When early man learnt to count, he did so by means of small pebbles (7) and later he used beads on a frame (8) for the same purpose. Tally sticks (9) were used when people did a business deal. The amounts were notched on a stick which was then split down its length, each man taking one as a record.**

Below **In coastal navigation, a line is charted showing the route to be taken. Another line drawn through the compass points on the chart, gives the compass bearing by which to steer.**

The earliest ways of recording facts was to knot string and notch wooden sticks.

It was natural for early man to use his fingers, thumbs and toes to calculate. Counting in tens and scores (twenties) has an obvious origin in the fact that we have ten fingers on our hands and ten toes on our feet. The old Roman numerals I, II, III etc., may be related to visual signs that can be made with the fingers and thumbs— one finger, two fingers, three fingers and so on. The very word 'calculate' comes from the Latin *calculus*, meaning a pebble, or little stone, and this is a link with early reckoning by means of seeds, counters or pebbles.

The numbers 1 to 9 in the system used today in the western world probably came from ancient India, although they are known as Arabic numerals. These numerals, which had been used by the Arabs for many years, were taken over by the people of Europe in the Middle Ages in place of Roman figures. The 0 or zero was added later. On early counting frames using beads, no beads at all meant nought.

In terms of measurement the length of various parts of the human body, such as the hand and the foot, were the basis for calculation. A natural yard is formed by the distance from the centre of the chest to the middle of a fully extended arm, and the fathom has its origin in the distance from hand to hand across the chest with both arms extended.

Below **This is a picture of Calder Hall, in Cumberland, England, the first industrial nuclear power station in the world. Opened in 1956, it has an output of 180 megawatts (180,000 watts) and uses uranium as its fuel. The cooling gas which flows up through the reactor at 400°C. boils water to produce steam for the turbo-generators.**

established an atomic theory about the nature of the basic elements, like iron and mercury, which make up the universe. His theory has long since been replaced by more detailed and accurate knowledge but the science of atomic physics has developed from such discoveries.

The tiny particles of matter are today called molecules, and molecules consist of atoms. Any familiar substance, like water, sugar or wood, is made up of atoms combined in different ways. Each piece of matter contains millions and millions of molecules and they all stick together, as

Below **Atoms consist of a nucleus (A), neutrons (B), protons (C) and electrons (D). Figure (E) shows an oxygen atom with its eight electrons moving around the nucleus. A molecule of water (F) contains two hydrogen atoms with an oxygen atom between them. They are held together by an electro-static charge.**

The atom

Everything in the world is made up of matter. That includes not only human beings and animals and the solid objects that surround us, like trees, houses and cars, but the earth itself, the water in it and the air we breathe. Matter may be solid, like a tree; or liquid, like water; or gaseous, like air. Matter does not always stay in the same state. Heat can alter it; for example, it can melt solid ice into liquid water.

All matter is made up of tiny particles. Ever since man began to think about the nature of things he has wondered whether these particles could be broken down into smaller and smaller pieces indefinitely. The ancient Greeks believed that matter was made from particles which they called atoms. For them the atom was the smallest thing, and existed as a tiny, solid object which could not be broken down any further: it was indivisible. In the 19th century an English schoolmaster, John Dalton,

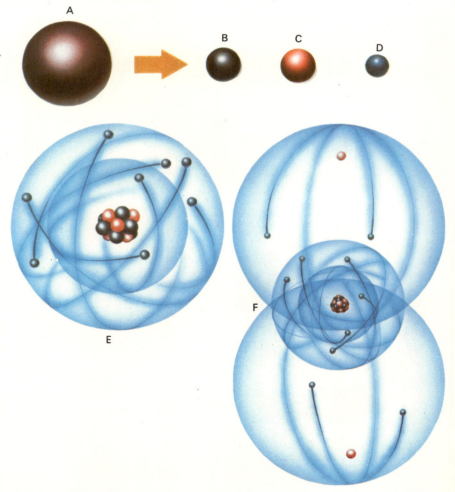

do the atoms inside them, because they are attracted to each other like little magnets.

Over the last 50 years scientists have been investigating the atom itself. They have, in fact, 'split' the atom, a thing which for many years was thought to be impossible. In 1911 the New Zealand physicist, Ernest Rutherford, first created a picture of the atom, more or less as it is known today. This picture shows that the atom is not solid but consists mostly of space, at the centre of which is a nucleus made up of protons and neutrons, around which circle a number of electrons. All these tiny things behave rather like a miniature solar system in which planets revolve around a central sun.

The simplest atom is that of the gas, hydrogen, and it consists of a nucleus of one proton with one electron spinning around it. At the other end of the scale is the complicated atom of uranium, which has a nucleus of 92 protons and 146 neutrons with 92 electrons around it arranged in seven layers.

Above **As sails were once superseded by mechanical power so one day will it give way to nuclear power. Here are two examples of nuclear power at sea – an ice breaker and a submarine.**

Right **Cockcroft's and Walton's 'accelerator'. These two British scientists were among the first to split the atom in 1931 using this kind of equipment.**

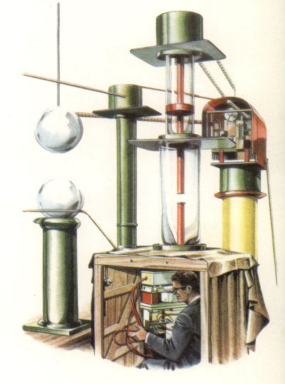

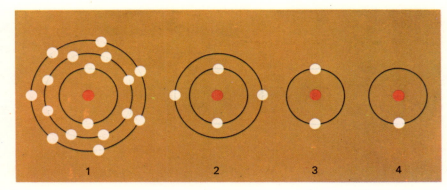

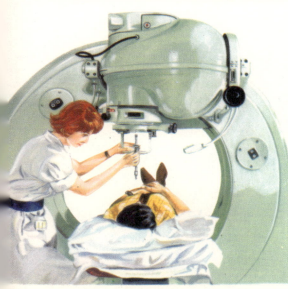

Above **The atomic structure of chlorine (1); beryllium (2); helium (3) and hydrogen (4), showing the electrons around the nucleus.**

Left **The discovery of nuclear energy has not only given us power, it has also provided us with a method of healing. The patient in the picture is being treated with radio-therapy. He is receiving radio isotopes – radioactive substances which kill diseased tissues of the body.**

In 1939 scientists in Italy and Germany succeeded in splitting the nucleus of an atom into two parts. This is known as nuclear fission and it led to the discovery of a new form of energy. It first demonstrated its power in a terrible way at the end of the Second World War when atom bombs were dropped on Japanese cities. Scientists continued to develop atomic energy for peaceful purposes and the first atomic power station was built in 1956 at Calder Hall in England. Such stations have now been built in many parts of the world to supply electricity and other forms of power.

Computers and automation

The earliest form of computer was probably a notched stick used to record some event in the life of primitive man. The practice continues in modern times in the emblems with which fighter pilots decorate their aircraft after each successful combat mission against an enemy.

The first counting machine was the abacus, invented in China, several thousand years ago. This is a device with beads strung on a series of wires which represent units, tens, hundreds, thousands etc. According to the position of the beads so a number can be

Top right **An abacus**

Above and right **Pascal and his mechanical adding machine.**

Below **Automatic gates at a car park.**

read off. It is possible with an abacus to add, subtract, multiply and divide, and this simple aid to calculation is still used in some parts of the world.

In 1617 the English mathematician John Napier produced some ingenious numerating rods which were the fore-runners of the modern slide rule, which is a type of pocket computer. One of the first mechanical adding machines was that made by the French scientist Blaise Pascal in 1642. In this a series of cogged wheels made it possible to add and subtract automatically, rather in the way that the modern device in a car works which notches up the miles travelled.

The first electronic computer began to work in 1946. This and subsequent computers used the binary system of

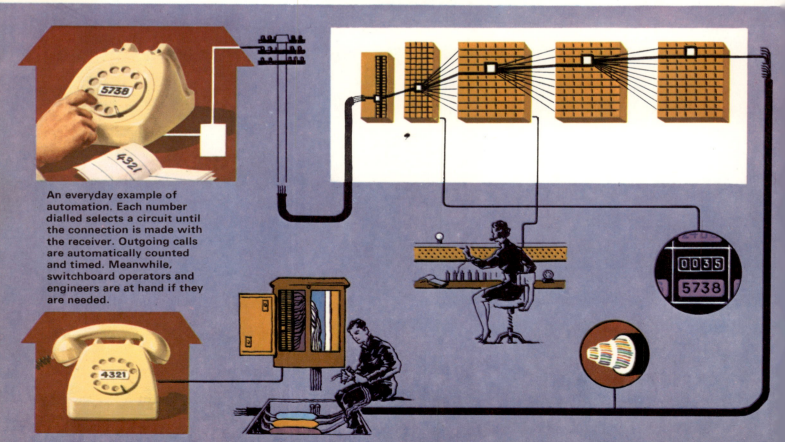

An everyday example of automation. Each number dialled selects a circuit until the connection is made with the receiver. Outgoing calls are automatically counted and timed. Meanwhile, switchboard operators and engineers are at hand if they are needed.

Left **A mechanical toy**

Above **The mechanism of the musical box (right). The pins on the revolving drum make a tune by plucking the 'comb'.**

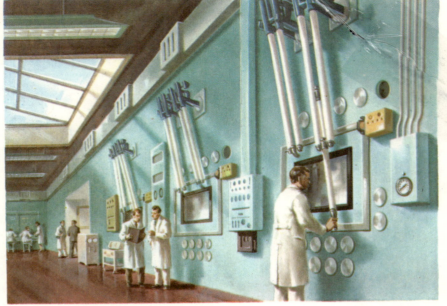

Above **Operators at a nuclear research station handle dangerous radio-active substances by remote control.**

Below **This is the control room at Houston, Texas, from which astronauts in space are guided by a complex remote control system.**

man from physical effort is really a product of automation. This applies to the very earliest inventions which took advantage of a natural source of power such as the wind, and in this sense automation has been with us for a very long time.

In the modern sense, the Industrial Revolution of the 19th century in Europe and America produced more and more machines which could mass produce articles previously made by hand. In the early part of this century the automobile industry, particularly in the United States, led the way in building factories which mechanised much tedious and repetitive work. After the Second World War all sorts of electrical devices came to the aid of industry. Now automatic control systems play a growing part in our everyday lives and are gradually doing away with the need for the unskilled worker. But the more complex the machinery becomes the more highly-trained the operators will have to be.

counting with the two symbols 0 and 1, which can be converted into the electrical impulses of negative and positive. Information has to be fed into a computer by means of punched tape or cards, and the machine can only solve those problems which are covered by the stock of calculations already stored in its memory bank.

Nevertheless, computers can be 'taught' to do a wide variety of things. The most celebrated examples of this are the computers programmed to play chess against human opponents, and another machine which is able to compose music to order. In a more serious way, computers play an increasingly valuable part in industry, business, education and scientific enquiry. Their greatest moments of triumph have been during the successful Apollo moon landings, in which they played so vital a part.

Automation is a word used to describe any process which can be carried out by a machine without human aid. Anything which relieves

Industry and Power

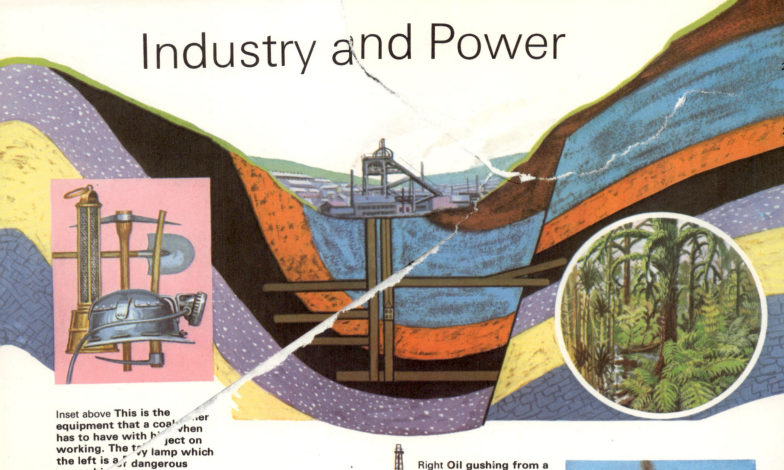

Inset above **This is the ...er equipment that a coal ... when has to have with h ... ject on working. The t... y lamp which the left is a ... r dangerous warns hi...he air. gases ...**

Right **Oil gushing from a well. Oil rigs are in the distance.**

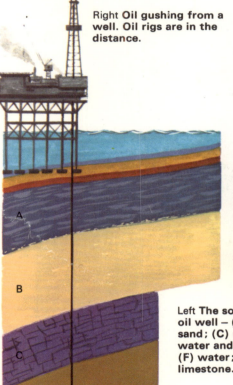

Left **The soil layers of an oil well – (A) shale; (B) sand; (C) rock; (D) salt water and sand; (E) oil; (F) water; (G) porous limestone.**

All industries obtain their power from fuel, and this comes from many sources. Some fuels are called fossil fuels because they come from the remains of plants and animals beneath the earth. Oil, perhaps the most important of all fuels, is a fossil fuel. With the use of an instrument called a seismograph, oil can be detected and its distance below the earth's surface measured. Drills are supported by a tall metal framework called a derrick. When oil is finally struck, the derrick is removed and the oil well plugged with a system of valves.

Oil has many uses and during the refining process it can be made into petrol, paraffin and benzine. It is also used as a lubricant to keep the wheels of industry turning. Some of the chemicals in oil go into making such varied things as perfume, polythene and aspirin. Altogether there are about 5,000 by-products obtained from oil. So valuable is oil to industry that no modern country could survive without it.

Coal is another important fossil fuel and is dug from the ground by miners. Sometimes explosives are used, and in modern mines automated machinery takes the place of picks and shovels. Coal is in fact the remains of plants that grew millions of years ago during the Carboniferous (or coal-bearing) period. Layer upon layer of plants rotted and formed large deposits of coal. There are three types of coal. Anthracite is the best, having the most minerals; it contains up to 95% carbon and has the greatest heating power. Bituminous coal is the type most used in households and industry. Lignite or brown coal is much inferior as a fuel.

Gas can be made from coal by heating it in ovens to a very high temperature. Valuable by-products are obtained from coal, and the coke that is left after processing is used in blast-

Left **A diagram showing soil layers of a coal mine — (1) top soil; (2) Triassic; (3) Permian; (4) coal seam; (5) millstone grit; (6) limestone and (7) old rocks. Inset — a primeval forest.**

Right **Logs are transported in Canada by letting them flow down the rivers. Lumberjacks often steer them through the rapids as the picture shows.**

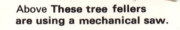
Above **These tree fellers are using a mechanical saw.**

Above **Lumber that has been pulped can be used for paper manufacture. The paper mill shown here is making newsprint for our daily newspapers.**

furnaces and in steel making. Most of the gas is used for domestic purposes.

Nowadays natural gas replaces coal gas. This natural gas was once looked upon as a waste product, and when drilling for oil the layer of natural gas seated on top of the oil deposits was allowed to escape. In industry, natural gas is used for burning under boilers, generating electricity, steel-making and as a raw material for the manufacture of chemicals.

Wood was once very widely used as a fuel but with the development of the oil industry, its use is now almost

entirely confined to the manufacture of furniture and to house-building. It might seem that in this age of iron and steel, timber would be of little use, but we are using timber faster today than ever before. Natural forests are disappearing at a tremendous rate as millions of trees are fed to the sawmills and pulping factories.

Timber from oak, walnut, plane, beech, teak and mahogany is all used in the construction of furniture. The elm, being resistant to decay in wet conditions, is used for all underwater constructions. Timber from oak, spruce, larch and some pines is used in the building of bridges, houses, pit-props, telegraph poles and boats. Pines are also used to make pulp for paper. Pear timber has an even grain and smooth texture and is used to make musical and geometrical instruments.

Huge logging camps exist in Canada and after the trees have been felled and branches removed, they are joined together and floated down-river to the sawmills where the bark is removed and the timber cut into planks.

Iron and steel

Iron is found everywhere on earth but it is used mostly in the form of alloys, that is, mixed with other metals to make it stronger than pure iron. Steel is a principal alloy and the percentage of iron used in its making is very high, except in special steels, such as stainless steel and steel used in toolmaking.

The modern steel industry began in the 1850s and immediately steel was used in the making of buildings and bridges. Now we have skyscraper buildings in steel reaching great heights and very long bridges.

Iron remains one of the most widely used metals, for the great manufacturing industries which make ships, aircraft and cars all need iron and its alloys for their products. The iron and steel industry is one of the largest in the world today.

Above and right **Steel is made by melting crude iron to a white heat until it is molten and mixing it with alloys. These pictures show furnaces in a modern steel mill.**

Plastics

Plastics are made up of molecules, or particles, which are called polymers. Although the natural raw materials that go into the making of plastics are in short supply, they are now being replaced by man-made materials which are often better than natural materials and are much cheaper to produce.

Plastics are light as well as being very strong. They do not rust, are very colourful and can be made into complicated shapes. Plastics do not conduct heat. This makes them suitable as covering for electric cables. When mixed with glass fibre, plastics are strong enough to be moulded into car bodies. Also many fabrics are made out of plastics. Polythene and polystyrene are plastics which melt when heated.

Left **Here are some of the many uses of modern plastics.**

Left **There are basically two ways of making plastics. One is by extrusion, by which molten plastic is forced through holes to make strips and the other is injection, by which it is pushed into a mould. This diagram shows a plastic injection moulder.**

Water

Water is very versatile and although it is a liquid it can also be made into a solid or a gas and can pass from one state to another more easily than other substances.

Like everything else, water is made up of molecules. When in a solid state the molecules in the ice move very closely together. When the ice melts the molecules move quickly and they roll and push against each other. That is why water has no particular shape except the shape of the vessel which contains it. When water is heated some of it changes into vapour, or gas. Then the molecules of water speed up and move further away from each other. Some are flung out of the liquid to disperse in the air. One of the most important industrial uses of water is in the generating of electricity, when it is used as a raw material at hydro-electric power stations.

Above left **A rubber tapper cutting back the bark so that the latex, from which rubber is made, can drip into the bowl.**

Below left **A latex plantation.**

Rubber

The raw material of natural rubber comes from certain trees grown in the tropics, the main tree being the *Hevea*. Latex, from which rubber is made, flows in channels in the inner part of the bark. Cuts are made in the bark and the latex runs into a cup attached to the trunk and is collected by a man called a rubber tapper. The bark will take from seven to ten years to grow again.

The important factors of rubber are its elasticity, resistance to wear and the fact that it is waterproof. Rubber is widely used in modern industry, especially in vehicle manufacture. So essential is it that synthetic rubbers are now made to keep pace with the ever-growing demand.

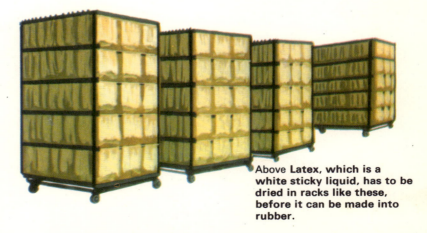

Above **Latex, which is a white sticky liquid, has to be dried in racks like these, before it can be made into rubber.**

The pictures at the top and on the right show wool shearing, preparation and traditional spinning. Above is a modern carding machine.

Above left **A mechanical cotton picking machine.**

Below **An English cotton mill.**

Above **Arkwright's spinning machine. It could spin a cotton thread which was strong enough to be used as warp as well as weft.**

Textiles

Textiles are made from both natural and man-made fibres. The natural fibres come from plants, animals and minerals.

Cotton and flax (the fabric from which is called linen) are the most common plant fibres, but hemp, jute and sisal are also used. The fibre from coconuts is used for making sacks and matting. Wool and silk are animal fibres. Most wool comes from sheep but the softest and shiniest wool comes from Kashmir (cashmere) and Angora (mohair) goats. Silk is obtained from silkworms and is the only natural fibre produced in a long, continuous thread. Asbestos, which is a rock mineral, is made up of fine fibres which can be woven into cloth. Most asbestos is mined in Canada and is a fire-proof material.

Among man-made fibres, rayon is produced by processing natural substances and reforming them. Synthetic fibres such as nylon are made entirely from chemicals.

To make textiles from the fibres, yarn is first spun and then interlaced in various ways. Weaving and knitting are the two most important methods of making textiles. Lace and netting are made by twisting the yarns, and felt is made by pounding hot, wet fibres together. Before the textiles are sold they go through a variety of processes.

Pottery

Ceramics is the name given to the art of making pottery and it refers to all types of pottery whatever the composition. The main raw material is clay, formed by breaking down natural rock such as granite.

Kaolin and ball clay are the two principal clays used in making pottery. Flint is an important substance which adds strength to the product, and to bind all the ingredients together various minerals are used. Other materials are added to the clay to stop shrinkage during the firing process.

To make ceramics, the natural rocks are first broken up and then reduced to powder form. Clay and kaolin are dissolved in water and placed in their correct proportions in a mixer. The watery clay is then sieved to remove unwanted particles. Further processing then takes place depending on the material, and the clay is then shaped either by hand or machine.

The products are dried and then passed through a huge heated oven. This process is called firing. Decoration is then added and the products are then glazed and fired again to fix the glaze. Sometimes further decoration is applied over the glaze and when this happens another firing is needed.

Above **A clay pot takes shape on the potter's wheel. The spinning lump of clay is gradually shaped into its final form entirely by hand.**

Above left **A factory kiln in which clay pots are 'cooked' at very high temperatures, converting the clay into pottery.**

Glass

The art of glass-making has been known since ancient times. In the Middle Ages, Venice was the centre for the manufacture of glass. So profitable was it to the state that a law was passed in 1547 prohibiting craftsmen from leaving the country and spreading their knowledge of the art. In spite of these laws, Venetian techniques gradually penetrated to other parts of Europe.

Glass is really a liquid, known as a 'super-cooled' liquid, which means it has a tendency to form itself into crystals. It is made from sand, soda, limestone and other substances. There are many different types of glass in use and several methods of making it. Blowing is the oldest-known way of forming glass vessels, and although some is still blown with mouth blow-pipes, machines are now more commonly used.

Sheet glass for glazing is processed by casting and rolling but this type does not have a very flat surface and 'ripples' in the glass can often be seen in windows. Plate glass is processed in the same way but it is afterwards ground and polished to give a perfectly flat sheet.

Above **An operator rolling a sheet of glass after casting.**

Right **Blowing molten glass into shape like a balloon.**

Food from the Land and Sea

Grain crops are the most important sources of food from plants. They can be used directly as cereals and they also help feed the farm stock which provides man with meat and dairy produce.

With one or two exceptions, all the grain crops belong to the grass family. In temperate climates wheats are the chief cereals, the most important being the variety used for making bread, cakes, biscuits and pastry. Durum wheat is used for making pasta, and there are other varieties now used mainly as food for livestock, although they were once very important to man as food.

Rye, oats and barley are other cereals used extensively for human consumption. Corn is the only crop which is American in origin. Since it was brought to Europe by Columbus it has been dispersed to many other parts of the world. Corn, which is also

Right **The invention of the wheel made ploughing easier. This type of plough, although primitive, is still in use in some parts of the world today.**

Above **Modern farmers use combine harvesters which reap, thresh, winnow and bundle the straw in one operation.**

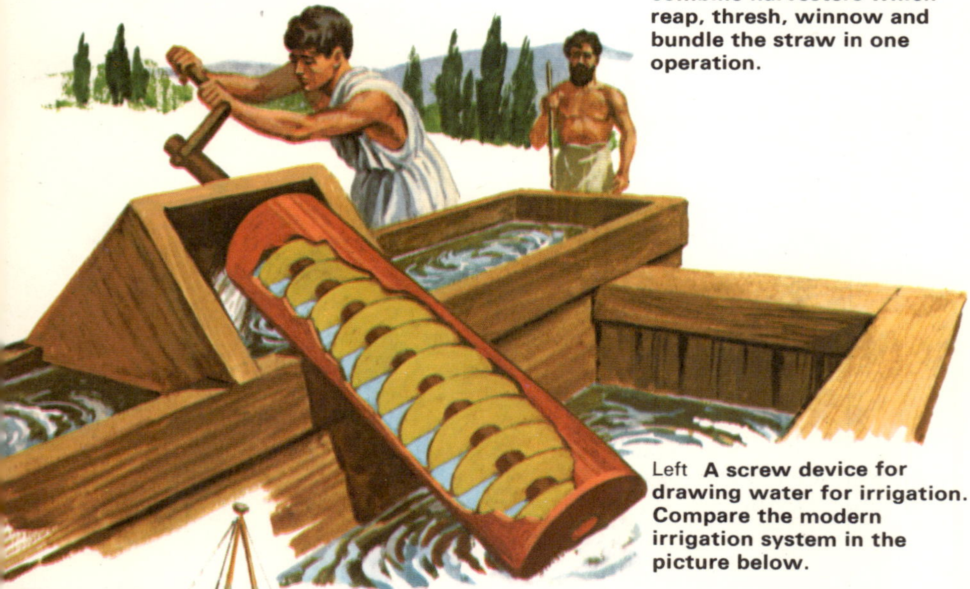

Left **A screw device for drawing water for irrigation. Compare the modern irrigation system in the picture below.**

called maize, is a good source of starch, but it has a lower protein value than the other grain crops.

Rice is one of the world's two most important food crops, the other being wheat. In countries where it is grown, rice provides a large proportion of the total amount of food eaten, so its value as a food is very high. Rice has been grown in China for nearly 5,000 years and it still dominates Chinese and other Asian agriculture. Rice growing in other continents is expanding steadily and it is now cultivated in Africa, South America, the United States and Australia on a commercial scale. Millets are grown in the tropics, for they can tolerate poor soil and drought. At the same time they have a high mineral content compared with other cereals.

Although all plants manufacture sugar, the sugar used by man comes mainly from sugar cane and sugar beet. Sugar is very important for it is an energy-producing food. Sugar gives its best yields in the tropics but it is also grown in the northern parts of the United States and in southern Spain.

Above **Fresh fruit is essential to us as it is a valuable source of vitamins. Oranges, which are one of the citrus fruits, grow in sunny climes. Other citrus fruits are limes, lemons and grapefruit.**

Above **These are some of our better-known cereals. They are important to us because they are made into flour and other items of food and provide us with starch and vitamins.**

Below **A modern dairy farming unit.**

Sugar beet is grown in the cooler temperate climates and although the plant was known in pre-Christian days, its use as a main sugar supply is a fairly modern development.

Coffee, chicory and tea are grown for use as beverages. Coffee is consumed by one-third of the world's population and tea by almost one-half. Although not of any special food value, these three beverages are important economically. Cocoa is another beverage which has a high food value.

Protein is essential to man's health and this comes mainly from beef, lamb and pork, which all come from animals bred by man to be eaten. Protein is also found in large quantities in fish. By far the greater part of the fish eaten as food is obtained from fish living in natural surroundings and caught with nets and lines. Fishing industries exist in every part of the world. Milk and cheese are other important sources of protein, so it is vital that the animals from which we obtain protein are, in turn, supplied with the right grain crops.

No plant can survive without water and as there is a shortage of food in the world, man is now taking pains to see that crops are grown even in areas where there is little water. To do this he uses various methods of irrigation to supply water to crops.

Below **Just as people in the West obtain starch from bread and potatoes, so in the East rice (left) is cultivated for the same purpose. It is grown in wet 'paddy' fields like the ones in the picture.**

Below **Three methods of obtaining food from the sea – (A) spear fishing; (B) dredge fishing and (C) trawler fishing.**

A

B

C

filtered and then heated to a temperature that will kill harmful bacteria. After this the milk is quickly cooled. Milk bottles are washed and sterilised on a huge machine. Conveyors are used to take the bottles to the machines that will fill them with milk and put the caps on.

Butter, cheese and yoghurt are all made from milk. To make butter the cream is removed from the milk in a machine called a separator. The cream then goes into large rotating churns which turn it into butter. Finally, the butter is salted if it is to be stored for a long time, and processed, then packed.

Bread has been a staple food of many people for thousands of years. At first, the wheat grain was dried, crushed and then roasted, but the bread was very hard. It was later discovered that if the grain was soaked in water for a certain time, a process called fermentation took place. The ancient Greeks knew about fermentation, but it was the Romans who improved the practice of bread making. Today bread can be baked or steamed, and the methods

Processing and packing

Special care has to be taken of natural food products, even after they have been harvested or reared, and many sciences are called upon to see that they arrive at their destination in good condition. Chemistry, physics, metallurgy, engineering and biology are important to the food industries. Most of New Zealand's lamb, for example, is exported to Britain, thousands of miles away, so it is imperative that the very best freezing methods are used in order to keep the meat fresh during its long journey.

Milk is nearer to being a complete diet than any other food but natural milk contains bacteria and it has to be processed to rid it of germs. Most milk germs are harmless but unhealthy cattle may contain the type of bacteria which can cause disease. The process most often used is pasteurisation, a technique developed by the French chemist Louis Pasteur. The milk is

Top **Scenes from a bakery showing mixing of the dough, baking and sorting of loaves prior to wrapping.**

Above **A bottling plant in an automated dairy.**

Right **A cheese factory. Once cheese making was confined to farms but today it has become an industrialised process.**

Above **When produce has been harvested from the land, it is handled expertly by workers like this porter at Covent Garden, London, and despatched to greengrocery shops.**

Above **(1) Cutting a joint of beef properly is a highly skilled undertaking. (2) Legs of lamb in a meat warehouse where the meat is kept under constant refrigeration.**

Right **If the produce has to be stored before sale, it has to be deep-frozen or processed and canned under extremely hygienic conditions, as in the picture on the right.**

of cooking it are highly developed. Modern bakeries are equipped with machines that slice and wrap bread.

Processing sugar cane, which has to be done almost as soon as the stems are cut, is a highly complicated business requiring the use of efficient modern machinery capable of producing sugar for direct consumption. When further refined, by-products such as 'golden syrup' are produced and this syrup is then canned.

Nuts and fruit can be processed to extract oil. Fruit can also be dried, bottled or canned. Fish such as salmon and tuna are also canned.

Chocolate is something most people like to eat and it comes from plants that produce cocoa beans. The beans reach the factories in powder form, where it is mixed with other ingredients and turned into a liquid. The liquid is poured into moulds which determine the shape of the finished chocolate.

All the grain crops have to go through a milling process. Because oats have a property in them that helps to delay deterioration, the flour is mixed with other foodstuffs such as ready-mixes for cakes.

Because of modern methods of processing, freezing and packing, man is now fortunate enough to be able to eat essential foods even when they are out of season.

Cooking our food

Before fire had been discovered, man ate his food raw. He hunted what he could and many people must have died through lack of the essential vitamins. It is believed that the burning of livestock in forest fires first gave man the idea of making fires to cook his food. When he was able to make use of fire, man probably just tossed a carcass into the middle of a fire and hauled it out when it was partly cooked. It is likely that many years passed before some prehistoric cook thought of skewering the meat and holding it over the flames.

In many primitive parts of the world ancient practices in cookery are still carried on. Although some civilisations had discovered how to preserve meat by drying and salting, it was the people of the eastern Mediterranean countries who studied food preparation as an art. The Greeks and Romans in particular were elaborate cooks.

Centuries passed and man ate a larger variety of foods, still cooked on open fires. People on the continent of Europe were eating cooked vegetables in the Middle Ages, while in Britain the pleasures of the table consisted of meat, pastry and sweetmeats. Medieval kitchens were very large and at banqueting time many cooks were employed. Cookshops were also in use at this time. They sold hot dishes or cooked customers' own food. Not until the 16th century did anyone seriously begin to plan kitchen aids.

The existence of vitamins in food was not established until 1912. This discovery was made by Sir Frederick Gowland Hopkins who demonstrated the presence of vitamins in milk. After this, studies of food and its value to man continued and we are now aware of the amounts of each type of food

Above **Early man roasting a fish in front of a fire.**

Above **Dinner in an Elizabethan manor house. Only the rich could dine like this. Note the minstrel with his lute.**

Right **Some common herbs and flavourings. They are (1) mint; (2) garlic; (3) rosemary; (4) oregano; (5) bay; (6) parsley; (7) thyme; (8) mustard; (9) black pepper; (10) salt; (11) brown and white sugar; (12) root ginger.**

Far right **The Chinese do not use knives and forks but chopsticks instead. These are often made of bone, and are just as efficient as knives and forks.**

Above **A quick way to cook is with a frying pan.**

Above right **Grilling is better than frying as it preserves more of the food's flavour.**

Right **Poultry and joints of meat are roasted in ovens.**

Far right **Some foods have to be boiled in a saucepan.**

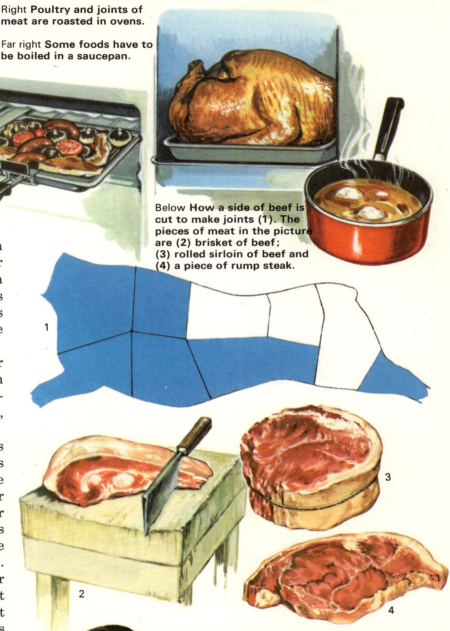

Below **How a side of beef is cut to make joints (1). The pieces of meat in the picture are (2) brisket of beef; (3) rolled sirloin of beef and (4) a piece of rump steak.**

needed to keep the body healthy. In the western world today it is rare for people to fall sick through lack of an essential food. Nevertheless, there is a world shortage of food and in less fortunate countries the people are grossly underfed.

Although most people do eat better food and are able to cook it on modern cookers, styles of cooking vary enormously. Food can be cooked by boiling, frying, grilling and roasting.

The British are fond of boiled meats and traditional steak and kidney pies and puddings, and stews. The Americans are renowned for their enormous steaks which are either fried or grilled, and in both countries roast joints of meat are popular. The French are also great beef-eaters. They cook it very lightly by frying or grilling, and garnish it with the most delicious sauces. They also use a great deal of butter in cooking. The Italians

love pasta and eat it in all shapes and forms, while the Spanish like to eat *paella* (a mixture of shellfish, chicken and rice), and cook their food in oil.

In Europe today there is a great interchange of recipes and it is not unusual for the people in one country to cook, as a matter of course, a traditional meal of another.

In eastern countries, rice, which is either boiled or fried, is the basic dish. The Chinese accompany their rice with pork, chicken or fish, and they have their own distinctive culinary vegetables which are always very finely sliced. They are masters at blending flavours together and Chinese food is enjoyed everywhere. In India rice is served with curried dishes containing spiced meats and vegetables.

Medicine and Hygiene

In primitive times medicine was connected with religion. The first people to study medicine as a science were the Greeks. Hippocrates, who was born about 460 BC, was the first true doctor, and during his lifetime Greek medical knowledge spread to other parts of the world. The Romans, always great organisers, built hospitals in all their major towns.

Galen, an outstanding Greek physician who practised in Rome lived from AD 130–201. His medical theories were followed for some 1,500 years. Galen was able to distinguish between nerve, muscle and tendon, but he made the mistake of thinking that food was carried to the liver and turned into blood. For hundreds of years after Galen there was no major advance in medicine and it was left to the Moslems in the East to make new discoveries.

By the 16th century surgery was more widely practised and doctors had learned a lot about anatomy. There followed a great revival of learning with doctors torn between the Arabian and Greek schools of thought.

Between 1590 and 1640 the thermometer was invented and methods of accurately timing the pulse rate had been introduced. In 1628 an Englishman, William Harvey, published his work on the circulation of the blood, completely disproving Galen's theories. Microscopes were invented by the 17th century and the Dutchman, Anton van Leeuwenhoek, had discovered bacteria with their aid.

By the 18th century much more had been learned about the heart, respiration, and the nervous and reproductive systems. Towards the end of the century it was at last realised how

Above **Primitive people believe that sickness is caused by evil spirits which must be driven out of a patient. To do this, they call in a medicine man like the one shown here.**

Left **The Greek scientist, Hippocrates, who was the first real doctor, was born about 460 BC. Today, new doctors still sometimes take the 'Hippocratic Oath' and agree to keep the code of conduct laid down by him.**

Below **Here, Achilles, who is one of the legendary figures of ancient Greece, is seen bandaging a warrior. Achilles is supposed to have been taught the art of healing by a centaur called Chiron.**

Left **A series of medieval drawings of surgeons and their patients.**

Above **Edward Jenner (1749–1823) the discoverer of vaccination which has almost eliminated smallpox from the civilised world.**

important hygiene was and drainage and water supply systems were installed. Louis Pasteur discovered the science of immunology and the advantages of vaccination against disease.

In 1847 James Young Simpson began the use of chloroform, a substance that prevented patients from feeling pain during an operation. This revolutionised surgery, which remained dangerous until Joseph Lister discovered that the use of antiseptics stopped infection in the wounds made by surgery. Penicillin, a drug which kills bacteria, and which we call an antibiotic, was discovered by Alexander Fleming in 1928.

Since the early years of the 20th century, much has been learned about medicine and surgery. The most spectacular advance has been in the field of transplant surgery, with the first attempts at grafting new kidneys and hearts.

Right **Thanks to radiology, it is possible to see inside people. Here, a surgeon is looking at the chest of the patient in the X-ray machine.**

Below **Here blood is being taken from a donor. It will then be classified and labelled and placed in a blood bank ready to save someone's life.**

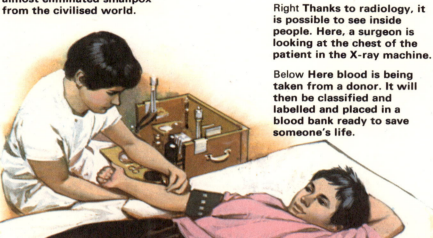

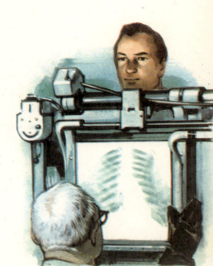

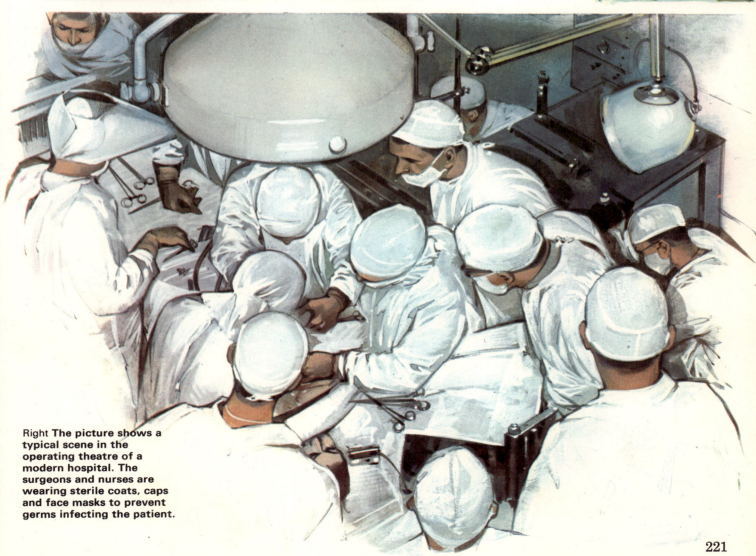

Right **The picture shows a typical scene in the operating theatre of a modern hospital. The surgeons and nurses are wearing sterile coats, caps and face masks to prevent germs infecting the patient.**

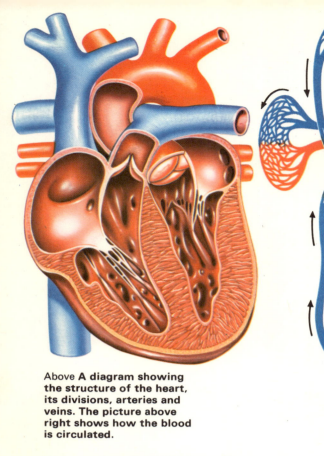

Above **A diagram showing the structure of the heart, its divisions, arteries and veins. The picture above right shows how the blood is circulated.**

How the body works

The human body is composed of several substances, such as carbon, nitrogen, hydrogen, oxygen, calcium, sugar and iron. The first four are in all parts of the body; calcium is mainly in the bones; sugar is mainly in the liver; and iron is mainly in the blood. To keep healthy our bodies must be supplied with all of these substances.

All living stuff, plant as well as animal, is composed of cells. People grow because some cells in their bodies increase by splitting into two cells, and these will divide and divide again as long as extra tissue is needed to enable the bones to grow. Cells wear out but the body can replace them. Cells group together to make tissue: skin is a tissue, and there is blood tissue and muscle tissue.

Several different types of tissue are arranged together to form an organ which is intended to perform a particular function. The eye, brain, liver and heart are all organs and when these organs work together in a special task they are called a system.

The digestive system is a machine which receives the food we eat and transforms it into a condition in which it can be of use to our bodies. The stomach takes four hours to digest

food before it is passed to other organs for further processing. The various parts of the digestive system work without interruption day and night.

The group of organs with which we breathe is called the respiratory system. It consists of the lungs and the various passages which pass the air to them. This system provides the blood with the oxygen it needs and lets the carbon dioxide escape from the blood to the air.

The cardio-vascular system is the one that deals with the heart and the circulation of the blood. It works with the respiratory system in the supply of oxygen to all parts of the body and the carrying away of carbon dioxide. The centre of this system is the heart.

The nervous system is the controller of everything we do both consciously and unconsciously, and it could not function without the brain. Not only does it control actions like thinking, speaking, moving and remembering, but it also looks after blood circulation, food digestion and all the other things that go on in our bodies.

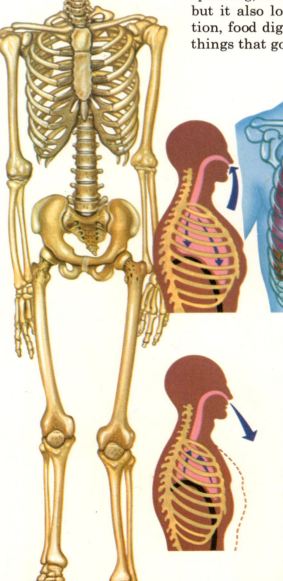

Above **This is the thorax. The lungs are enclosed by the ribs.**

Far left **The bones of the body to which are attached the muscles and tissues. The rib cage and the pelvis at the bottom of the spine, protect the vital internal organs.**

Left **When we breathe correctly the diaphragm, shown immediately below the lungs, moves up and down and the bottom of the rib cage expands and contracts. At every ingoing breath, our lungs take in about 20 per cent oxygen and 79 per cent nitrogen.**

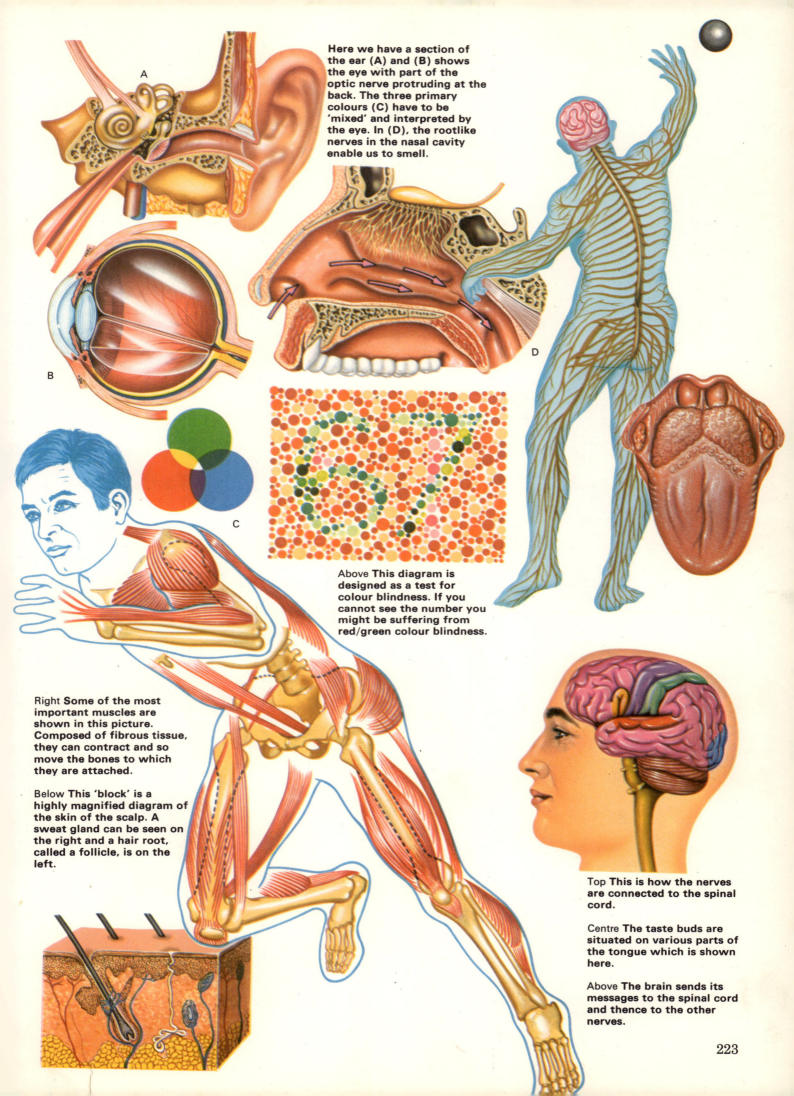

Here we have a section of the ear (A) and (B) shows the eye with part of the optic nerve protruding at the back. The three primary colours (C) have to be 'mixed' and interpreted by the eye. In (D), the rootlike nerves in the nasal cavity enable us to smell.

A

B

C

D

Above **This diagram is designed as a test for colour blindness. If you cannot see the number you might be suffering from red/green colour blindness.**

Right **Some of the most important muscles are shown in this picture. Composed of fibrous tissue, they can contract and so move the bones to which they are attached.**

Below **This 'block' is a highly magnified diagram of the skin of the scalp. A sweat gland can be seen on the right and a hair root, called a follicle, is on the left.**

Top **This is how the nerves are connected to the spinal cord.**

Centre **The taste buds are situated on various parts of the tongue which is shown here.**

Above **The brain sends its messages to the spinal cord and thence to the other nerves.**

Primitive people carried their burdens on poles or dragged them along the ground. Canoes were carved out of fallen tree trunks found near the rivers.

Travel by Land, Sea and Air

One of man's earliest needs was to find a way of transporting himself and his belongings on land from one place to another. This was particularly so at the time before man became a farmer, when he lived a nomadic, or wandering, life. At first, he travelled on foot and carried everything with him on his back. At least, the womenfolk did, since it was generally necessary for men to keep their hands free to use their weapons to defend themselves against wild beasts or other men.

Probably the earliest form of transport was some kind of sledge made very simply of two trailing sticks fastened together with cross-pieces. This contraption would originally have been hauled by man himself, but later the idea of harnessing the sledge to an animal would have occurred.

The greatest single invention in the whole history of transport is the wheel. No one knows how it was first thought of, but it is most likely that it developed from the wooden rollers or tree trunks used in ancient times to move large blocks of stone.

In the world in which primitive man lived, water was a great natural element, and sooner or later he would have wished to travel across it. Whether it be to traverse the seas or simply to reach from one bank of a river to another his need was the same: something which would float and support the human body. One theory is that man used instinctively a fallen tree trunk or branch to assist him while he swam in the water. From this, it was an easy step to the moment when he clambered on to the log and

Above A sedan chair, popular transport in the 18th century.

used it as a simple boat. Fallen tree trunks may also have formed the first bridges.

When man actually began to make boats he used the material that lay to hand around him. In wooded areas trees were fashioned into dugout canoes, whereas in other places the dried skins of animals were stretched across rough wooden frames to make canoes or kayaks.

In the ancient world transport across land on a horse, or some other animal, or in a kind of vehicle hauled by an animal, was the privilege of the few. Most people walked, and for this reason few moved about very much except within the confines of their own home and village. Unless, of course, you happened to be in the army: one thinks of the epic journeys on foot of Alexander's soldiers, or of the 10,000 Greek mercenaries who walked 1,500 miles *2413 kilometres* back from Babylon to the Black Sea after a battle.

The first roads were tracks worn by men or animals. These might have been simply short cuts through a forest from one village compound to another, or the mighty trade routes, hundreds of miles long, worn down by the constant traffic of merchants. The first bush trails in Africa followed the paths of animals, and it is interesting to know that the route for the Canadian Pacific Railway through the Rocky Mountains in Canada follows the course of ancient passes discovered and trodden by thousands of American bison.

Below **Camels are called 'ships of the desert' because they are used as beasts of burden in desert areas. They have great powers of endurance, being able to withstand intense heat and cold and they can live without water for several days.**

Left **An Indian elephant carrying a maharajah on a ceremonial occasion.**

Above **The stage coach was a familiar sight in 18th- and 19th-century England.**

Below **Rickshaws were often used in the Far East to carry people about.**

Above **A cart like this was a common mode of transport until the coming of the motor.**

Travel by road

Man's first attempts to travel by a mechanically propelled vehicle began in the 18th century. One of the first successful designs was a three-wheeled steam cart built by a French army officer, Nicholas Cugnot, in 1769. Two designers in England who worked on steam wagons were William Murdock and Richard Trevithick. Murdock's model steam carriage which he built in 1784–6 would almost certainly have been efficient on the roads had a full-sized vehicle ever been tested, but his employers, Watt and Boulton, seem to have discouraged him from continuing his experiments. Both Murdock and Trevithick switched their attention to rail transport, in which they were among the early pioneers.

After 1820 large numbers of steam coaches were built. These heavy monsters needed good smooth surfaces of road on which to run and men like Telford and McAdam were ready with new methods of road construction. The steam coaches kept up the tradition of a regular, reliable service for passengers and goods which the horse-drawn stagecoach had established. Yet, despite improved speeds of up to 20 m.p.h. *32 k.p.h.* and a generally high level of performance, the steam carriage was forced out of existence by savage road tolls and the opposition of many people to machinery. As with so many inventions in the 19th century, the working man saw the introduction of any form of machinery as a threat to his job and attempts at sabotage were frequent. Nevertheless, the steam car continued to be popular right up to the end of the 19th century and only faded from the scene because it could not be produced cheaply and easily by mass-production methods.

The most notorious Act in the history of motor transport was passed in England in 1865, when the Road Locomotives (Red Flag) Act put a speed limit on vehicles of 4 m.p.h. *6·4 k.p.h.* in the country, and 2 m.p. *3·2 k.p.h.* in towns, and demanded that each vehicle should have a man walking in front of it carrying a red flag. This effectively stopped the development of the motor car in Britain.

Below For centuries, wild African elephants have trampled their way through the jungle to drink at the water holes, keeping faithfully to the same routes. These paths are called bush trails.

Below In this picture, the rocks have crumbled, exposing the tree's roots so that it has fallen across the gorge and made a convenient bridge.

Above The Romans found that flat stones used in this way made wonderful roads

Below Stepping stones can span a river for people to cross.

Above Large pieces of granite are hewn and trimmed and laid on piles to make a bridge.

Above **A Roman bridge in Spain.**

Below **William Murdock experimented with a steam carriage for road use in 1786.**

These three pictures show how the bicycle has evolved since 1790. The hobby-horse (1) had no pedals. The rider sat on the frame and propelled himself by pushing along with his feet. About 80 years after this, the penny-farthing (2) was invented and the Moulton bicycle (3) is a familiar sight on the roads of Britain today.

Although early motorists had to suffer many restrictions, the craze for motoring soon caught the imagination of adventurous people. The use of mechanised transport in the First World War did much to prove its worth but cars like the one in figure (4) were already on our roads. Between the wars, motor cycle racing (5) was becoming popular and enthusiasts were racing their cars round tracks like Brooklands in England.

Below **Today's traffic needs modern systems of flyovers, underpasses and filter lanes. One such system is shown here.**

Above **The entrance to a dual-carriageway motor tunnel.**

Progress in the design of vehicles propelled by the internal combustion and diesel engines was continued on the continent of Europe.

The originators of the modern motor car were two Germans, Carl Benz and Gottlieb Daimler. Benz's three-wheeled petrol-driven car was built in 1885 and the first Daimler motor carriage was on the road by 1886. When the Red Flag Act was repealed in Britain in 1896 and the speed limit on the road raised to a maximum of 12 m.p.h. *19.2 k.p.h.* the famous London to Brighton run, which still takes place annually, was held in

Top right **The famous Golden Gate Bridge in San Francisco.**

celebration. From a field of thirty-three entrants, which included the top motor cars in Europe and the United States, the race was won by Léon Bollée's tri-car from France.

Electric cars were first built in 1888 and although they proved silent, smooth running and easy to drive they were never popular. One reason for this was that they had to carry large batteries which needed recharging after the car had covered only a short distance.

The history of the motor car since the beginning of the 20th century has been one of rapid change from year to

Above **A motor cycle and (below) a long-distance Greyhound coach. These Greyhound coaches travel all over the United States.**

Right **Here is one of London Transport's Routemaster buses.**

and even electronic highways which will control the movements of cars automatically. The manual clutch and gearbox will finally disappear and once the driver has switched on, his vehicle will need only to be steered.

Now that a very high percentage of people in the western world are motor car owners, the problems of providing adequate roads, sufficient parking places and safe vehicles are vital. Much research has been done to try to find out the causes of car accidents in order to make driving safer.

Left **The Jeep made its name in the Second World War because it was very tough and could be used on almost any kind of terrain.**

Above and left **A 1930 Duesenberg motor car and a former Glasgow tramcar.**

year. At first, quality and reliability were the aims, as in the famous Rolls-Royce *Silver Ghost* of 1907. This classic car remained in production for nineteen years and the original model was still in excellent working order in 1939, having travelled over 400,000 miles *643,750 kilometres*. Then, when the popularity of motoring spread, the most important things were cheapness and speed of production. This led to the revolutionary methods of men like Henry Ford in the United States and William Morris in England, who mass-produced good, simple cars down to a price that ordinary people could afford. On the Continent, Renault, Volkswagen and Fiat cars, among others, also catered for the mass market.

Motor racing as a sport has been responsible for many new developments in cars. The demands of the high-speed world of Grand Prix racing, and the toughness and reliability needed to stand up to rally and endurance tests, has brought technical advances which are eventually passed on to the ordinary motorist.

In the future motor cars are likely to become even easier to drive. There are experiments with jet engines, rotary engines, hovercraft engines,

Top **The Mini, one of the most popular family cars of the post-war years.**

Above **One of the finest cars of all, the Rolls-Royce Silver Shadow.**

Above **The Formula I Grand Prix Ferrari 312B. This fine racing car has a design which reduces wind resistance and its broad tyres give very great stability on the track.**

Above **A horse-drawn passenger train. The first railway, opened in 1803, was like this but it carried only goods. It was not long before steam locomotives were taking over from the horses.**

Travel by rail

The earliest records of railways date from about the 16th century. In the mining districts of central Europe wheeled carts hauled by horses used to carry coal. Their wheels wore ruts into the ground and to strengthen these ruts someone had the idea of laying strips of timber along them: in this way the first rails were invented. The standard gauge of track used in the first iron railways in Britain was probably determined by the average width of the old coal carts. The gauge also corresponds roughly to the width of a Roman chariot and it is possible that railed tracks of this sort existed in the ancient world. Cast-iron rails date from the 1760s and sleepers, made from stone and later from wood, were in use before the steam engine appeared.

The first true public railway was the Surrey Iron Railway in southern England which was opened in 1804. It carried only goods, and its wagons were hauled by horses. In the same year the first steam locomotive to run on rails, built by the English engineer, Richard Trevithick, was tried out at Pen-y-darran in Wales.

The most famous of all railway engineers, George Stephenson and his son Robert, developed the first successful railways to transport passengers as well as goods. George Stephenson was appointed engineer to the Stockton and Darlington Railway and he persuaded the directors of the company to use locomotives powered by steam engines as well as horses. He and Robert founded their own company to build the locomotives. Despite much opposition from the public and a general disbelief in the efficiency of the steam

Above **George and Robert Stephenson's famous 'Rocket'. In 1829, the Liverpool and Manchester Railway offered a prize of £500 in a competition for the best steam locomotive. 'Rocket' won as it pulled a full load at an average speed of 24 m.p.h. 38.5 k.p.h.**

Below **The 'Catch-me-who-Can' railway invented by Richard Trevithick in 1808. The public would pay a shilling to ride on a circular track in an open carriage.**

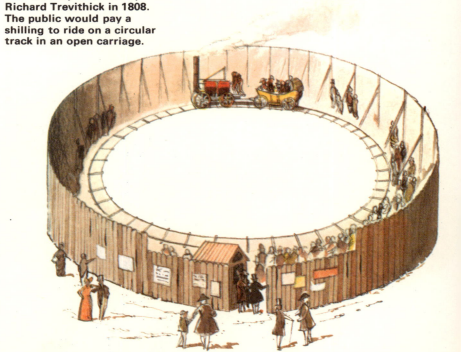

engine, the opening of the Stockton and Darlington Railway in 1825 was a great success. The engine, *Locomotion No. 1*, driven by George Stephenson himself, hauled no less than thirty-eight wagons at a speed of 15 m.p.h. *24 k.p.h.*

In 1829 the celebrated Rainhill Trials were held to decide which locomotive should have the honour of pulling the trains on the new railway from Liverpool to Manchester.

The winner was the most famous of all railway engines, George and Robert Stephenson's *Rocket*. The Liverpool and Manchester Railway became the first complete railway in the world, in the sense that it ran regular scheduled services and was entirely steam-hauled from the beginning. Those who attended the opening ceremony witnessed the first fatal rail accident, when William Huskisson, who was a member of parliament for Liverpool, was run over and killed by the *Rocket*.

Very soon after the first locomotives were running successfully in England, railways powered by steam began to operate in other parts of the world. The Stephensons were responsible for the design of many of the first engines exported from Britain to other parts of Europe and the United States. In 1829 Marc Seguin built the first French locomotive, while in the United States the first steam-powered locomotive to run on rails was built by John Stevens in 1825.

Below This picture shows how some engines had strange designs at the beginning of the railway era. Here is 'The Best Friend of Charleston', the first steam locomotive to run on a regular service in the United States in 1830.

Left An American locomotive of the last century. It shows the 'cow catcher' on the front which prevented buffaloes from falling beneath the wheels. It was the coming of the railways in America that enabled large tracts of land to be developed by settlers.

Above A Post Office van which made its appearance on the London and Birmingham Railway in 1838. The basket on the side was for picking up mail bags without stopping the train. Carrying the mail has been an important part of the work of the railways since 1830. Eight years later, letters were being sorted in the mail van as the train sped along the track.

Railways in Britain grew up at the time of the Industrial Revolution. There was a 'railway mania' in the 1840s when new lines sprang up almost overnight and, in some cases, there were two, or even three rival routes between towns. In other parts of the world during the 19th century, railway building went ahead on a grand scale. In North America, lines were built from east to west over the continent, and in Russia the vast distance of 6,000 miles *9,656 kilometres* which separated St. Petersburg from Vladivostok was linked by rail.

Underground railways, now so familiar a part of the city scene, were first built in the 1860s. The earliest of them, the Metropolitan line in London, opened in 1863.

The era of the steam engine is now over. Diesel and electric engines have taken over the job of hauling the world's trains. Railways today face great competition from road and air transport. Many railway lines do not pay and some have had to be closed. But the quest for higher speeds, greater comfort and safety continues, and new methods of traction are always being tested.

Above A Stirling engine on the East Coast route to Scotland. It is called a 'single' as it has only one driving wheel coupled to the cylinder.

Below Ever since the railways began, its engineers have been striving to increase engine speeds. The picture shows the 'Mallard' which, in 1938, set up an unbeaten record for a steam locomotive of 126 m.p.h. *203 k.p.h.*

Right In 1955, the French National Railways set up a world record of 205 m.p.h. *330 k.p.h.* with this electric train.

232

Right Until recent years, trains were run on two or more rails. Now, however, monorails – one-rail trains – are being taken seriously especially in Japan. Here is the Alweg monorail system in which the train straddles the rail. In some other systems, the train hangs suspended from the rail rather like a basket.

Left The funicular railway to the famous church of the Sacré Coeur in Montmartre, Paris. Funicular railways are pulled up the steep gradients by cables. The two carriages are joined to the same cable so that when one is ascending, the other is going down.

Right Londoners call their underground railway the 'tube'. Here is one of the tube's latest trains made in unpainted aluminium.

Right The Canadian National Railways' revolutionary new turbo train for very fast cross-country journeys. The turbines, which provide the motive power, have been undergoing extensive trials and it is hoped that the train will shortly be in regular service.

Left An indication of what trains may look like in the future. The picture shows the prototype of British Rail's new advanced passenger train.

Left **The reconstruction of an Egyptian ship which was in service about 1300 BC. It is based on a model found in the tomb of Tutankhamen. As the picture shows, it is a sailing ship steered by two oars at the stern acting as rudders.**

The first great sea-faring and trading people, the Phoenicians, founded colonies all along the shores of the Mediterranean, yet there is little known about their ships. The Greeks and Romans had large merchant fleets, but the most familiar ships from these civilisations are the war galleys, light and elegant in Greek days, and sturdy and powerful in Roman times.

From the waters of northern Europe the seamen of Scandinavia explored the world in their longships. There was little contact with the people of Mediterranean countries and the boats of the Norsemen developed independently. It is now believed that the Vikings crossed the Atlantic in their open boats to land on the shores of North America in about the year AD 1000, nearly 500 years before Columbus 'discovered' the continent.

Travel by sea

Many early forms of boats continue to be made and used in various parts of the world where people still live in primitive conditions. The earliest boats with sails, oars and rudders of which we have a record are those of the ancient Egyptians. Models of ships which journeyed up and down the Nile have been found in tombs of the pharoahs dating from about 2000 BC. Drawings from an even earlier period suggest that the Egyptians had properly built boats of a crude sort as long ago as 4000 BC. But the shape and design of boats altered very little in the ancient world.

Above **A Greek war galley. The fighting platform can be seen on the side above the oars.**

Left **'Henry Grace à Dieu', a massive warship armed with 186 guns, built by Henry VIII in 1514 to meet the ever-growing challenge of Spain.**

Above **Ships' figureheads were believed to contain spirits who acted as the ships' eyes for protection. This one is on the 'Cutty Sark'.**

Sea-power was important in the Middle Ages, as the Danes and others who invaded England and central Europe demonstrated. King Alfred built the first English navy, which was so neglected after his death that in 1066 William the Conqueror was able to land his great fleet of warships and transports on the shores of England with little opposition.

During medieval times ships in northern Europe began to rely entirely on the power of sail, and high castle-like platforms developed fore and aft. In the Mediterranean, galleys continued to be used and it was not until the 16th century that these oar-propelled vessels died out. The last important sea battle in which galleys played a major part was the Battle of Lepanto between the Turks and the forces of the Christian League in 1571.

The voyages of discovery into the New World, around Africa, and far away to the East, were made in three-masted carracks and caravels which, despite their smallness, mastered the perils of the oceans. Voyages such as the three-year expedition of Magellan's fleet around the world are a wonderful tribute to the ship-builders

Above **Capt. Cook's 'Endeavour'.** In 1768, Cook sailed this ship to the South Seas to observe the movement of the planet, Venus, for the Royal Society. He returned by the unknown eastern coastline of Australia and charted it brilliantly.

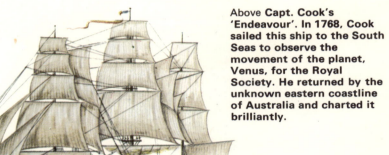

Above **An old American frigate, 'The President'.** A frigate's main function was to find the enemy and to report its position to the battle fleet.

Below **The 'Cutty Sark'** the famous tea clipper built for the tea trade in 1869. She made several record runs between Australia and England.

of Portugal, Spain and the Netherlands, who led the way in these epic journeys.

The English warships of Henry VIII's fleet were the first to mount cannon effectively between the decks and fire them through portholes. This revolutionary step led to the great sea battles of the Elizabethan era which ended in the dramatic defeat of the Spanish Armada by the small, manoeuvrable ships of England. Over the course of about 250 years ships grew bigger but did not alter greatly in design. The tactics of sea warfare continued to be based on the effective use of wind and sail and maximum fire power from broadsides of cannon.

The last great days of sail belonged to the graceful frigates and clippers of the 18th and 19th centuries, until the power of steam was harnessed to a ship for the first time.

No one man can be credited with the design of the first steamship. There were many early experiments in Europe and the United States in the 18th century but the first effective steamboat is generally taken to be the *Charlotte Dundas* built in Britain by William Symington in 1801. The boat was not given a fair trial and progress switched to the United States where Robert Fulton, who was much interested in the design of submarines, successfully launched the *Clermont*, a steamship powered by a Boulton and Watt engine.

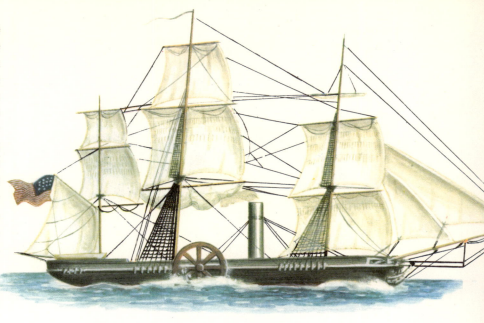

Probably the most famous steamships of the 19th century were three vessels built by I. K. Brunel. These were the *Great Western*, the first steamship to be built specially for service between Europe and America; the *Great Britain*, the first iron-built transatlantic liner with screw propellers; and the mighty *Great Eastern*,

Above **The 'Savannah' which came into service when sails were giving way to steam.**

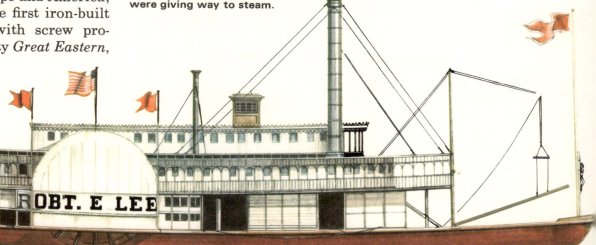

Above **The deep south of the USA once had unusual theatres called showboats. These were floating music halls which plied the Mississippi river. Here is the 'Robert E. Lee', the most famous showboat.**

Below **The 'Campania', an early aircraft carrier used in the First World War. The picture shows a Sopwith Pup circling before landing on the flight deck in front of the bridge.**

launched in 1858, then the largest vessel ever built, over five time bigger than anything that had gone before. She was intended to be the finest passenger-carrying ship in the world, but was a failure. Her size made a smooth passage difficult and many of the world's ports could not accommodate so vast a ship. She finished her days as a cable-layer and was scrapped in 1888.

Fighting ships continued to be made of wood until the middle of the 19th century. The first iron-clad battleship was the *Devastation*, built in Britain in 1873. The two world wars brought great advances in the design of ships. Before the coming of the aeroplane, command of the seas was supremely important and all the big powers in the First World War had powerful fighting fleets. Although command of the air became more important in the Second World War the development

Left **A modern aircraft carrier – the US Navy's 'Enterprise'. The deck is large enough for fast jets to land on it and many hundreds of planes can be housed below decks.**

of underwater craft was vital. Britain, during a period when she fought alone, was nearly starved out of existence because of the destruction wrought upon her merchant convoys by submarines.

Between the wars the great transatlantic liners battled for the Blue Riband, an award made for the fastest trip between Europe and North America. The last of these enormous luxury liners was the 80,000-ton *Queen Elizabeth*, launched in 1938.

Nuclear power is now being used to propel ships on and under the seas, and one of its great advantages is the fact that a vessel is able to stay at sea for long periods without refuelling.

Above right **A modern cruise liner, the 'Nordic Prince'.**

Far right **A container ship fully loaded. Modern container ships are capable of carrying many thousands of tons of cargo.**

Below **A cross section of a container ship showing the engines, crew's cabins and bridge.**

Travel by air

Man has dreamed of flying ever since he first looked up into the sky and watched the easy progress of the birds through the air. At first he did not think of flying as a means of transport but as a spiritual experience, a release from the earth-bound troubles of his life. This is understandable since he looked upon the sky as the natural home of the gods. Although flying was one of man's earliest basic desires it is only in the last 70 years that science has come to his aid and helped him construct machines which permit him to travel safely in the air.

Most early attempts at flying were doomed to failure because men tried to imitate the flapping wings of birds. Leonardo da Vinci designed a machine to be propelled by the arms and legs,

Above An 11th-century British monk thought he could fly by using bird's feathers and flapping his arms about.

Right Centuries ago, inventors thought that 'sky ships' would be like those on the sea. Here are two of them – the one with balloons was invented by Francesco de Lana in 1670. The other is the 'Convertiplane' designed in 1843 by Sir George Cayley, a Yorkshire squire.

although he realised that a heavier-than-air machine could not be kept in flight by physical effort alone. The first successful experiments to lift people off the ground were with lighter than-air machines, or balloons.

The fixed-wing model gliders designed by Sir George Cayley in England in the early 19th century gave the first practical demonstrations of the true principles of flight. Then in 1891, Otto Lilienthal, the German 'bird-man', built his first glider. He went on to make over 2,000 remarkable flights over short distances in single and double fixed-wing

Below In the last century, a series of gliders was made by Otto Lilienthal, a German. One of them is shown here in flight.

Top A Montgolfière hot-air balloon which made the first manned flight over Paris in 1783.

Above Part of the original plan of Wolfmüller's flying machine showing the elevator.

Americans, Orville and Wilbur Wright, made four flights, the last of which covered 852 feet *259 metres*: a short enough distance for such an enormously important event.

The progress in the practical application of the science of aeronautics since that date has been astonishing. Even allowing for the fact that two world wars brought unusual pressures to bear on inventors – and unlimited funds – to move from the flimsy struts and wires of the *Flyer* to the supersonic aircraft of today is a vast leap in a period of 70 years.

When one looks at the sleek shapes of modern aircraft it is difficult to understand how designers managed to produce so many of the weird and unlikely-looking aircraft which followed the Wright brothers' achievement. But some of them, such as the French *Antoinette* monoplane of 1911, are elegant and graceful machines.

aircraft which he controlled by movements of his body.

The historical moment when man made his first sustained flight in an aeroplane powered by an engine took place on 17 December 1903 at Kittyhawk in the United States. In the *Flyer* driven by a 12 h.p. engine the

The daring and skill of the early pioneers were soon put to the test during the First World War. The aeroplane grew up almost overnight from a design experiment into a deadly weapon of war. Apart from its immense importance as a fighting machine, the aeroplane has also quickly established its place as the chief means of long-distance transport. The first passenger airlines were formed in the 1920s, and today the network of their routes penetrates into the remotest corners of the world. Now the scientist and the explorer have moved on from aeroplanes to rockets and seek to journey to other planets.

The fastest and most exciting way to travel in the modern world is by air. What used to be, only sixty years ago, an adventure full of risk and uncertainty, which only brave people would undertake, is now safe and comfortable. Millions of passengers pass through the airports of the world every year. The modern airport has become almost a town in miniature, with shops, restaurants, car parks, even its own fire brigade and policemen. Everything exists for the comfort and safety of the passengers. The central point of any airport is the control tower from which the constant stream of aircraft is organised. In the busiest airports there may be an aircraft taking-off or landing every minute of the day and night.

Left When passengers arrive at an airport after their journey, their baggage is opened and checked by a customs officer.

Below Before boarding an aircraft, passengers' tickets are checked and their baggage weighed and sent to be loaded aboard the aircraft.

Above Ground plans of three of the world's leading airports at (from top to bottom) Paris, Hong Kong and London.

Below The basic principle of the jet engine is that air is taken in through the front of the engine and mixed with fuel which is set on fire. The resulting gases are pushed out through the rear of the engine. The force of this drives the aircraft through the air. The engine below is one of the latest types of turbojet, called a turbofan.

Right The Concorde is a supersonic airliner built by Britain and France and is designed to fly at twice the speed of sound, about 1,400 m.p.h., 2,250 k.p.h.

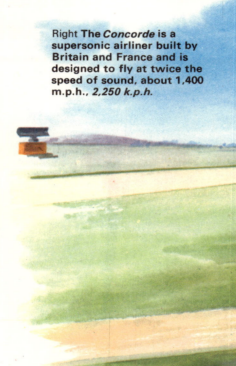

Fan   Combustion chamber

Air →

Air →

→ Hot exhaust

→ Hot

Above **The flight deck of the *Concorde* contains a mass of complicated instruments and gauges, all of which are necessary to ensure safety in the air at the very high speeds at which it flies.**

Flight controllers in the control tower of an airport make sure that the aircraft take off and land safely by organising their movements in the air and on the ground.

The Hovercraft was invented by the British scientist, C. S. Cockerell in 1955. It works on a simple principle. A large rotor blade mounted in the centre pulls down air and forces it out under the craft, creating a cushion of compressed air on which the Hovercraft rides along just above the surface of land or water.

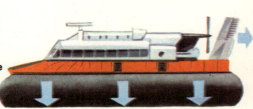

Left **In this view of a typical modern airport are seen some of the aircraft used by leading airlines. On the left in the background is a VC-10, while in front of it being refuelled and loaded with passengers' baggage, is a Super VC-10. On the right is a Trident. The airport control tower and a hoverport can also be seen. The large cutaway drawing is of a Boeing 747 Jumbo-jet, which can carry nearly 400 passengers in comfort.**

Right **It takes all these people to crew the enormous Boeing 747; 3 pilots, 1 engineer, 7 stewards and 8 stewardesses.**

The Journey into Space

The journey into space really starts with the Chinese in the 13th century, for they were the first people to use the rocket as a means of offence and defence.

Weapons of this type were used by the Chinese in all sorts of shapes and designs and were fired in salvoes from conical cylinders or boxes that contained many missiles. They were manned by either a single operator or even two or three artillerymen specially trained in this type of warfare.

The rocket made its appearance again in 1258 during the capture of Baghdad by the Mongols and then later in the 15th century. With the gradual improvement of cannon and other firearms, the rocket weapon, because of its comparative inaccuracy was then discarded.

It was during the 18th and 19th centuries that the rocket made a comeback, and the name of an English colonel, William Congreve, is linked with the military rocket weapon.

On this page we show an example of one of his bombardment weapons, this particular one weighing no less than 300 lb. *136 kilogrammes.* Even 150 years ago these rockets had the most devastating effect and produced hideous wounds when launched against an enemy.

Congreve could be described as the early 19th-century equivalent of Wernher von Braun, for his designs were a vast improvement on previous rockets and they weighed anything from 18 to 300 lb. *8 to 136 kilogrammes.* For their time they had great destructive power in addition to producing a crushing effect on the morale of enemy troops.

Another Englishman, William Hale, developed a spin stabilised rocket and this weapon became standard equipment in both British and American armies during the mid 19th-century.

The revival of the rocket started again in the 1920s and Hermann Oberth is remembered as an engineer who inspired the great men of rocket

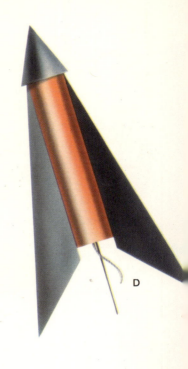

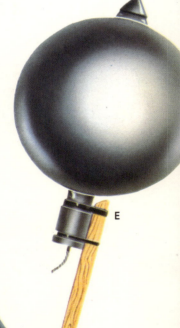

Right **Some weapons of the 18th century – (D) a rocket with fins; (E) an artillery rocket with an explosive head and (F) Congreve's 300-lb. *136 kilogrammes* rocket.**

Left **All these objects come from 13th-century China. The quiver (A) holds fire arrows. The man with the torch is about to launch a salvo from the multi-rocket launcher (B). The disc fire arrow (C) has three spear heads and is fired by a rocket.**

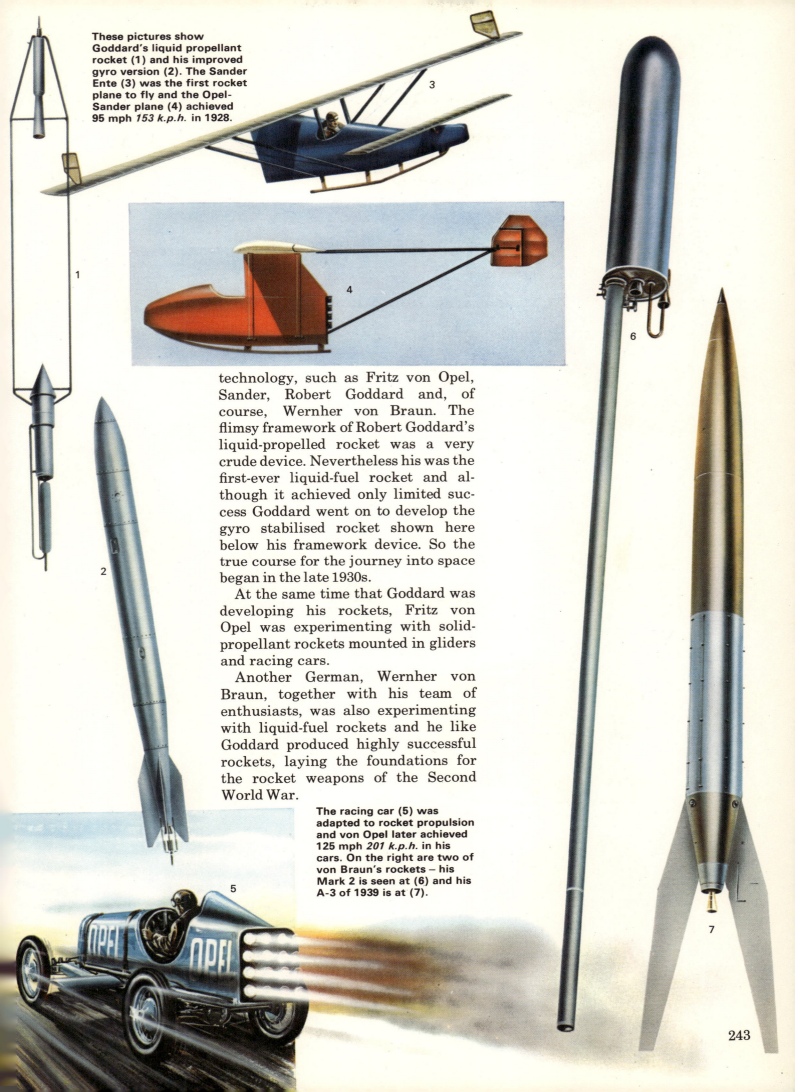

These pictures show Goddard's liquid propellant rocket (1) and his improved gyro version (2). The Sander Ente (3) was the first rocket plane to fly and the Opel-Sander plane (4) achieved 95 mph *153 k.p.h.* in 1928.

technology, such as Fritz von Opel, Sander, Robert Goddard and, of course, Wernher von Braun. The flimsy framework of Robert Goddard's liquid-propelled rocket was a very crude device. Nevertheless his was the first-ever liquid-fuel rocket and although it achieved only limited success Goddard went on to develop the gyro stabilised rocket shown here below his framework device. So the true course for the journey into space began in the late 1930s.

At the same time that Goddard was developing his rockets, Fritz von Opel was experimenting with solid-propellant rockets mounted in gliders and racing cars.

Another German, Wernher von Braun, together with his team of enthusiasts, was also experimenting with liquid-fuel rockets and he like Goddard produced highly successful rockets, laying the foundations for the rocket weapons of the Second World War.

The racing car (5) was adapted to rocket propulsion and von Opel later achieved 125 mph *201 k.p.h.* in his cars. On the right are two of von Braun's rockets – his Mark 2 is seen at (6) and his A-3 of 1939 is at (7).

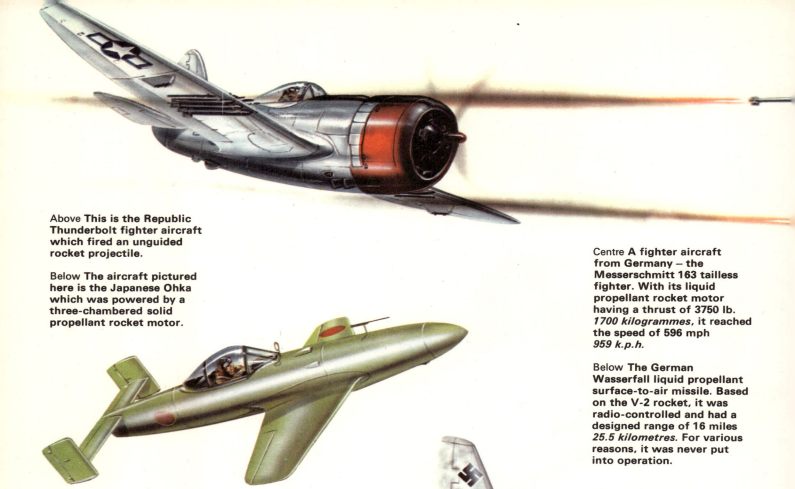

Above **This is the Republic Thunderbolt fighter aircraft which fired an unguided rocket projectile.**

Below **The aircraft pictured here is the Japanese Ohka which was powered by a three-chambered solid propellant rocket motor.**

Centre **A fighter aircraft from Germany – the Messerschmitt 163 tailless fighter. With its liquid propellant rocket motor having a thrust of 3750 lb. *1700 kilogrammes*, it reached the speed of 596 mph *959 k.p.h.***

Below **The German Wasserfall liquid propellant surface-to-air missile. Based on the V-2 rocket, it was radio-controlled and had a designed range of 16 miles *25.5 kilometres*. For various reasons, it was never put into operation.**

The Second World War saw the development of all types of rocket weapons and on this page we show only a small selection of them. However, they are the most important ones and trace the story from the unguided rocket projectile fired from the Republic Thunderbolt fighter aircraft to the V-2. A similar aircraft, the Hawker Typhoon, was also used to great effect as a rocket-fighter.

The Wasserfall was a liquid-fuel surface-to-air missile, having a range of 16 miles *25·6 kilometres* and controlled by radio, but it did not become operational.

Yet another weapon which looked very futuristic was the multi-winged two stage solid-fuel surface-to-air missile known as the Rheintochter R-1. This weapon was designed to have a range of 25 miles *40 kilometres*, but like the Wasserfall did not become operational.

The Germans also experimented with weapons by wire, which they controlled successfully. The one shown on this page is known as the Ruhrstahl X-4, originally designed as main armament for the M.E. 262 jet fighter.

The H.S. 293 we show on this page was carried in bomber aircraft and was a radio-controlled rocket-powered bomb. This weapon was used operationally and proved highly successful.

Looking rather like a modern delta-winged aircraft, the Feuerlilie was an experimental rocket missile.

V-2, perhaps the most successful of all German rocket weapons, carried one ton of high explosive and reached a speed of 3,800 m.p.h. *6,115 k.p.h.* less than 5 minutes after lift-off. The range

The rocket missiles on this page are (A) Rheintochter R-1 two-stage surface-to-air missile with a 25-mile *40 kilometres* range; (B) Ruhrstahl X-4 air-to-air missile was intended for the Me 262 jet fighter; (C) a German Hs 293 radio-controlled bomb powered by a rocket; (D) the Feuerlilie experimental rocket and (E) the largest missile used by Germany, the V-2 rocket.

of the V-2 was about 190 miles *306 kilometres* and it attained an altitude of approximately 60 miles *96 kilometres*. There was no defence against this form of attack and although it was conceived as a terror weapon, the V-2 helped rocket engineers to develop the complicated spacecraft of today.

The next four pages show how the use of the rocket has progressed from its early beginnings in the 13th century to become a gigantic industry employing tens of thousands of people helping mankind in his never ending quest for knowledge.

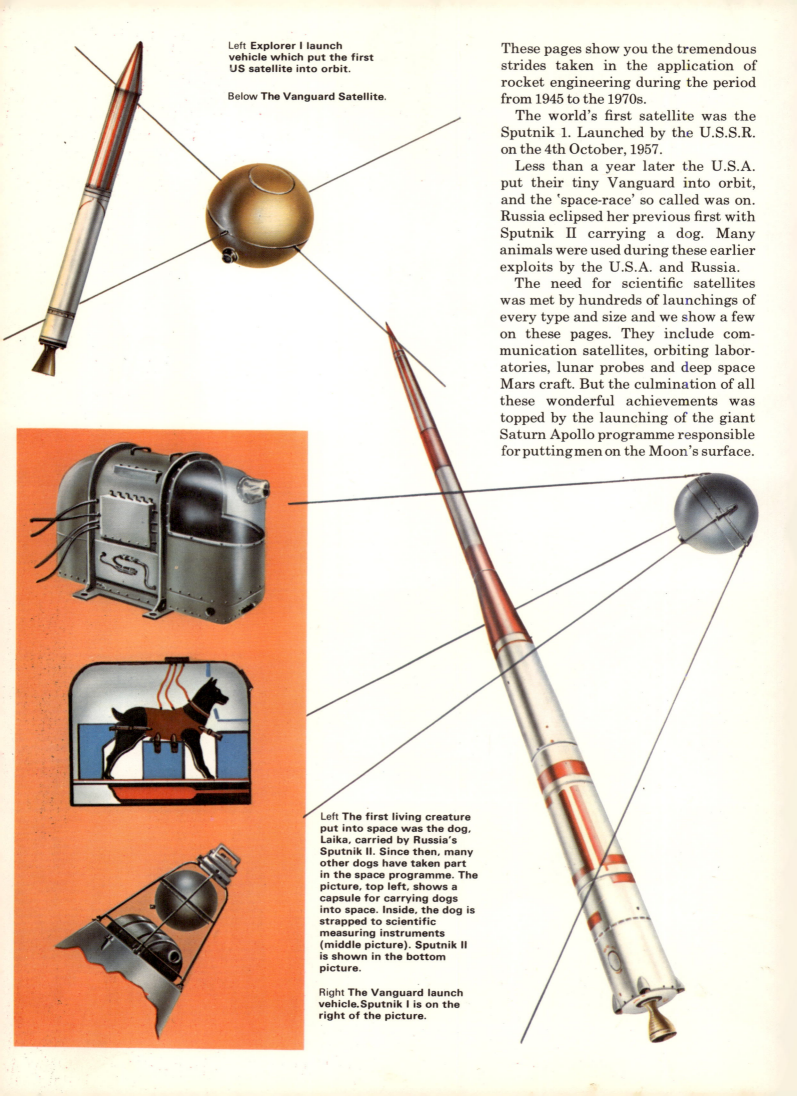

Left **Explorer I launch vehicle which put the first US satellite into orbit.**

Below **The Vanguard Satellite.**

These pages show you the tremendous strides taken in the application of rocket engineering during the period from 1945 to the 1970s.

The world's first satellite was the Sputnik 1. Launched by the U.S.S.R. on the 4th October, 1957.

Less than a year later the U.S.A. put their tiny Vanguard into orbit, and the 'space-race' so called was on. Russia eclipsed her previous first with Sputnik II carrying a dog. Many animals were used during these earlier exploits by the U.S.A. and Russia.

The need for scientific satellites was met by hundreds of launchings of every type and size and we show a few on these pages. They include communication satellites, orbiting laboratories, lunar probes and deep space Mars craft. But the culmination of all these wonderful achievements was topped by the launching of the giant Saturn Apollo programme responsible for putting men on the Moon's surface.

Left **The first living creature put into space was the dog, Laika, carried by Russia's Sputnik II. Since then, many other dogs have taken part in the space programme. The picture, top left, shows a capsule for carrying dogs into space. Inside, the dog is strapped to scientific measuring instruments (middle picture). Sputnik II is shown in the bottom picture.**

Right **The Vanguard launch vehicle. Sputnik I is on the right of the picture.**

Above **(A)** Relay communication satellite; **(B)** lunar orbiter; **(C)** orbiting astronomical observatory and **(D)** Mariner 9 Mars probe.

Below **These pictures show what happened when man landed on the moon. (1) The service and command module in orbit round the moon; (2) the lunar module on the moon's surface; (3) the lunar rover, the first 'car' on the moon and (4) the return to earth.**

Right **The rocket shown here is the Saturn V used for the conquest of the moon. With the Apollo spacecraft in position, it stands over 353 feet** *107 metres* **in height — almost as high as the cross of St. Paul's Cathedral in London. And it weighs no less than 2725 tons.**

1

2

3

4

On now to the late 1970s and on this page we show some of the exciting spacecraft now being planned by the U.S.A. These are the gigantic space shuttles to link the earth with the large space stations due to be launched in the mid-70s. To give you some idea of the size of these vehicles we show you a comparison between a typical heavy road transport lorry and say a Volvo or Scania Vabis, the enormous shuttle craft with its pay-load air-spacecraft orbiter mounted above it.

When the current series of Apollo missions ends in 1972, the U.S.A. expect to have the next phase of space exploration well under way. Space stations in orbit, carrying out experiments with materials and manufacturing processes, will need to be manned with large crews of scientists and technologists. The requirement for these men to be ferried in large numbers will be met by the shuttle.

A space shuttle will consist of an orbiter vehicle and a booster element. The orbiter vehicle will contain crew, passengers and cargo, together with fuel for the orbital mission.

The booster will also be manned and have a power system that will enable it to return to earth and make a horizontal landing on an airport. The whole plan for this challenging series of missions will be under the impressive title of the United States Space Task Group.

Left This picture shows how the shuttle space craft would appear at the moment of launching.

Right A diagram which shows the enormous size of the pick-a-back unit compared with an ordinary articulated truck.

Below An experimental HL–10 lifting-body research aircraft riding pick-a-back in space flight.

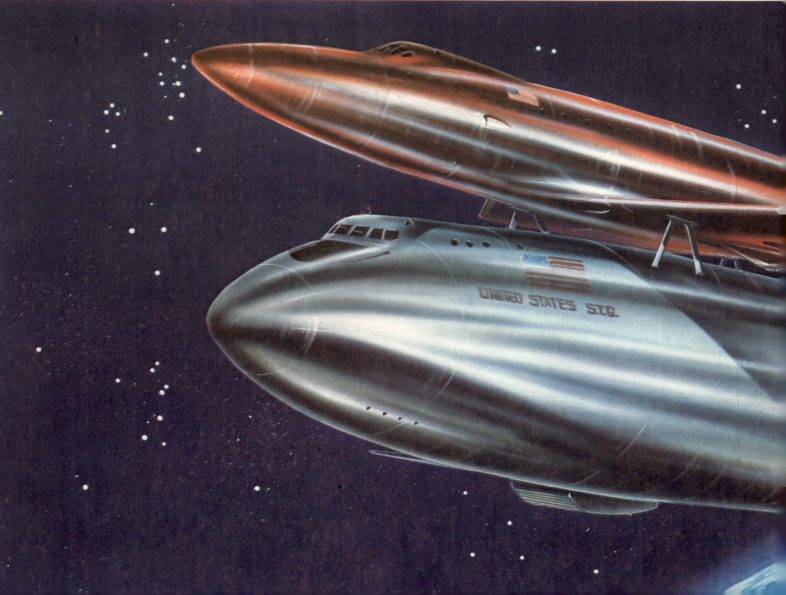

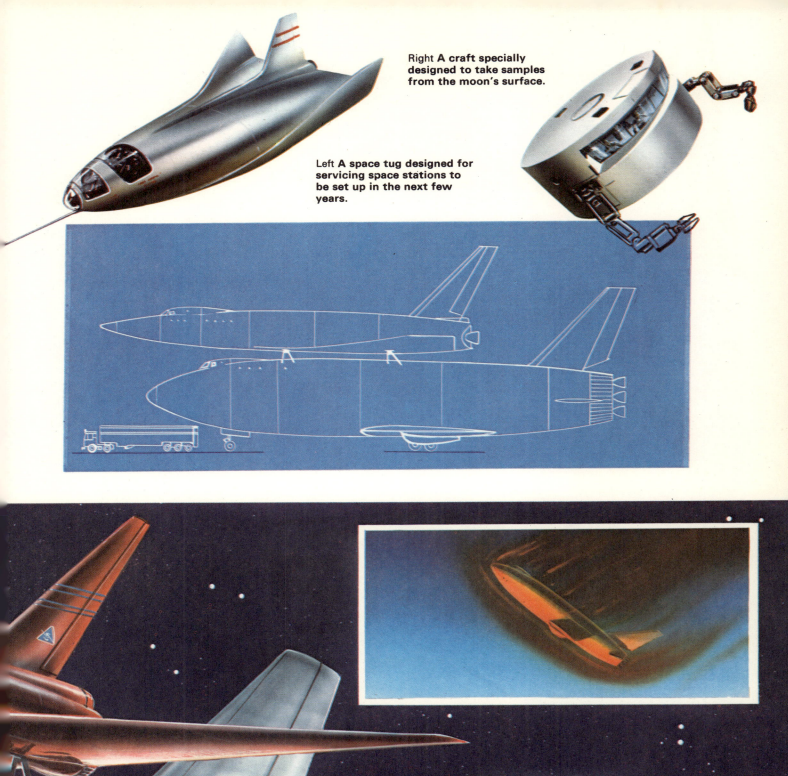

Right **A craft specially designed to take samples from the moon's surface.**

Left **A space tug designed for servicing space stations to be set up in the next few years.**

INDEX

ACKNOWLEDGEMENTS

P.8. top right. Syndication International, London;
P.8. bottom right. British Leyland (Austin-Morris);
P.9. top. Aerofilms Ltd. London; P.9. centre. H.G.P.L.;
P.9. bottom. Central Office of Information; P.10.
H.G.P.L.; P.11. Picturepoint Ltd. London; P.13.
bottom right. E.M.I. Ltd; P.15. top. Aer Lingus, Irish
International Airlines; P.15. centre. Ulster Office,
London; P.16. top & centre. Picturepoint Ltd.
London; P.16. bottom. H.G.P.L.; P.17. top. F. W.
Davidson; P.17. centre. Picturepoint Ltd.; P.17.
bottom. H.G.P.L.; P.28-29. The Press Association Ltd.
P. 29. top right. Courtesy Her Majesty's Stationery Office,
London; P.31. bottom. Fox Photos Ltd. London; P.37.
left. H.G.P.L.; P.37. right. National Aeronautics &
Space Administration, Washington D.C.; P.44.
H.G.P.L.; P.46. Picturepoint Ltd.; P.106. top
right. French Government Tourist Office, London;
P.106. centre. Italian State Tourist Office,
London; P.106-107. Mr. W. F. Davidson; P.107. top
right. H.G.P.L.; P.107. centre. Swedish National
Travel Association, London; P.107. bottom right.
H.G.P.L.; P.110. top left. Hong Kong Gov. Tourist
Office, London; P.110. right. Japan Information
Centre, London; P.110. bottom. Serena Fass
Photography; P.111. Marketing Services, (Travel &
Tourism Ltd.); P.113. top. H.G.P.L.; P.113. centre.
British Overseas Airways Corp; P.113. bottom.
Syndication International, London; P.115. top.
H.G.P.L.; P.115. bottom left. Varig, (Brazilian
International Airlines); P.115. bottom right.
Picturepoint Ltd. London; P.117. left. H.G.P.L.;
P.117. right. South African Tourist Corp. London;
P.119. left. Australian News & Information Bureau,
London; P.119. right. H.G.P.L.; P.129. bottom left.
Tate Gallery (H.G.P.L.), London; P.129. bottom
right. J. E. Dayton; P.136-137. Syndication
International, London; P.139. right centre. Musée
Guimet, Paris (H.G.P.L.); P.140. bottom right.
National Museum, Athens, (H.G.P.L.); P.142. top left.
Scala, Florence; P.142. top right. Board of Trinity
College, Dublin; P.142. bottom. H.G.P.L.; P.143. top
left. Universitetets Oldsaksamling, Oslo. (H.G.P.L.);
P.143. centre. National Museum, Copenhagen
(H.G.P.L.); P.143. bottom left. Musée Condé,
Chantilly; P.144. top left. Scala, Florence; P.144. top
right. Kupferstichkabinett, Berlin; P.144. right.
Victoria & Albert Museum, London. (Copyright
Reserved); P.144. centre. British Museum, London;
P.144. bottom left. Victoria & Albert Museum, London;
P.145. top left. Louvre, Paris (H.G.P.L.); P.145. centre
right. Prado Museum, Madrid. (H.G.P.L.); P.145.
bottom left. Metropolitan Museum of Art, New York;
P.146. top right. Tate Gallery, London, (H.G.P.L.);
P.146. bottom right. Victoria & Albert Museum,
(H.G.P.L.); P.146. centre. Rodin Museum, Paris
(H.G.P.L.); P.146. top left. Musée de
L'Impressionnisme, Paris, (H.G.P.L.); P.146. bottom
left. Tate Gallery, London. (H.G.P.L.); P.147. top
right. Courtauld Institute Galleries, (H.G.P.L.); P.147.
bottom centre. St. Matthew's Church, Northampton
(H.G.P.L.); P.147. bottom right & left. Tate Gallery,
London. (H.G.P.L.); P.149. bottom right. Musée
Guimet, Paris. (H.G.P.L.); P.150. Country Life. (by
permission Marquess of Exeter); P.152. top left.
(H.G.P.L.); P.170-171. British Broadcasting
Corporation.

P.146. top left. P.146. centre & P.147. bottom right.
© by S.P.A.D.E.M. Paris. 1972.

Abbreviation: H.G.P.L. = Hamlyn Group Picture
Library.